IMAGES
of America

ASHLAND

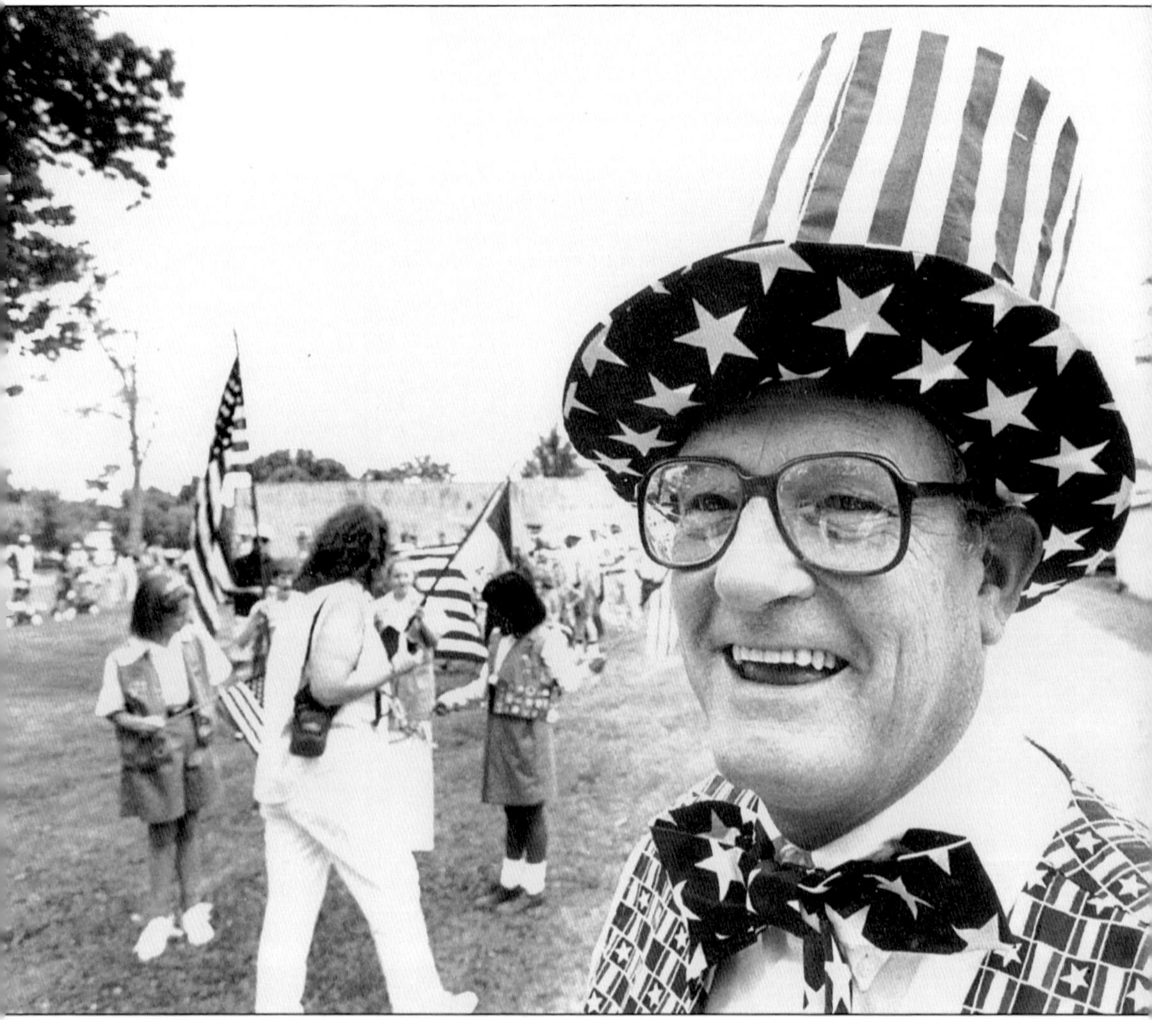

JAY MALCOLM PACE. It is impossible to tell the story of Ashland without remembering J. Malcolm "Jay" Pace III. As editor and publisher of Hanover's community newspaper, the *Herald-Progress*, Pace was a shining star in the "Center of the Universe." He took pride in Ashland and Hanover and considered the community his family. In addition to his roles as editor and publisher of the local paper of record, Pace always made time to wear the many hats the people of Hanover threw at him. From Uncle Sam in the Ashland Fourth of July parade to the musical director of the Ashland Variety Show, Pace was an integral part of the county he cherished. Pace left his beloved community behind on April 12, 2004, when he died unexpectedly at the age of 58 after a brief illness. (*Herald-Progress.*)

IMAGES
of America

ASHLAND

Dale Paige Talley

ARCADIA
PUBLISHING

ISBN 978-0-7385-1770-4

Published by Arcadia Publishing
Charleston, South Carolina

Printed in the United States of America

Library of Congress Catalog Card Number: 2004116050

For all general information contact Arcadia Publishing at:
Telephone 843-853-2070
Fax 843-853-0044
E-mail sales@arcadiapublishing.com
For customer service and orders:
Toll-Free 1-888-313-2665

Visit us on the Internet at www.arcadiapublishing.com

Contents

Acknowledgments

Projects like this can be daunting. It is often difficult to make a choice about which photograph to include and which to leave out. In the main, I have tried to choose images that represent the town's lifestyle rather than highlight prominent political figures, families, or structures. I hope we can do a second volume to include some pictures I was simply unable to find that could be reproduced, like Eddie Rakeleaves, Lester Jackson, and Miss Mary Beirne.

The town opened its vaults to me as I put this together. In particular, I would like to thank Dorothy Jones and Sarah Wright, who know more about Ashland and Hanover County than I could ever hope to know. Without them, the project would have been impossible. Woody and Susan Tucker were absolutely tireless in their efforts to put this project together. I will always be grateful for their kindnesses. Todie Grattan and Gene Luck supplied fabulous stories and invaluable photographs. Eloise Piccolo is nominated as the most organized keeper of photographs. Pen and Betty Carol Stevenson were very diligent in researching the identities of group photos. Ann Curtis Palmore provided many images and insights. Marion Herget's fine book *The Watkins Years* provided vivid local color. Inez Gray spent a long afternoon reminiscing and sharing her collection. The jolly P.K. Perrin handed me 12 photo albums one afternoon. Cabell Luck lent a nice collection. Terry Barnes Shaw and Mildred Smeeman Davis went beyond the call of duty to find old photos. Judee Showalter at Randolph-Macon is ever helpful. Laughlin Spencer, Liz Stiles, and Lelia Palmore Weyman made significant contributions. Tom Willis lent his collection from Cross Brothers. Pat Pace and Anne Peters provided photos that are utterly unique. Judson Vaughan provided anecdotes and photos. The Hughes family was extremely generous. Kathleen Clark made special efforts to provide a long sought-after photo of her aunt. Rick Gran's memorabilia was key in illustrating old businesses. Lynn Taylor helped in a last-minute crisis. As always, the *Herald-Progress* never fails to be supportive.

If I have left out anyone, I apologize. Thanks, Ashland. This is your book.

INTRODUCTION

There is no place like Ashland. The official history could be said to be that of the Richmond, Fredericksburg, and Potomac Railroad and Randolph-Macon College. But in truth, Ashland is more than the sum of its parts. It is the realized vision of what a small town can be. Close and protective of its own, Ashland is today as it was in the beginning, looking to the future with an eye on its remarkable past.

In 1837, almost as soon as the first trains began running in America, the Richmond, Fredericksburg, and Potomac Railroad (RF&P) laid tracks from Richmond to Fredericksburg. Passengers could speed along at 10 miles per hour over iron-capped wooden rails from Richmond to Aquia Creek. There, they could board a stagecoach that bore them to the railroad-owned steamship line and a cruise up the Potomac to Washington. Between Richmond and Fredericksburg lay the boggy and overgrown area known as the Slashes.

By 1858, the Slashes was renamed in honor of native son Henry Clay's estate in Kentucky—Ashland. The town that began as a fueling stop for the RF&P had a resort hotel complex complete with bowling alley, ballroom, and race track that brought gamblers and sportsmen from up and down the East Coast.

By 1868, the Civil War had devastated Southern America and nowhere as completely as Hanover and Ashland. Economic collapse and a resultant depression saw the literally newborn Ashland, still guided by the iron-fisted railroad, faced with serious challenges to its very existence. A town that had relied on money spent in pursuit of gambling, horseracing, and other leisure activities could no longer expect revenue from the same sources. In Mecklenberg County, Randolph-Macon College, also suffering from the war, saw its student population dwindle. The railroad persuaded the college that being located on a rail line would help to save it from extinction, so the oldest Methodist college in the country moved to its present location in Ashland.

By 1903, Randolph-Macon College, the RF&P railroad, and tough-minded Ashlanders had reinvented the town. Each day, nearly 40 trains rumbled through, including the Accommodation Train that stopped for bank executives on their way to work in Richmond. It stopped to pick up passengers at street corners or to pick up a sample of fabric to be bought in Richmond for a waiting housewife. One could hear the clip-clop of horses' hooves pulling wagons that delivered groceries, mail, and passengers all over the tiny town. On Hanover Avenue, the ring of the blacksmith's hammer echoed above the tree tops and over the Randolph-Macon College campus. In town along the tracks, people visited the dry goods store, the ice cream parlor, and the new Hanover National Bank.

By the early 1900s, Frank Jay Gould built an electric trolley line from Richmond to Ashland that ran like clockwork every hour on the hour. By 1917, his Chesapeake Bay Railway Company had collapsed and stock was issued for the Richmond Ashland Railway line, which ran until 1938.

Eventually, the gas lights were replaced by streetlights and the trolley supplanted by a bus line. Cars began to ply the rutted streets, and ordinances were passed to manage roaming livestock. Taken at face value, Ashland may have seemed just a railway stop. But the intellectual life of the college and the irrepressible spirit of the residents brought a vitality to this community that remains a delight for all who remember the past—the plays and parades and dances and the Tucker and Wightman Minstrel Show, in which many members of the town played a part. Men's clubs and women's clubs sprouted up not for philanthropic efforts but to keep intellectual life alive.

Throughout Ashland's history, Ashlanders have retained a sense of humor, a strong dedication to each other, and a fierce desire to preserve what is locally known as the "Center of the Universe."

One

TRAINS

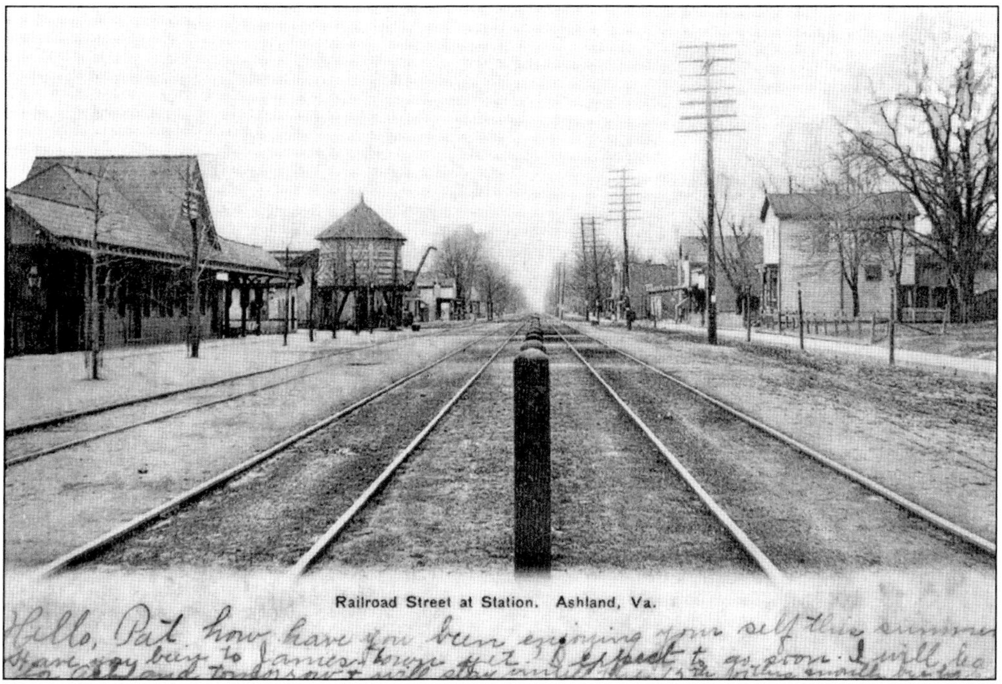

THE OLD TOWN. The fact that there are double tracks through town indicates this picture was taken after 1903. By 1906, the entire line of the RF&P had been double tracked. Standing out on the left is a fine example of the old water tower that filled the trains' boilers. Towers like this were constructed at regular intervals along the line. (Woody and Susan Tucker.)

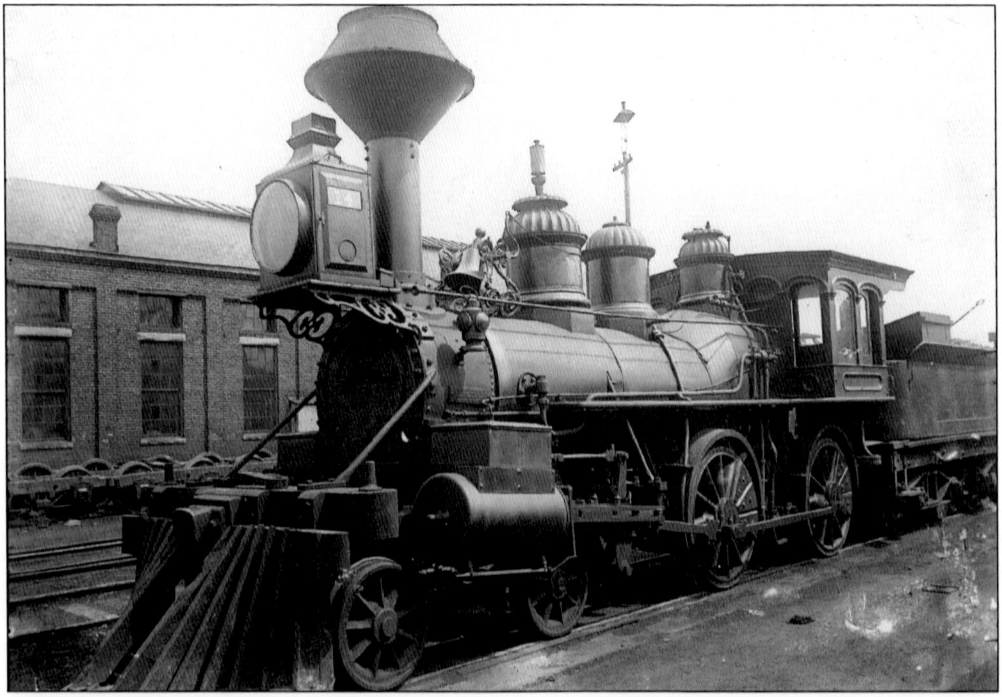

CIVIL WAR–ERA RF&P. The RF&P was chartered in 1834. By February 1837, tracks were laid and the first trains passed through what is now Ashland, then called Adams Shanty, to Fredericksburg. Passengers left Richmond at 4:30 a.m. and arrived in Washington by 6 p.m. the same day. This was rapid transit considering the traveler had to take a stagecoach from Fredericksburg to Aquia Creek and a steamship from there to the capital. Before 1815, travelers had to set aside 38 hours to make the trip. (Dementi Studios.)

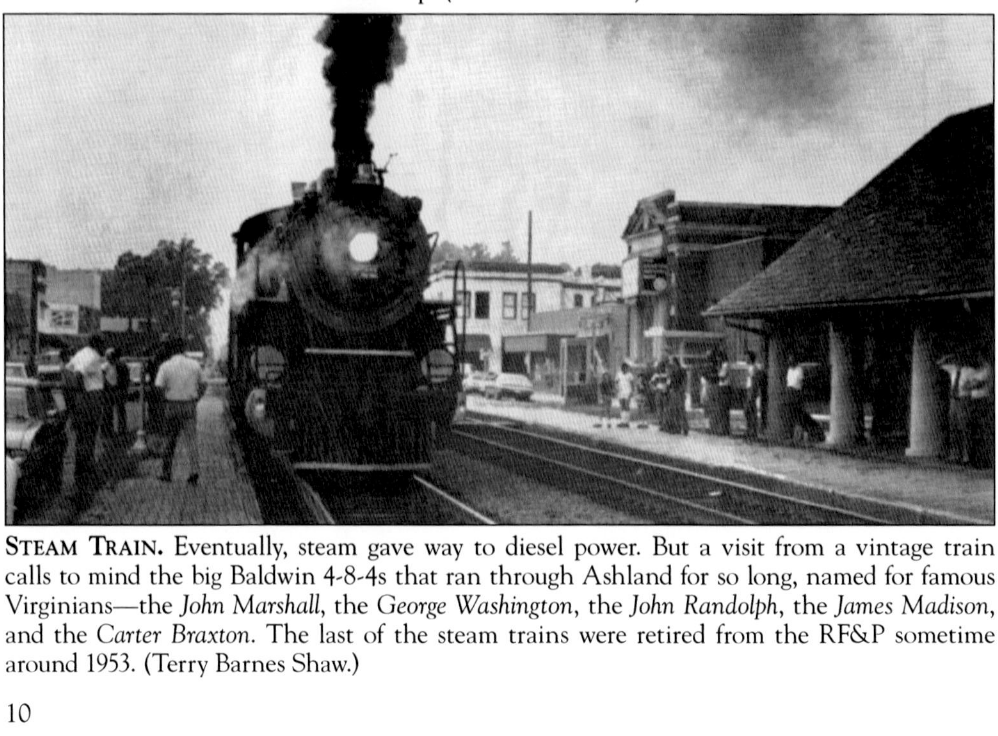

STEAM TRAIN. Eventually, steam gave way to diesel power. But a visit from a vintage train calls to mind the big Baldwin 4-8-4s that ran through Ashland for so long, named for famous Virginians—the *John Marshall*, the *George Washington*, the *John Randolph*, the *James Madison*, and the *Carter Braxton*. The last of the steam trains were retired from the RF&P sometime around 1953. (Terry Barnes Shaw.)

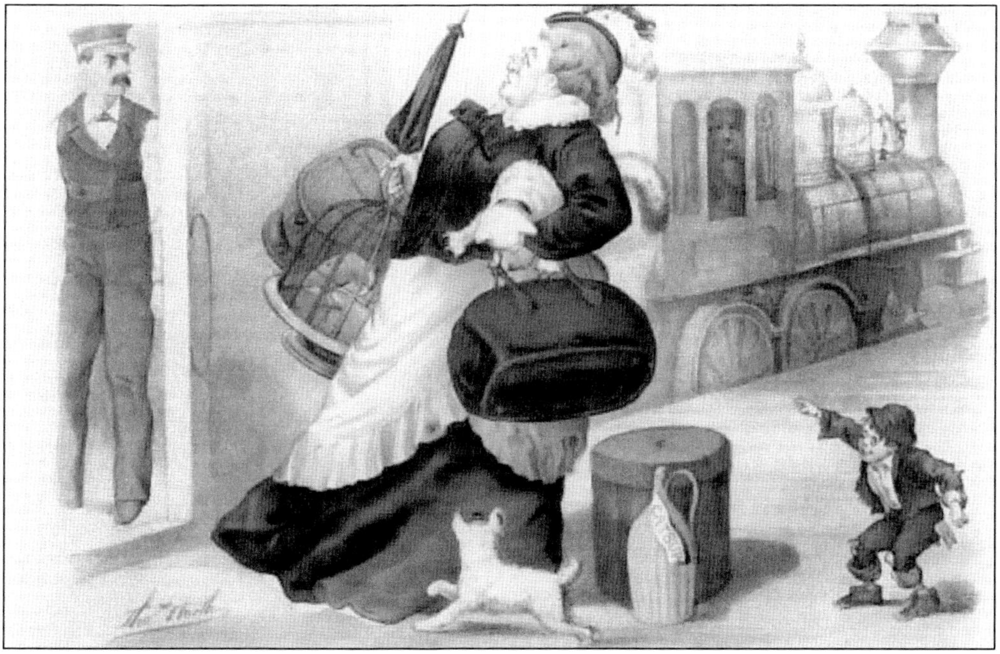

ACCOMMODATION TRAIN. As early as 1881 and until after World War II, the RF&P operated an accommodation train that stopped nearly everywhere between Ashland and Richmond. Businessmen could take the train at 7:30 a.m. and return to town by 7:15 p.m. The afternoon train linked Ashland ladies with Richmond shopping. They could leave at 11 a.m. and be home by 5 p.m. Purchases from such stores as Miller and Rhoads, Thalhimers, and Kaufman's could be delivered to Richmond's Elba Station and put on the baggage car to Ashland. Rebecca Grattan remembered running for the train every morning to get to town in time for school with a biscuit in her mouth and her coattails flying. (*Harper's Weekly.*)

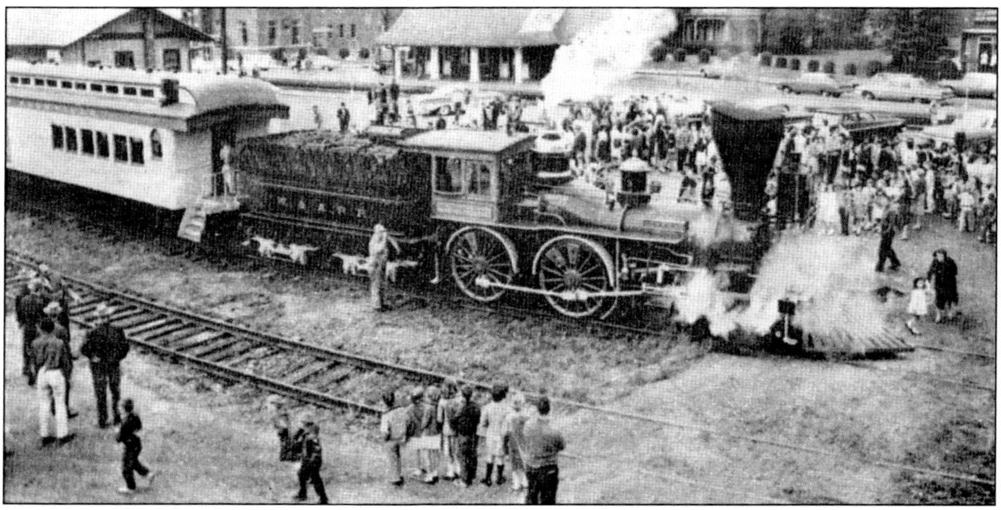

HISTORIC TRAIN VISIT. This photograph suffers from age, but the sight of this Civil War–era train pulling off behind the RF&P freight depot in the 1960s brought out townspeople. Railroad Avenue runs between the freight depot (upper left) and the Ashland passenger depot (top center). A parking lot for Randolph-Macon College has taken place of the old depot. (Lynn Taylor.)

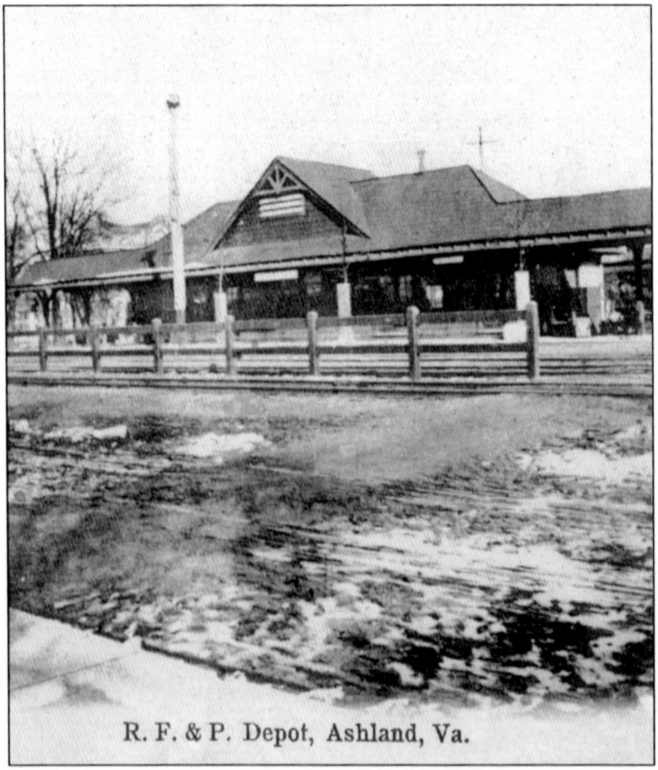

OLD ASHLAND DEPOT. The depot was often a hub of activity as townspeople traveled there to pick up packages from a day's shopping in Richmond. (Gene Luck.)

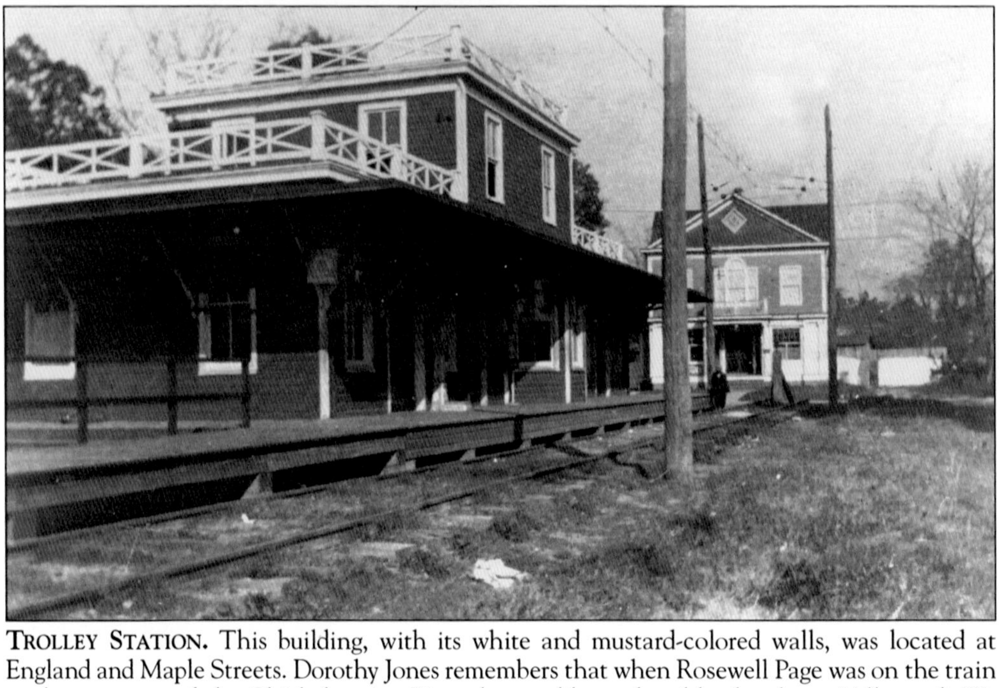

TROLLEY STATION. This building, with its white and mustard-colored walls, was located at England and Maple Streets. Dorothy Jones remembers that when Rosewell Page was on the train as the cars crossed the Chickahominy River, he would stand and lead a cheer: "All stand! We are in Hanover County! God bless her!" The Masonic Building is in the background. (Mildred Smeeman Davis.)

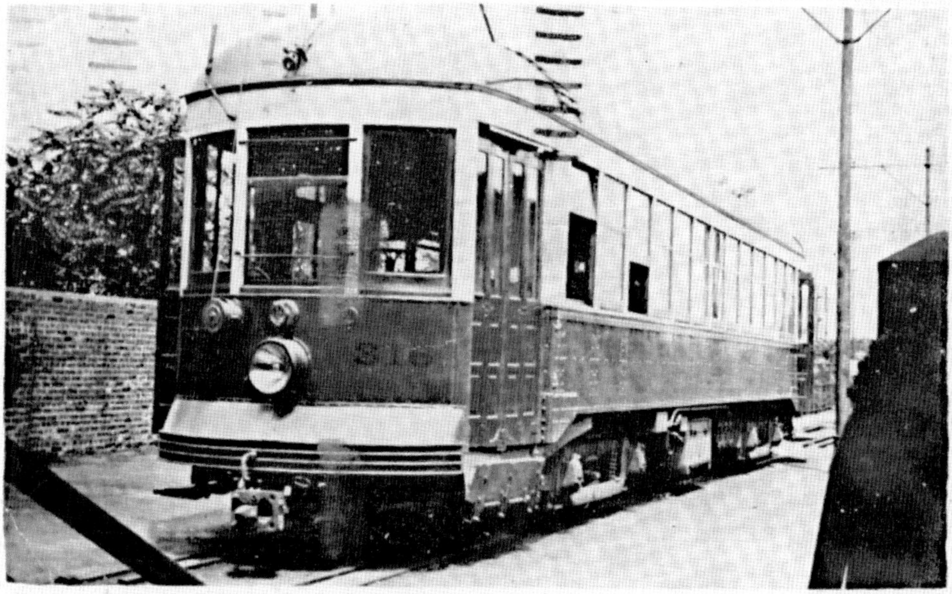

Richmond-Ashland Railway Car 316 at Richmond Terminal 1934

NO. 316 TROLLEY. Frank Jay Gould built the Richmond and Chesapeake Railway Company. By 1907, trolleys took passengers 14 miles round-trip from Ashland to the terminal at Laurel and Broad. In 1917, Gould sold the line that became the Richmond-Ashland Railway. In 1938, the last trolley left Ashland at 11 p.m., driven to its final destination by two locals. The copper wire and 2,800 tons of rail were sold for $35,000. Much of the steel went to Japan. One Ashlander remarked, "They probably hurled it back at us at Pearl Harbor!" (Woody and Susan Tucker.)

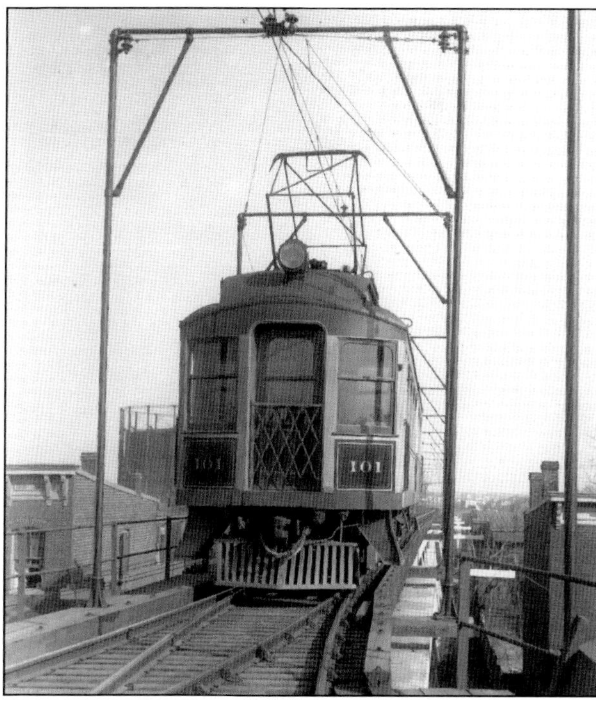

MARSHALL STREET VIADUCT. A half-mile-long bridge crossed Bacon's Quarter Branch of Shockoe Creek to join Brook Turnpike in Henrico County as well as the double tracks of the Seaboard Air Line Railway. The bridge was so ruggedly built that 50 years later, it was difficult to dismantle. Dorothy Jones remembers: "That trestle was probably as high as a house. But it looked like it was as high as Mt. Everest. You just looked down at your death. I think there were lots of people who closed their eyes during that part of the trip." (Woody and Susan Tucker.)

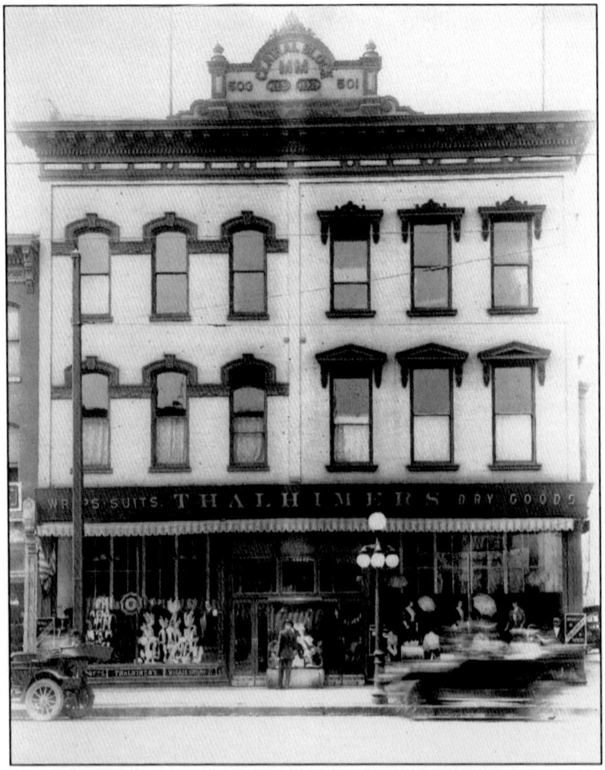

THALHIMER'S. Opened in 1842 as a dry goods shop, Thalhimer's eventually grew to a huge department store chain selling everything imaginable. Richmonders and Ashlanders alike still remember the six-layer chocolate cake, meeting under the clock, and shopping in white gloves. (Dementi Studios.)

MILLER AND RHOADS. Throughout its 105-year life span, Miller and Rhoads played an active role in the extended community, frequently working to better the community and to promote downtown. The store was incorporated in 1906, at the same time the trolley line was being used between Richmond and Ashland. By 1909, it had acquired nearly half a city block fronting Broad Street. (Dementi Studios.)

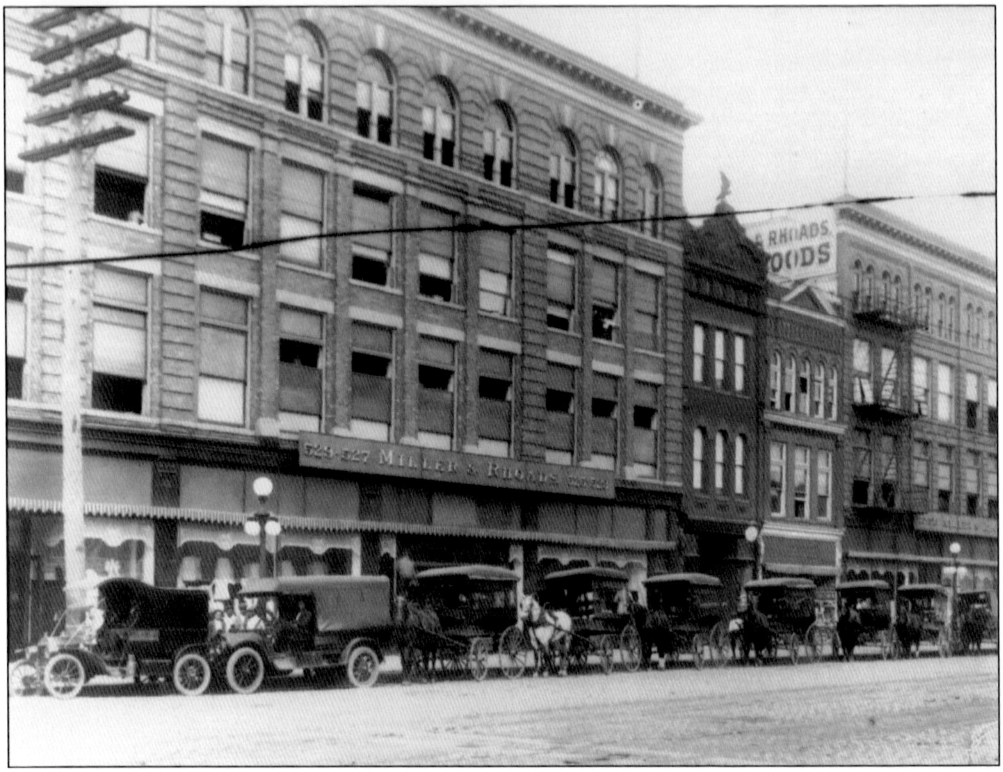

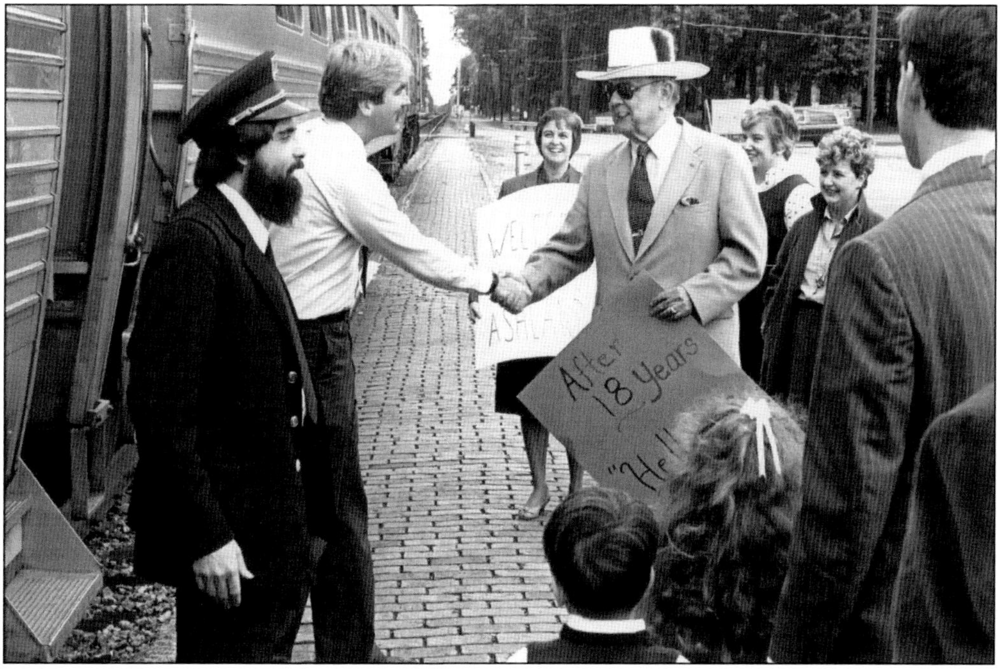

REOPENING PASSENGER STATION. Passenger service was suspended in Ashland in 1967. For 18 years, the old train station, once crowded with passengers, languished and fell into neglect. In the early 1980s, passenger service was resumed. Mayor Dick Gillis made a point to be there the day the trains stopped in Ashland once again. (*Herald-Progress.*)

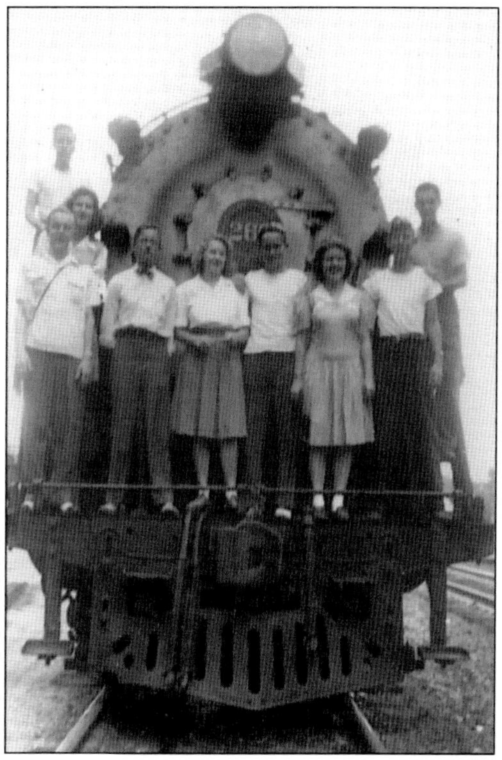

A MOMENT IN TIME. Visible from left to right are Eloise Goddin Piccolo, Adolphus Shepherd, Curtis Palmore, Gladys Coulter, Leslie D. Campbell Jr., Doris Harlow Quarles, A.B. Vaughan Jr., and J.D. Cichielo. Partially obscured in the back on the far left is thought to be T. Roy Jarrett. In 1942, they asked the engineer's permission to pose for this picture while the train was stopped in Ashland. (Eloise Piccolo.)

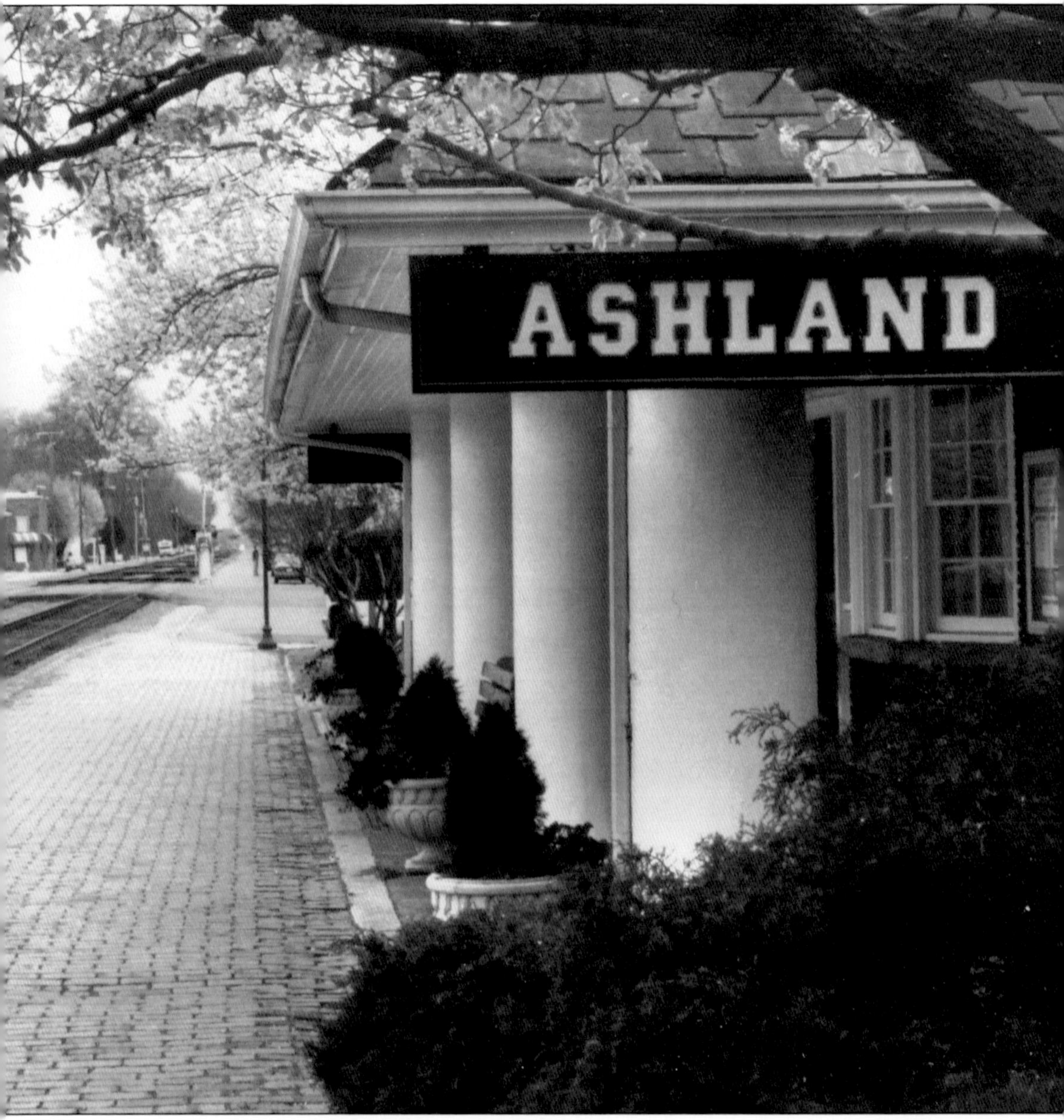

ASHLAND STATION. The heartbeat of this old railroad town is, naturally, the Train Station Visitors' Center. Thick white columns accent the prominence of this handsome depot built in 1923 in the Dutch colonial style. Duncan Lee—designer of the Governor's Mansion—designed the station. (*Herald-Progress.*)

Two

RANDOLPH-MACON

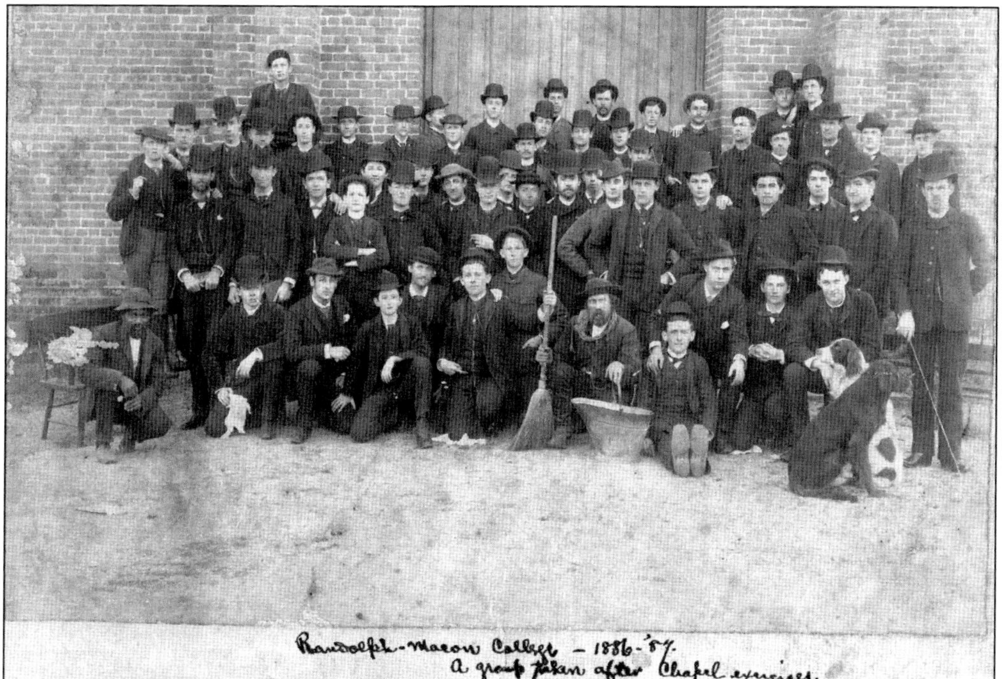

RANDOLPH-MACON STUDENT BODY, 1886. Chartered by the General Assembly of Virginia in February of 1830, Randolph-Macon is the oldest Methodist college in America. The depression following the Civil War was one of the leading factors in the college's 1868 move from its original home in Mecklenburg County to the resort village of Ashland, where the train provided easier access to more students, who could provide revenue to the college. The college brought a new vitality to Ashland, which saw local merchants, restaurants, and boarding houses flourish from the infusion of cash from the student body. (Randolph-Macon Archives.)

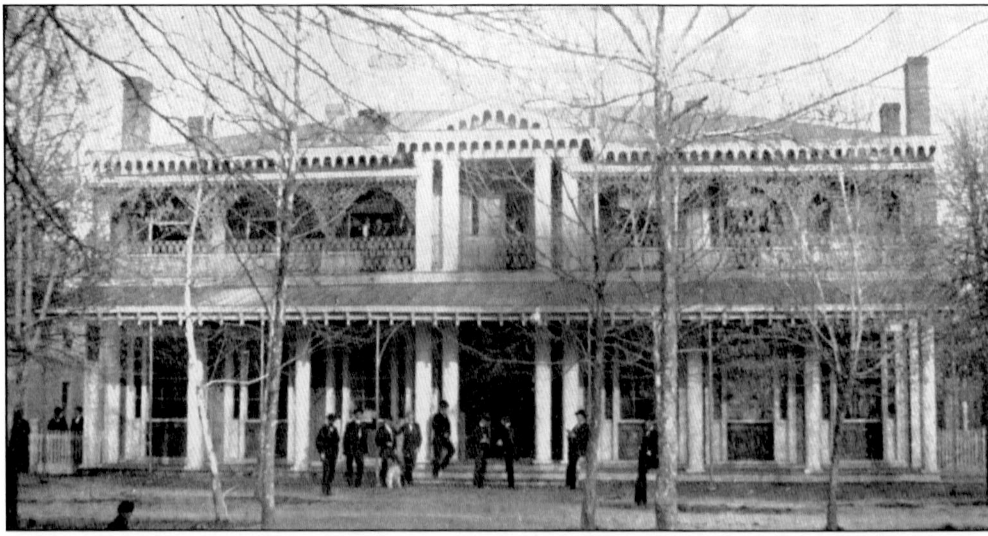

Slash Cottage. Between 1845 and 1848, the RF&P created a resort north of the intersection of what is today College and Railroad Avenues. Rail travel was a novelty, and Richmond residents came for the ride and to picnic and dance. When Randolph-Macon (RMC) opened on October 1, 1868, this building was converted into a chapel and halls for the two literary societies. The hotel became the main dormitory, and the lower floor was made into lecture rooms; the bowling alleys and shooting galleries became dormitories. (Woody and Susan Tucker.)

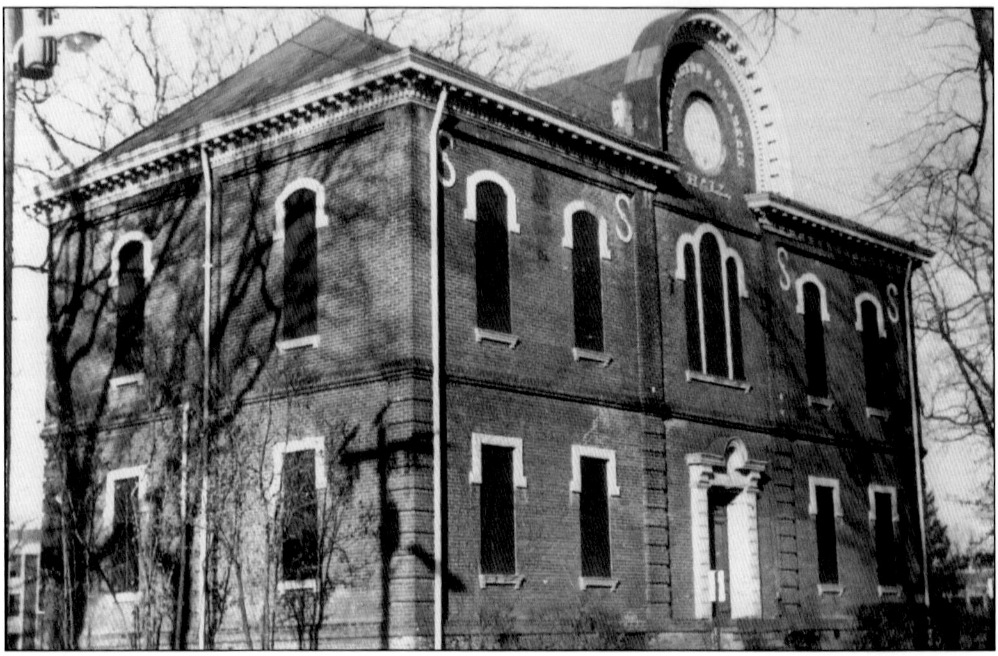

Washington Franklin Hall. The first brick structure erected in Ashland and the first permanent structure on the RMC campus was built by the Washington and Franklin Literary Societies to house the two groups and provide a debating venue. A successful drive was conducted in the late 1970s to restore this much-loved structure on the RMC campus. (*Herald-Progress.*)

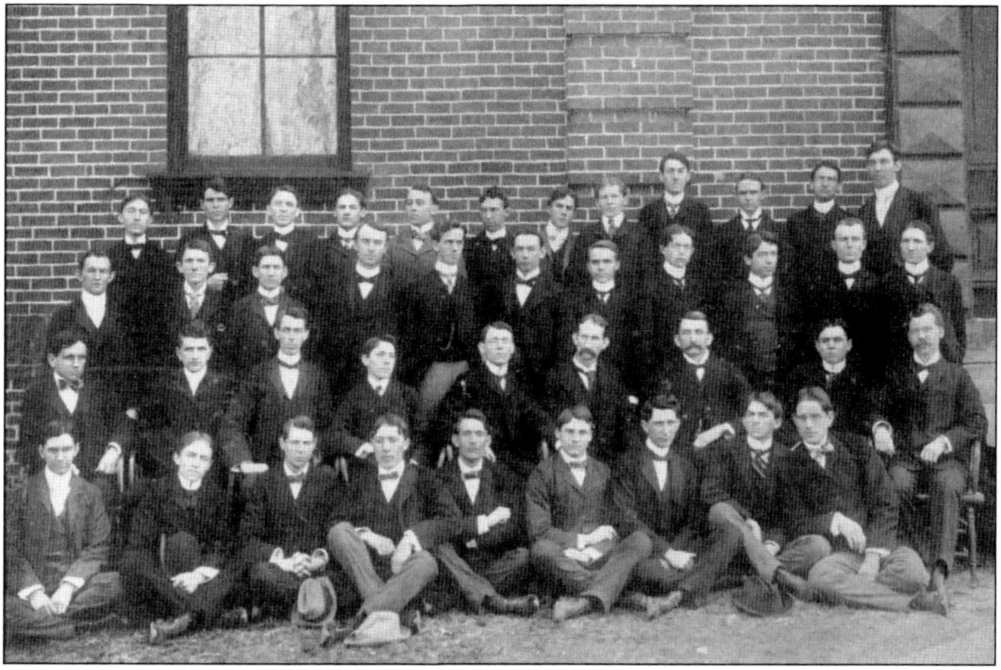

The Washington and Franklin Literary Societies. These debating societies were influential campus organizations. Tired of boarding houses and cramped facilities in the old hotel, they set out to build their own meeting rooms and libraries. Raising the funds themselves and finding it difficult going, the societies nevertheless completed the hall in 1872. Above is the Washington Society and below the Franklin in 1900. (Randolph-Macon Archives.)

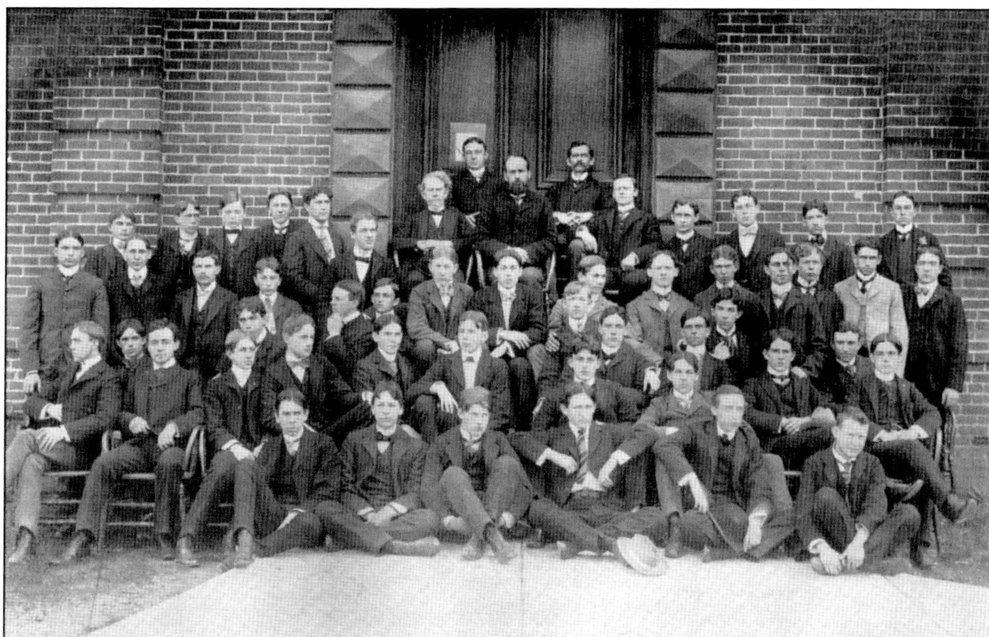

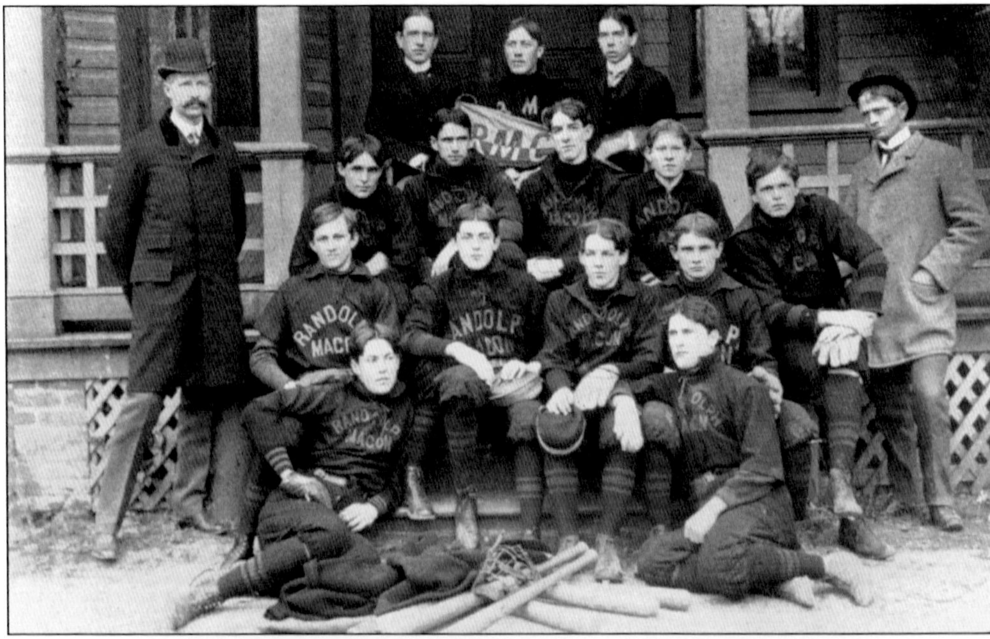

Baseball Team. The college had teams for baseball, football, gymnastics, and tennis, among others. In 1900, officials from Randolph-Macon, Richmond College, Hampden-Sydney College, Virginia Military Institute, Washington and Lee University, Virginia Polytechnic, and the University of Virginia (UVA) met at UVA to form the Virginia Intercollegiate League. (Randolph-Macon Archives.)

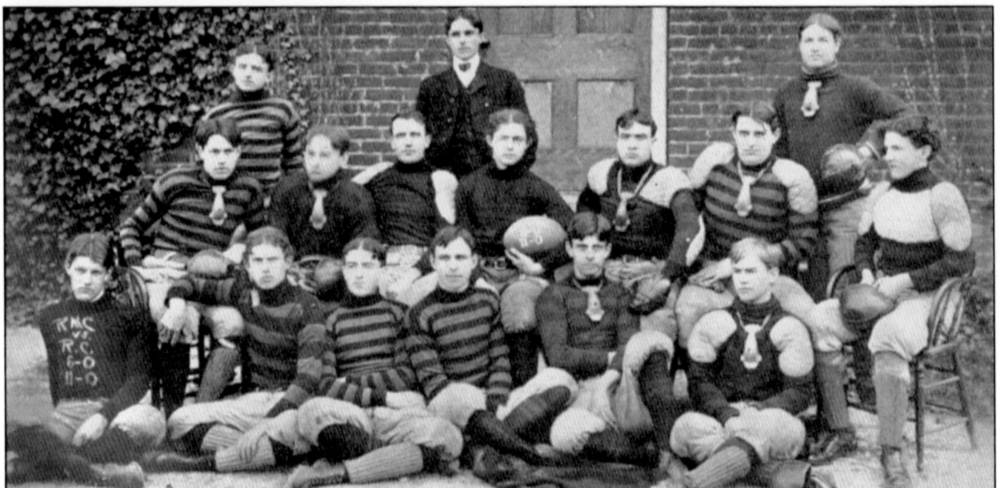

Football Season, 1902. Randolph-Macon defeated Richmond College in a game that was described in local papers as "a beauty." Four thousand enthusiastic spectators watched the contest, which was won by the visiting team during the first half. The 1902 *Yellow Jacket* said, "Richmond boys braced up in the latter half, but without avail. The final score was R-MC 6, Richmond College 0. The LINE UP—Center, C.E. Williams, Left Guard, R.T. Wilson, Left Tackle, W.B. McNeal, Left End, W.T. Edwards, Right Half Back, F.M. Bond, Right Guard, R.E. McCabe, Right TACKLE W.F. Kellam, Right End, J.M. Lear, Quarter Back, J.T. Robinson, Left Half Back, J.M. Leake, Full Back James Woodward." (*Yellow Jacket.*)

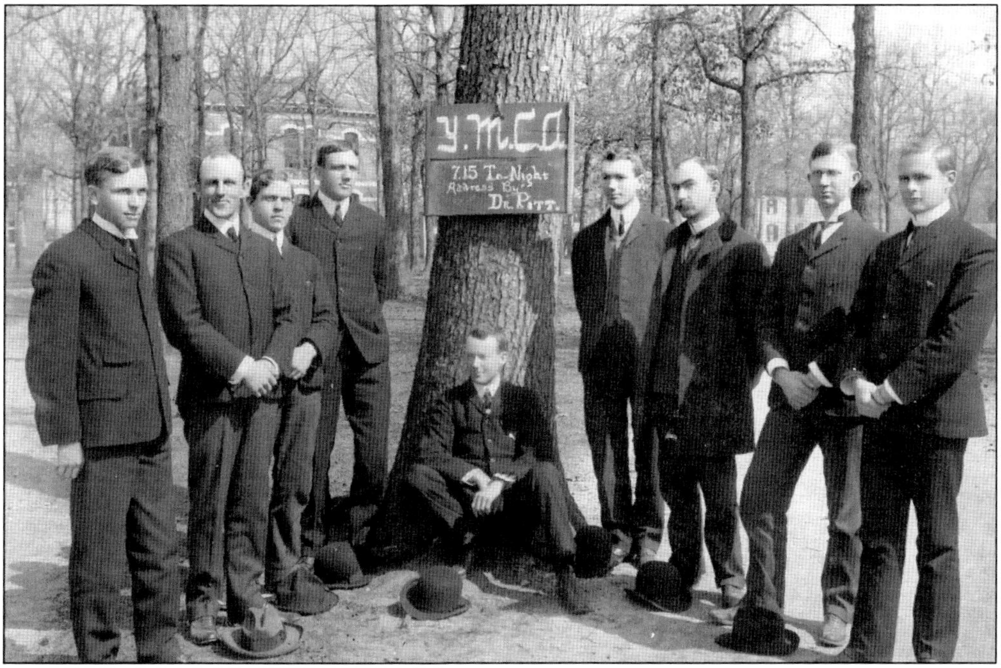

YMCA. The YMCA was a robust organization in 1902 and only one of many organizations that were popular on the Randolph-Macon campus. Here it is advertising a lecture by Dr. Jacob Pitt. (Randolph-Macon Archives.)

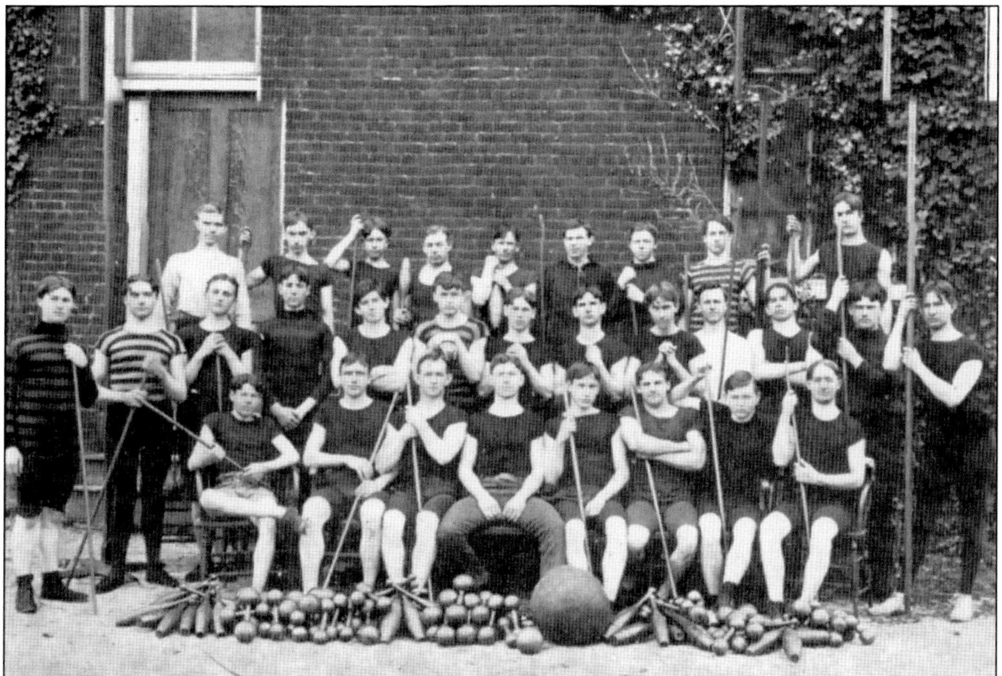

ATHLETIC CLUB. Without the elaborate equipment of today's gymnastic teams, this 1901 Athletic Club honed their skills with medicine balls and Indian Clubs. (Randolph-Macon Archives.)

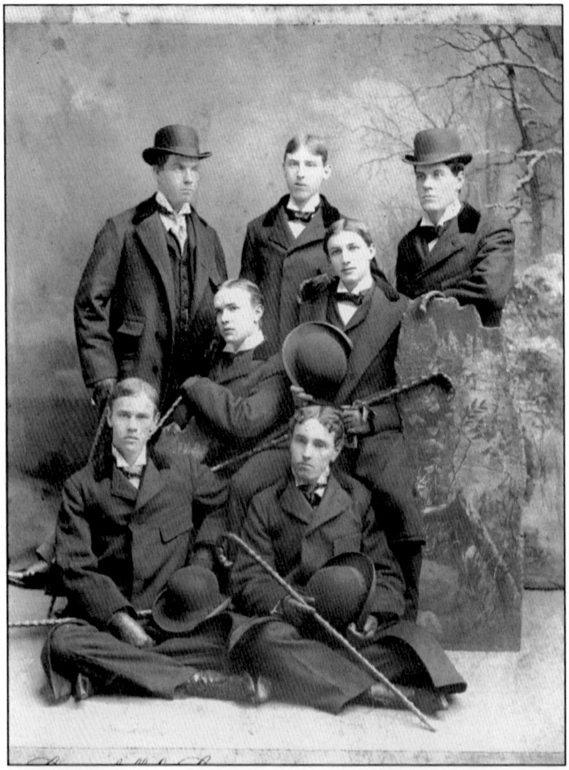

GAMMA GAMMA CHAPTER. From school year 1895–1896 comes this photograph of the members of the Gamma Gamma chapter of the Sigma Chi fraternity. Shown from left to right are (front row) Henry A. Christian and Albert H. Licklider; (middle row) A.C. Southall and P.H. Drewry; (back row) W.S. Denna, James Muller, and S.H. Watts. (Randolph-Macon Archives.)

THE DELTAS. RMC and the town were tightly woven in 1901. Many local families sent their boys to school here. Women were fraternity sweethearts but not resident students until 1971. Shown here from left to right are (front row) Annie Lee Blincoe and Leonidas Arnold Haden; (back row) Garnett Peatross, James Marcellus Cox, Louis Fielding Tysinger, Conde Roy Bridges, and William Benjamin Gates. (Pen and Betty Carol Stevenson.)

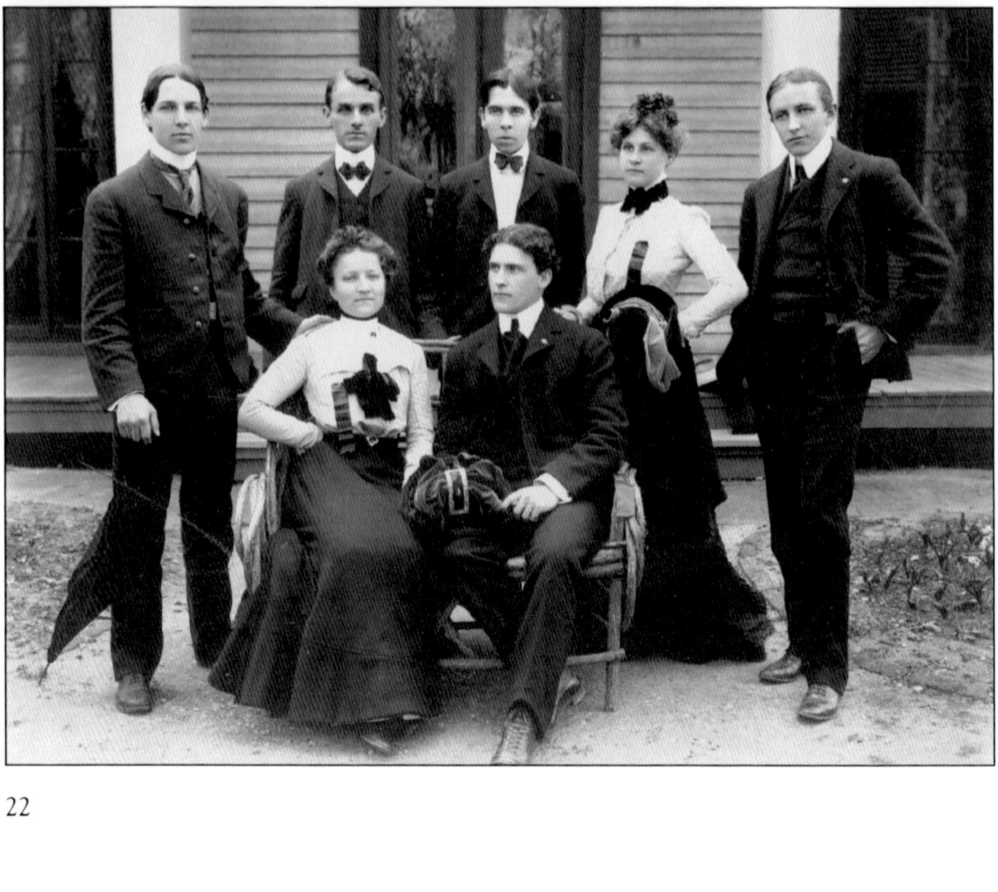

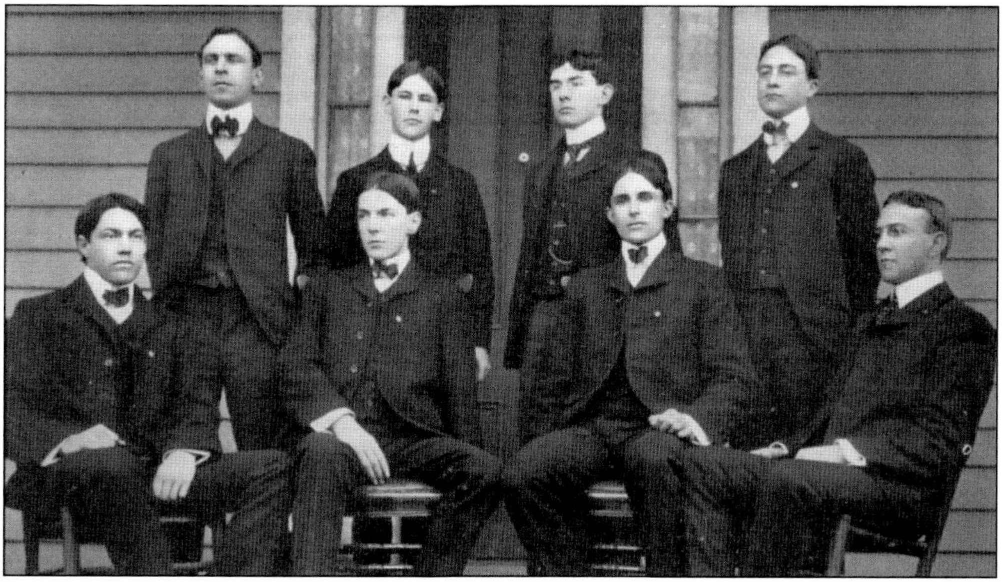

PHI KAPPA SIGMA (TAU CHAPTER). Established in 1872, this fraternity's colors were old gold and white, and their flower was the carnation. Members were Herbert Cannon Lipscomb, Robert Beale Davis, Richard Taylor Wilson, Francis Osgood Smith, Joseph Merritt Lear, Thomas Russell Jones, and Edward Leonidas Green. Unfortunately, they are not individually identified in the picture. (Randolph-Macon Archives.)

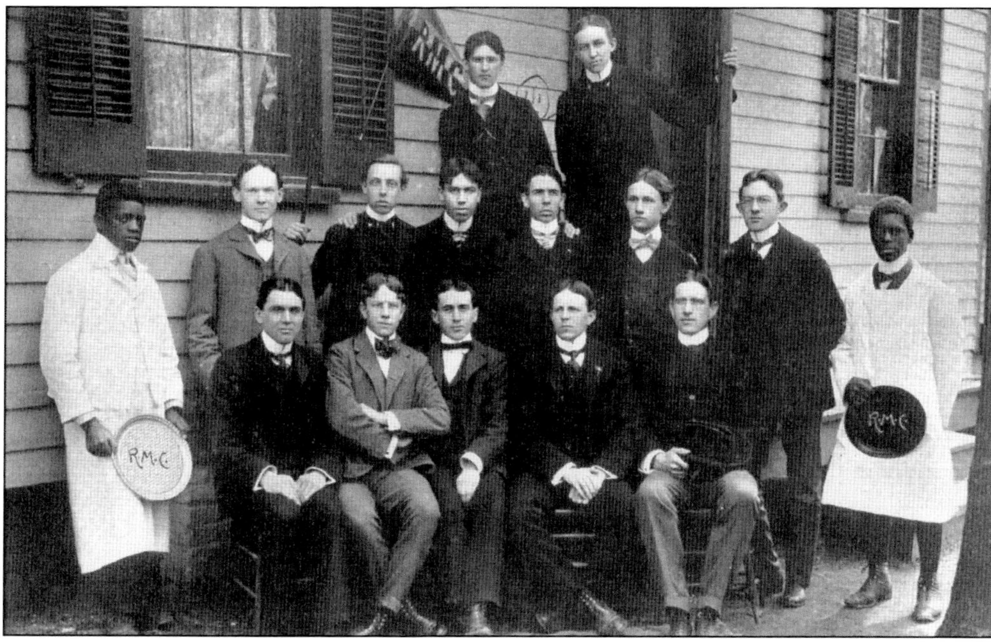

THE SATURDAY NIGHT EATING CLUB. They drank Paregoric and Jamaica Ginger as their "drinks." Their motto was "One, two, three! Who are we? Red-hot members of the S.E.C.!" Their club song was "There Are Moments when We Would Like to Be Alone." Their clubhouse was at 1313 Crocodile Alley. The group had such members as Lord High Chief Epicure (James Vickers in 1900), Lord High Eat-What's in Sight, and Lord High Distributor of Big Pieces. (Randolph-Macon Archives.)

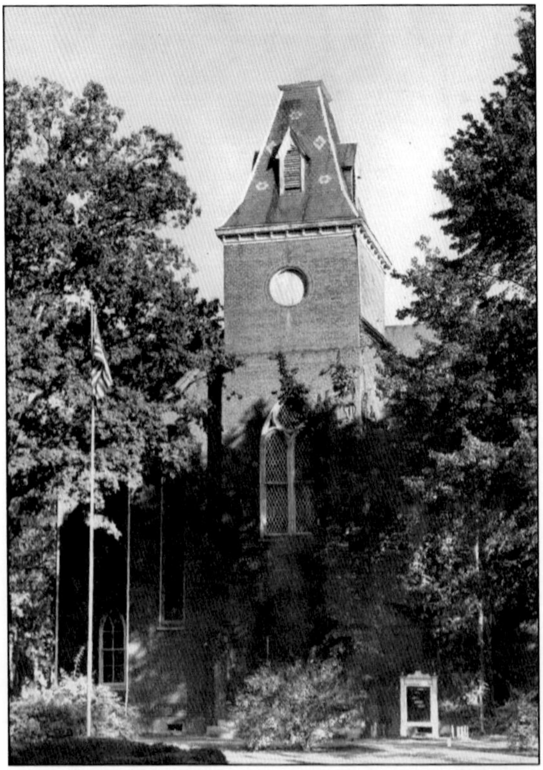

DUNCAN MEMORIAL CHAPEL. At the death of President James A. Duncan in 1877, the Methodists of Ashland joined with the college to erect a chapel as a memorial to him; this building burned and was replaced with the Duncan Memorial Chapel in 1879. The church sanctuary was upstairs, and the Randolph-Macon Chapel was downstairs, as well as classrooms. In 1955, the present Duncan Memorial Church was built on the northeast corner of College Avenue and Henry Street. (Randolph-Macon Archives.)

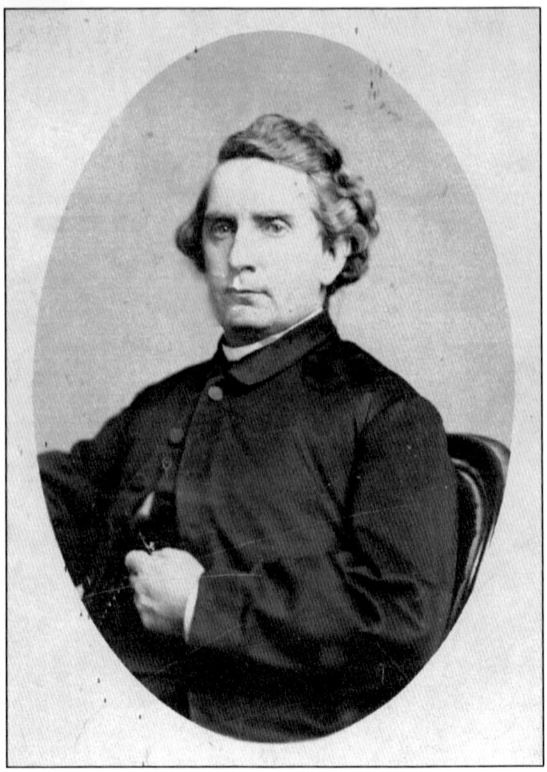

REV. JAMES A. DUNCAN. A leader of unusual gifts and an alumnus of the class of 1849, he brought a small but distinguished faculty to Ashland, and the college began to enjoy an influence as one of the inspiring intellectual centers of the South. His administration extended over the years 1868 to 1877. (Randolph-Macon Archives.)

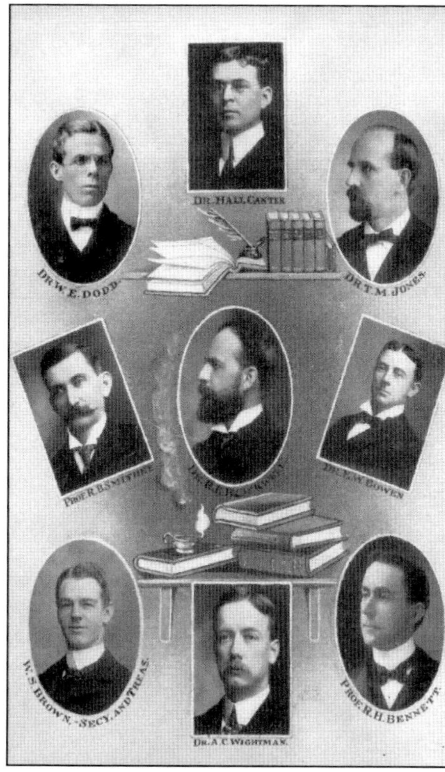

RANDOLPH-MACON COLLEGE FACULTY. At center is Dr. Emory Blackwell. Clockwise from top are Dr. Hall Canter; Dr. T.M. Jones; Dr. W.D. Bowen; Prof. R.H. Bennett; Dr. A.C. Wightman; W.S. Brown, secretary-treasurer; Prof. R.B. Smithey; and Dr. W.E. Dodd. (Randolph-Macon Archives.)

DR. ROBERT EMORY BLACKWELL. During his administration, Dr. Blackwell made notable contributions to the cause of higher education and came to be recognized as one of the South's great educational leaders. His humanitarian outlook was reflected in many activities but particularly in the field of race relations. From its establishment until his death, he was chairman of the Virginia Commission on Interracial Cooperation. Blackwell (standing fourth from left) and his wife, Epia Duncan Blackwell (third row at left), relax with Randolph-Macon students on the front steps of the Blackwell home at 403 South Center Street in Ashland. (Randolph-Macon Archives.)

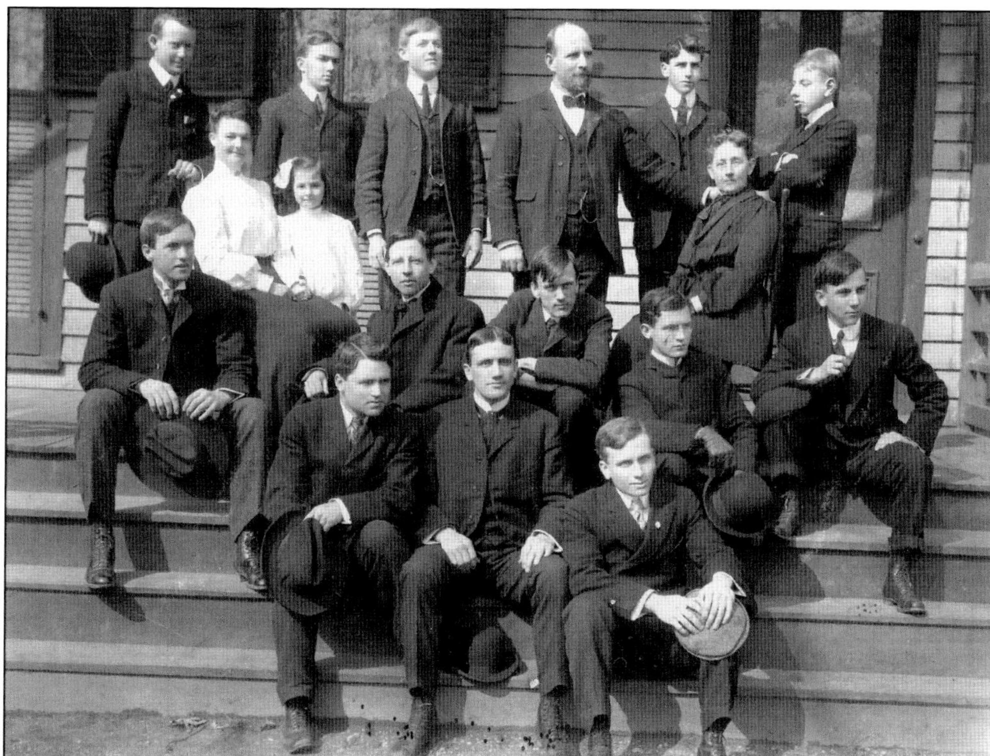

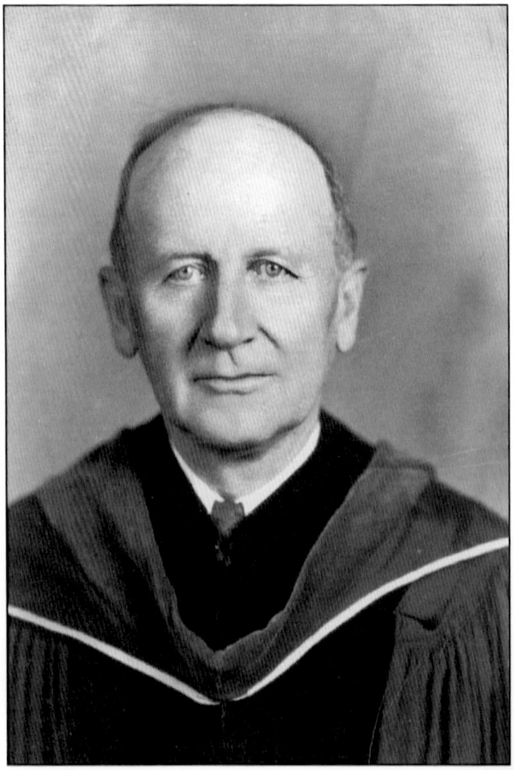

S.C. HATCHER. S.C. Hatcher was acting president of Randolph-Macon during the 1938–1939 session. (Woody and Susan Tucker.)

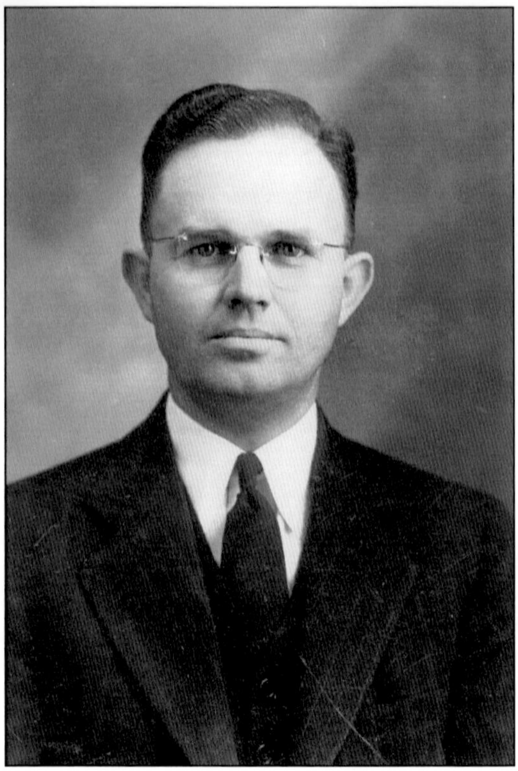

J. EARL MORELAND. A well-known and respected member of the community for many years, Moreland became the 11th president in June 1939. (*Herald-Progress*.)

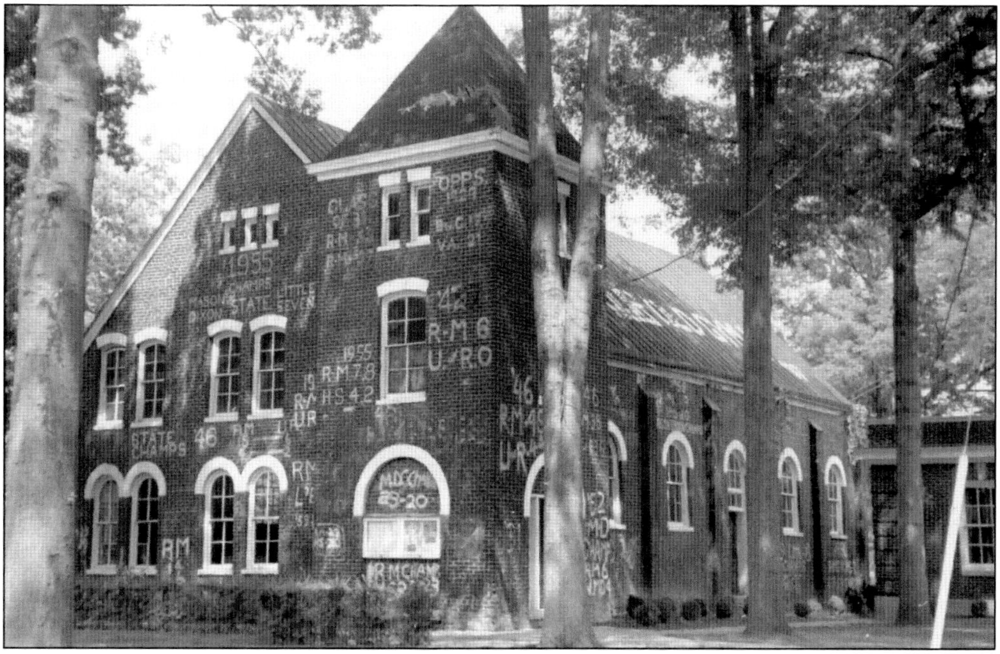

PACE GYM. J.B. Pace donated $3,000 to build this gymnasium in 1887 to promote "health, vigor and manly grace." It is said to have been the earliest building in the South erected for the exclusive purpose of a gymnasium. The building has also served as a post office, a hall for the Commons Club, and an artist's studio where John Temple Witt modeled the statue of "Bojangles" Robinson, the famous African-American dancer from Richmond. It was used as a Yellow Jackets scoreboard before it was torn down in 1974. (Randolph-Macon Archives.)

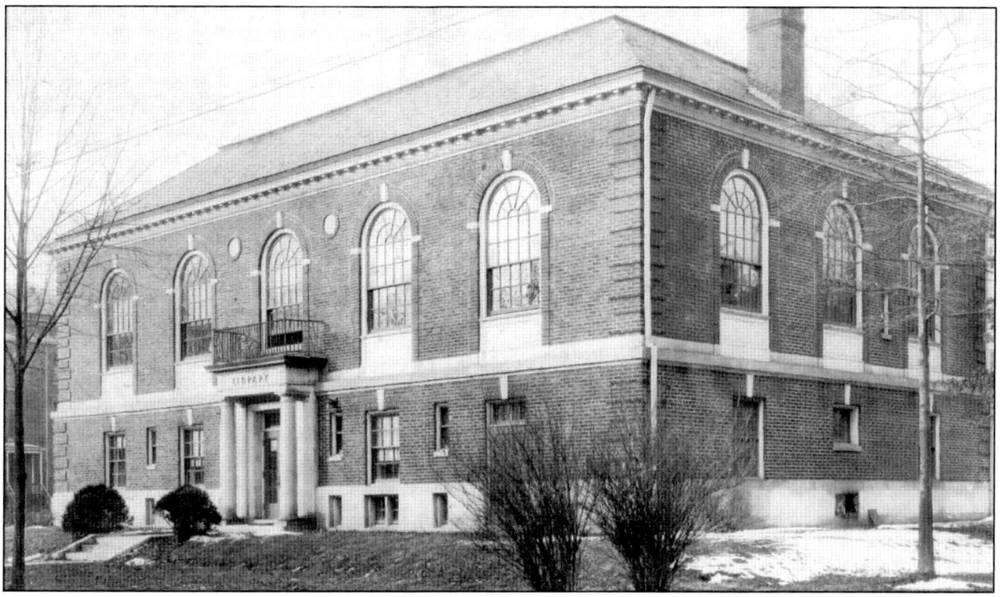

WALTER HINES PAGE LIBRARY. When a new library was built across the street, this building was named Peele Hall and used for administrative offices. Todie Grattan remembers when the students formed a human "conveyor belt" to transfer books from the old library to the new. (Terry Barnes Shaw.)

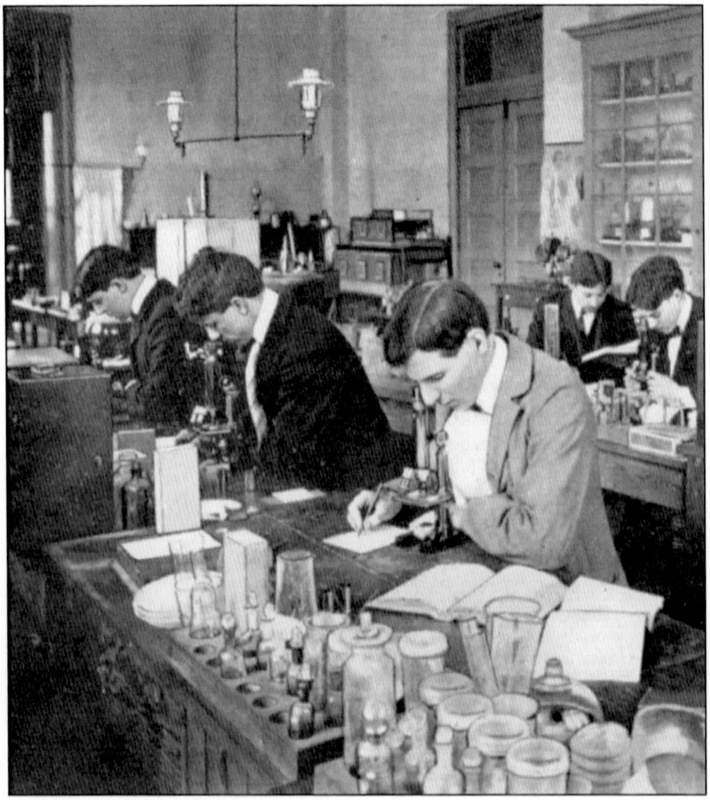

A FULL CURRICULUM. Perhaps it was in a laboratory like this that J.W. Lambert, Randolph-Macon student and president of the literary society, invented Listerine and conceived the beginning of his pharmaceutical company. (Randolph-Macon Archives.)

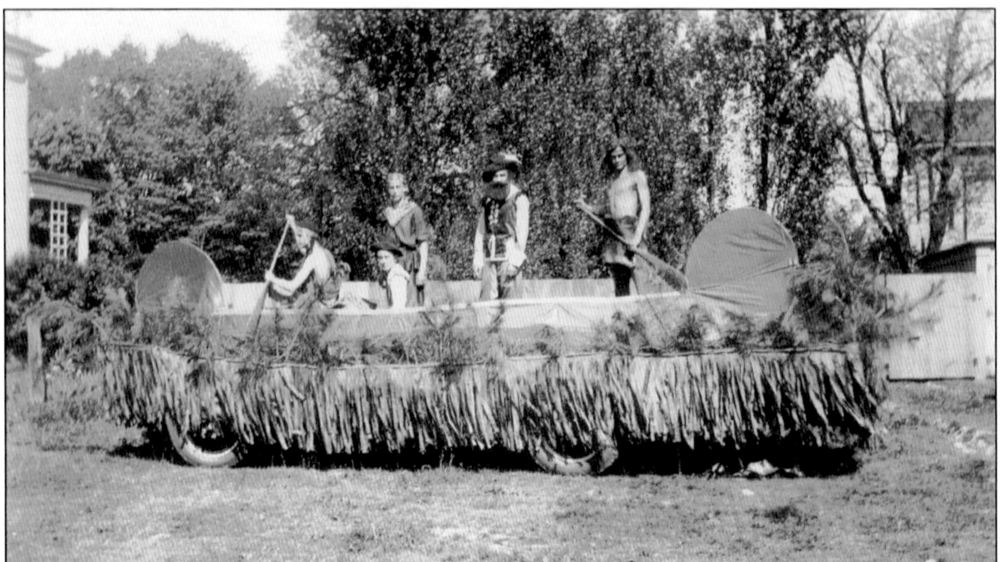

PARADE FLOAT TELLS HANOVER HISTORY. The story of early Hanover is re-enacted in this 1930s Randolph-Macon parade. (Terry Barnes Shaw.)

Three

BUSINESS

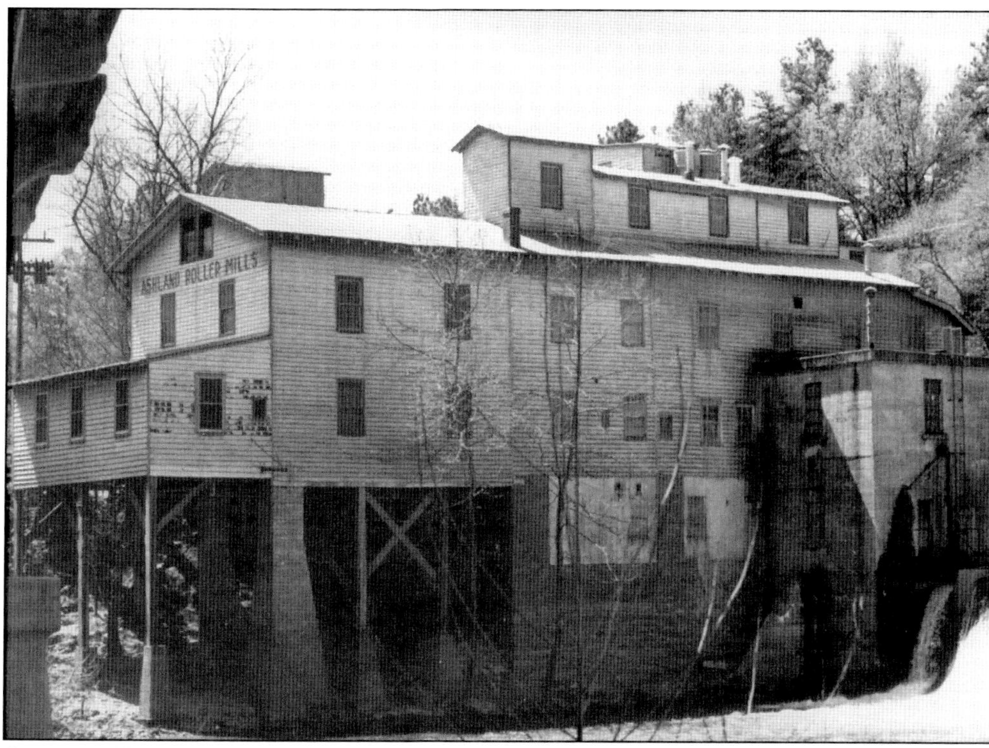

ASHLAND ROLLER MILLS. The home of Patrick Henry flour, meal, and feed, one of the oldest mill sites in the county is Ashland Roller Mills on the South Anna River. Originally known as Darracott's Mill, it was bought by W.W. Newman in 1872. During the devastation of the Johnston Flood in 1889, the mill was washed away, but the milldam remained. The mill was rebuilt in 1892. Newman's son, E.W., became the owner of the mill and president of the Piedmont Miller's Association. (Virginia Department of Alcohol Beverage Control.)

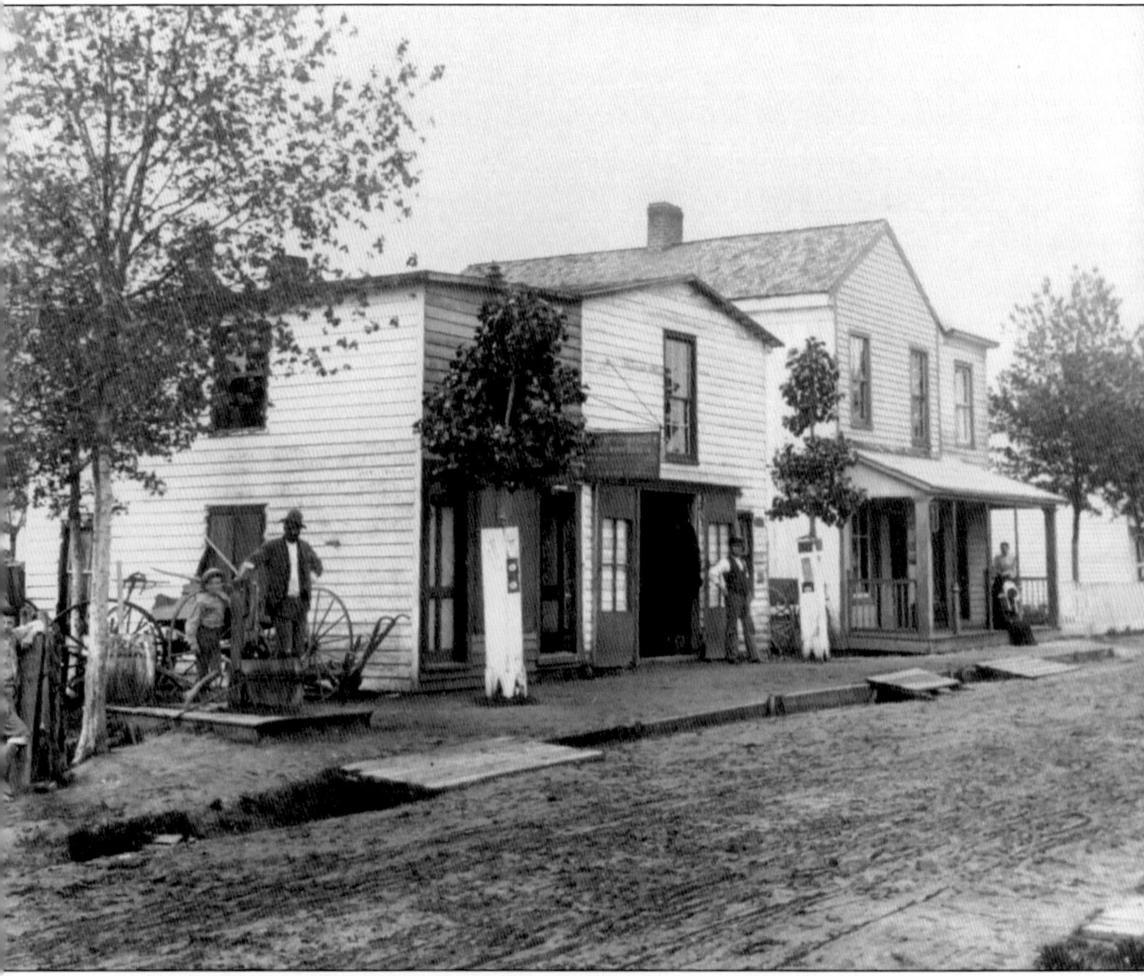

CLINTON WINSTON'S BLACKSMITH SHOP. Beginning in 1887, Winston's shop on Hanover Avenue, across from where the town office is today, provided several services. Customers entered the blacksmith's shop through the large doorway in the middle. Above the entrance on the second floor was an undertaker's facility and Alice Trotter's beauty salon. Next door to the right, the taller structure was the Winston family home. On the porch are Annie Cross (seated), who cooked for Dr. Day, a professor of religion at the time. Ethel Winston leans against the bannister. In the far background was another Winston home, where Hattie Winston was born in 1909. When Henry Dabney opened his funeral home, he offered Clinton Winston a partnership. Winston refused because he "liked things the old way." The shop was torn down in the spring of 1958. (Inez Gray.)

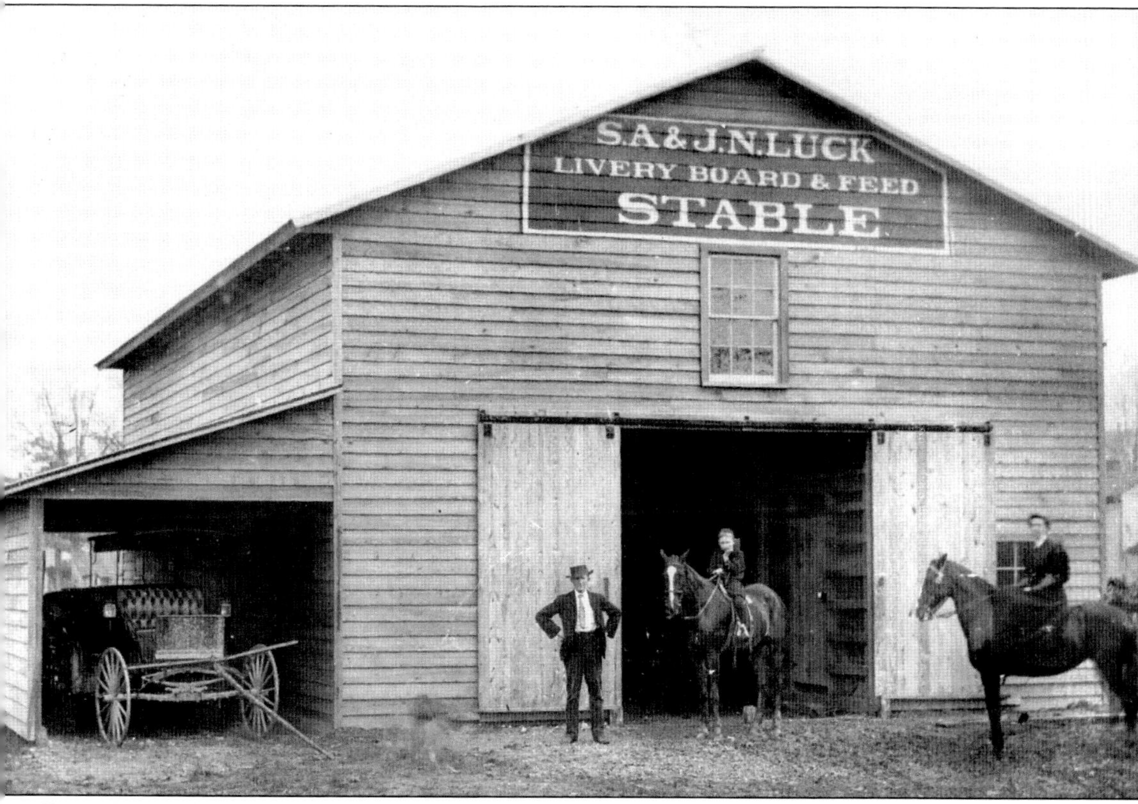

Luck Livery Stable Car Dealership. James Napoleon "Jimmy" Luck and his brother Samuel Apollos began a livery stable in Ashland as early as 1908. The dealership has moved several times, and it is one of the oldest continuously operated Chevrolet dealerships on the East Coast. (Ron Luck.)

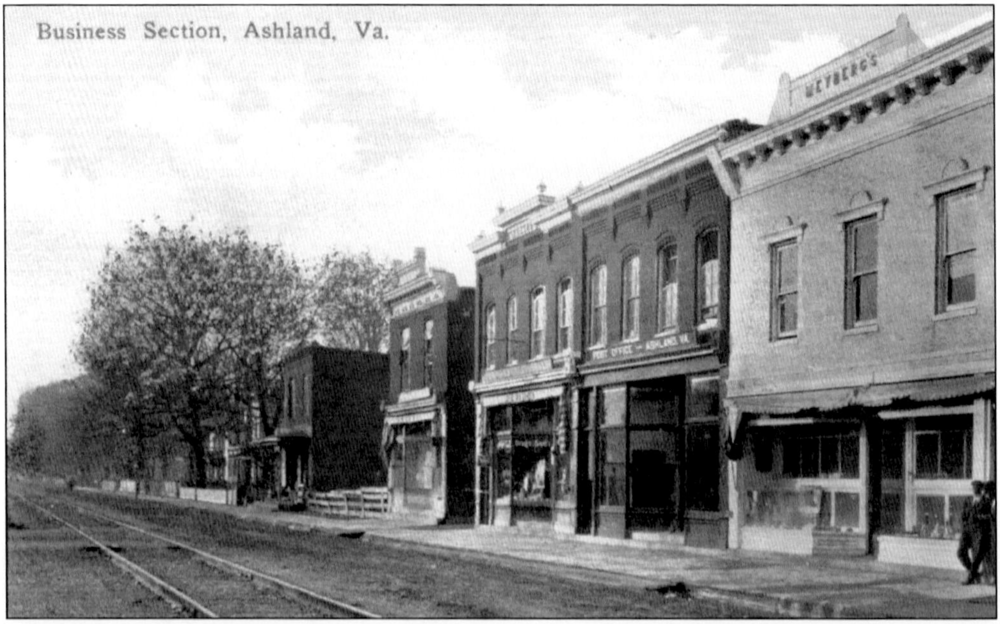

TURN-OF-THE-CENTURY ASHLAND. This photo was taken before double tracks were laid through Ashland. Meyberg's store, a children's favorite for penny candy lovingly dealt out by the gentle Mr. L.E.W. Meyberg, is flanked on the left by the old post office and then Hughes Drug Store. (Woody and Susan Tucker.)

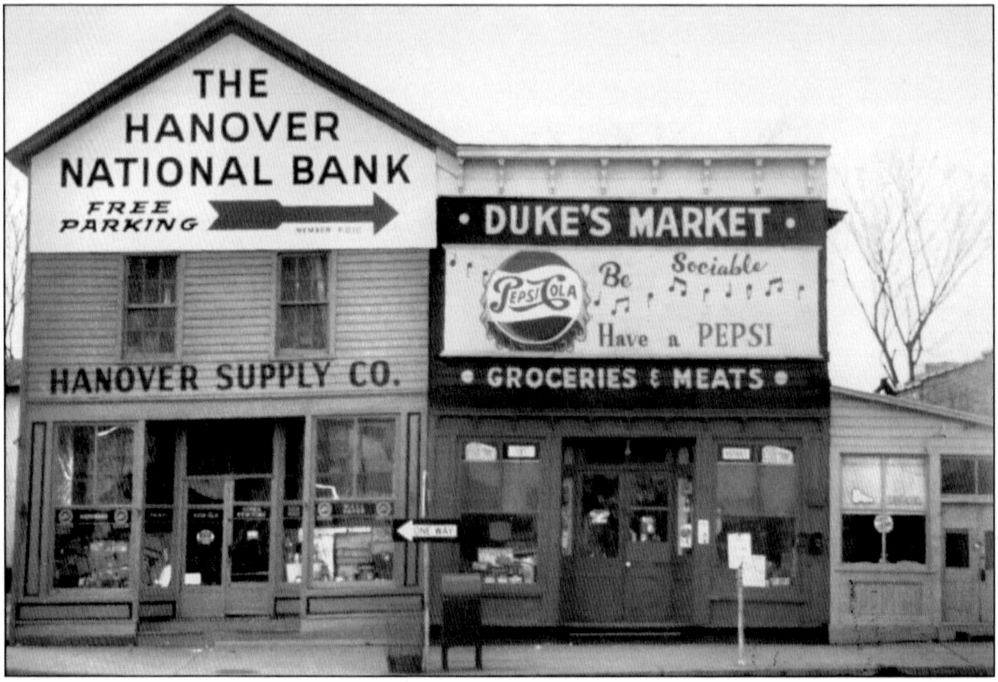

HANOVER SUPPLY COMPANY, 1959. Also known as Bumpass Hardware, the familiar landmark was located near the corner of Railroad Avenue and Thompson Street, once called Stebbins Corner, where Stebbins Store stood. The Hanover National Bank, located north of this cluster, was begun in 1903. (Eloise Piccolo.)

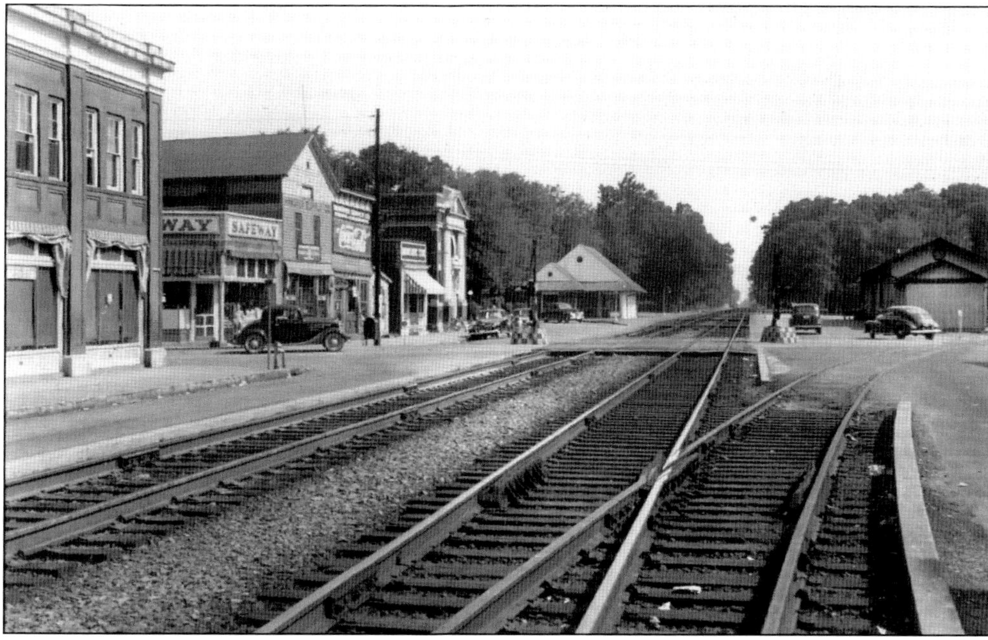

ASHLAND, LATE 1940S, HEADING NORTH. D.B. Cox's store is on the left. The Safeway has replaced the old Sanitary Market at Thompson and Railroad Avenue. The old freight depot is still visible on the far right, as is the long-since-departed spur that went behind the depot. (Terry Barnes Shaw.)

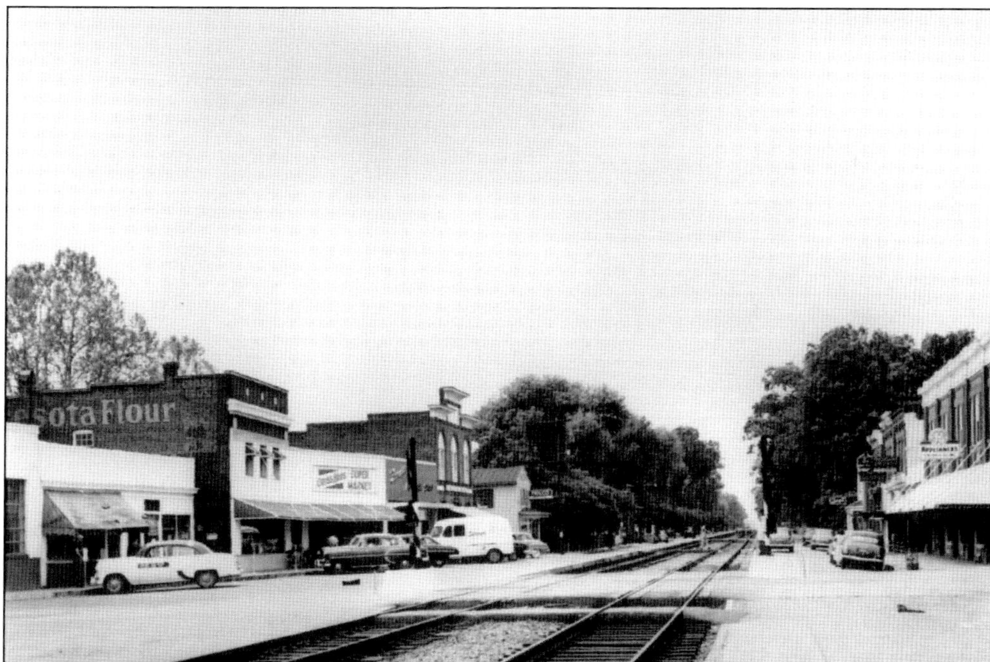

LOOKING SOUTH, 1950S. The painted sign on the side of Cross Brothers Grocery advertises flour, and the one on the front Pepsi. On the right, the awnings are unfurled in front of Cox's Store. (Virginia Department of Alcohol Beverage Control.)

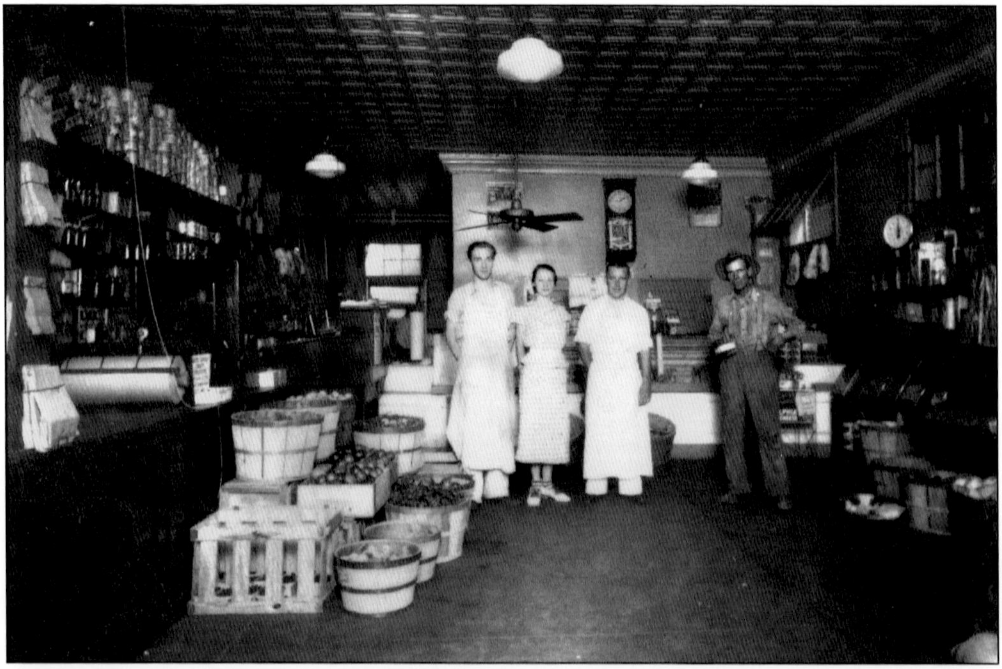

INSIDE CROSS BROTHERS. Cross Brothers Grocery has been in continuous business for almost 100 years. During the Depression, the store was the community's best friend, offering credit and friendship that helped some weather the storm. This photo was taken sometime in the 1930s. From left to right are Walter Lee Cross, Roberta Gilman, Pat Patterson, and Mr. ? Duke. Roberta Gilman remembered her dress well. She bought three for $1 at a Thalhimer's basement sale in Richmond. (Tom Willis.)

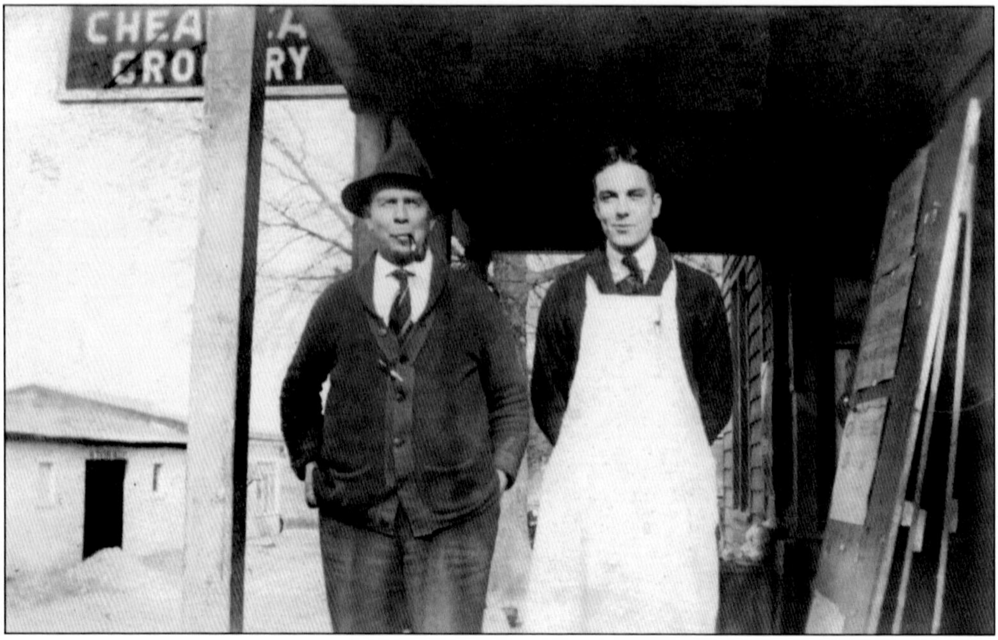

EARLY GROCERY STORE. Bill Perrin (left) and Aubrey Harlow are pictured in 1919 at an early grocery store on England Street. (P.K.Perrin.)

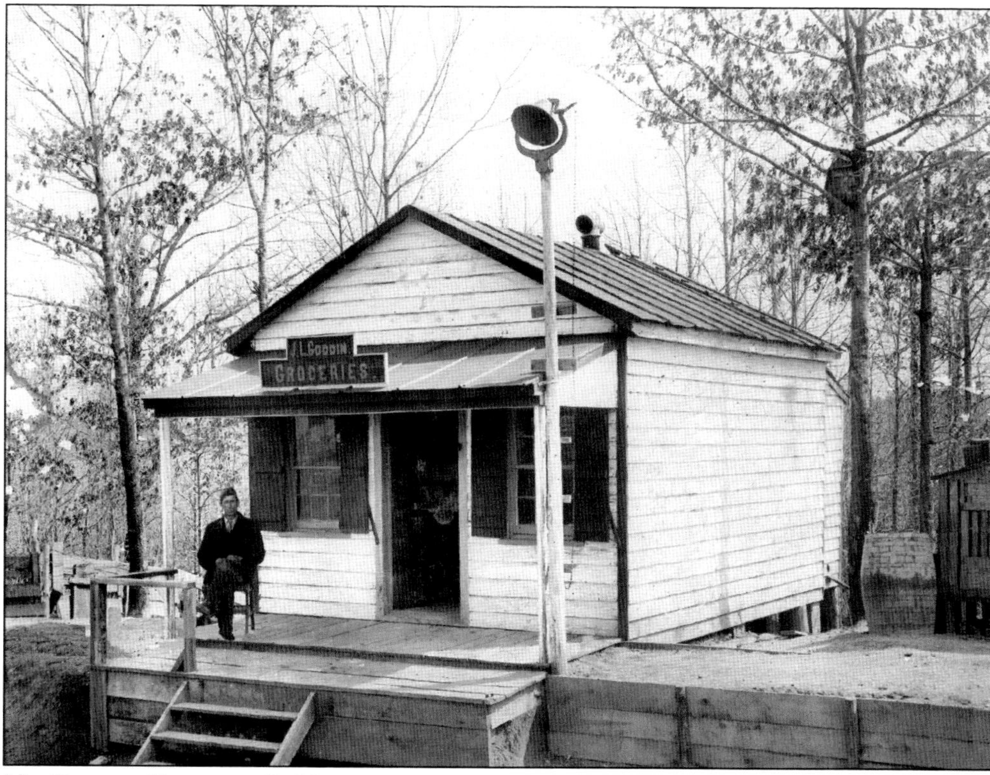

J.L. GODDIN GROCERY. Goddin opened his general store sometime around the turn of the century at Goddins' Hill, the area's premier sledding venue. The store provided a convenient shopping place for both black and white community members from nearby farms such as Hickory Hill. Although there was no large-scale refrigeration, Mrs. Goddin kept cream, milk, and her own churned butter in an icebox just in case anybody ran out. (Eloise Piccolo.)

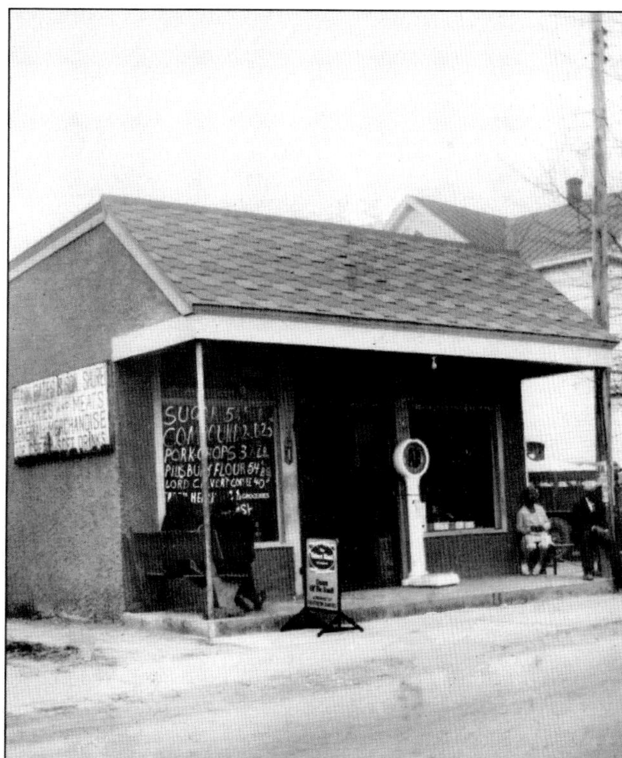

BATES STORE. Located on England Street near the Masonic Lodge and next door to the Octagon House, this general store was a local gathering place. It is thought the store was open until the mid-1930s. (P.K. Perrin.)

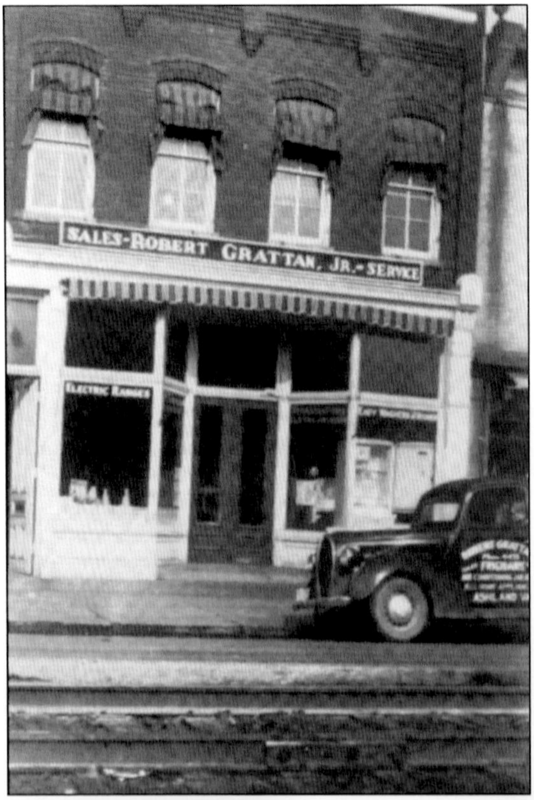

GRATTAN APPLIANCE STORE. Robert Grattan operated his Frigidaire dealership on Center Street for many years. It was also the place to buy RCA Victor and Columbia records and albums. (Harvey "Todie" Grattan.)

IVY'S BECAME BILL'S. Bill and Dick Piccolo came from New Jersey to visit their brother "Pic" and fell in love with Ashland. They bought Ivy's Restaurant from Ivy Blue. They hired Marie Harper to prepare Italian dishes. When the brothers sold the restaurant to Marie, she named it after her husband, Bill Taylor. It was a "hangout" for Randolph-Macon students. (Rick Gran.)

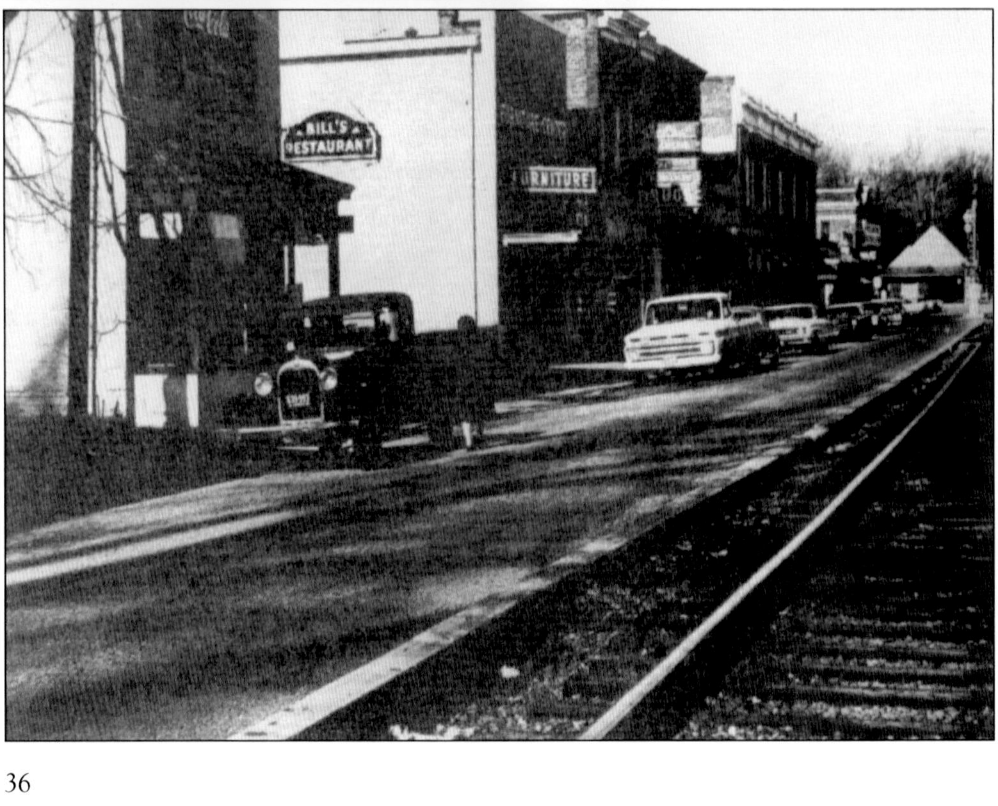

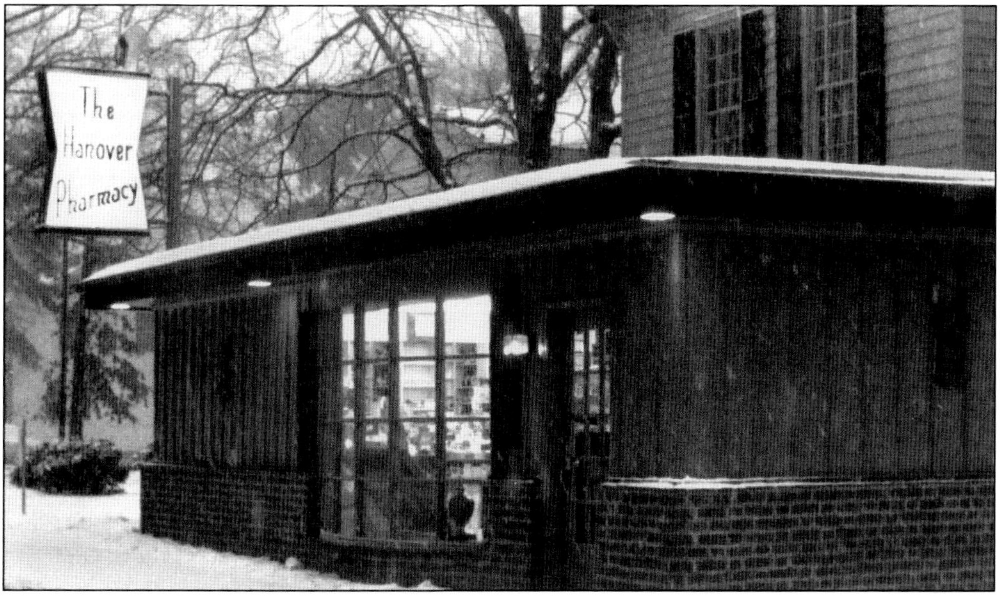

HANOVER PHARMACY. Though not one of the oldest stores in town, this pharmacy was run by Bob "Pic" and Eloise Piccolo in an old Colonial-style home with an extension added right on the sidewalk where the Henry Clay shopping center stands today. (Eloise Piccolo.)

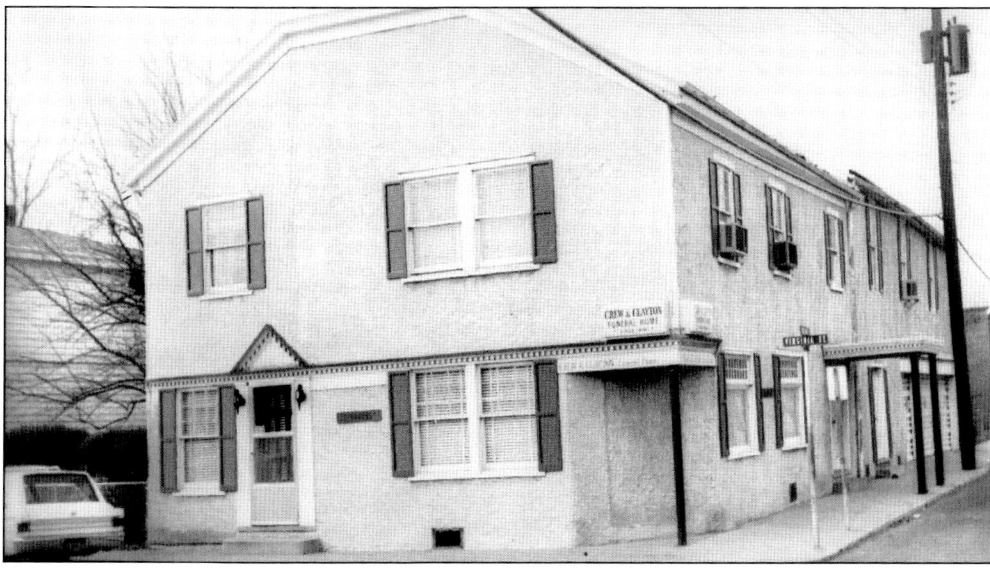

CREW AND CLAYTON FUNERAL HOME. This funeral home closed in 1977 after 103 years of service. The business was for many years the only funeral home in Hanover County. It was actually a coffin making business. "In that day and time, most bodies were taken care of in the home. An undertaker would come from Richmond and prepare the body in the home," recalls Mrs. Hope Ellis. "Mr. Crew and his daughter, Miss Christy, would make the coffins out of wood. Sometimes they'd put a varnish finish on it, and sometimes they'd cover it in black cloth. Then he used to take the coffin out to the house in a horse-drawn hearse." When Mr. Crew died in 1925, Miss Christy Crew took over the business. Mrs. Ellis played the organ at Crew and Clayton for about 25 years after it became a funeral home with services more like today. (*Herald-Progress*.)

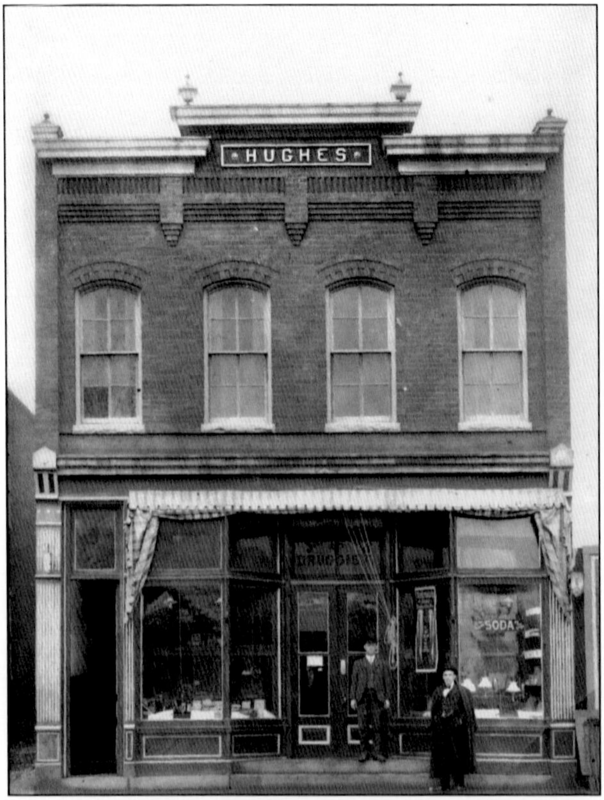

HUGHES DRUG. Hughes Drug advertised: "People of Hanover County. Bring your Doctor's prescriptions to our store. Here they will be filled promptly with absolute accuracy and best quality drugs. This is our tried and true policy that has made possible continuous operations for the past 57 years." The store opened its doors in 1889. This building is within the Ashland Historical District and is listed on the National Register of Historic Places and the Virginia Landmarks Register. (Hughes family.)

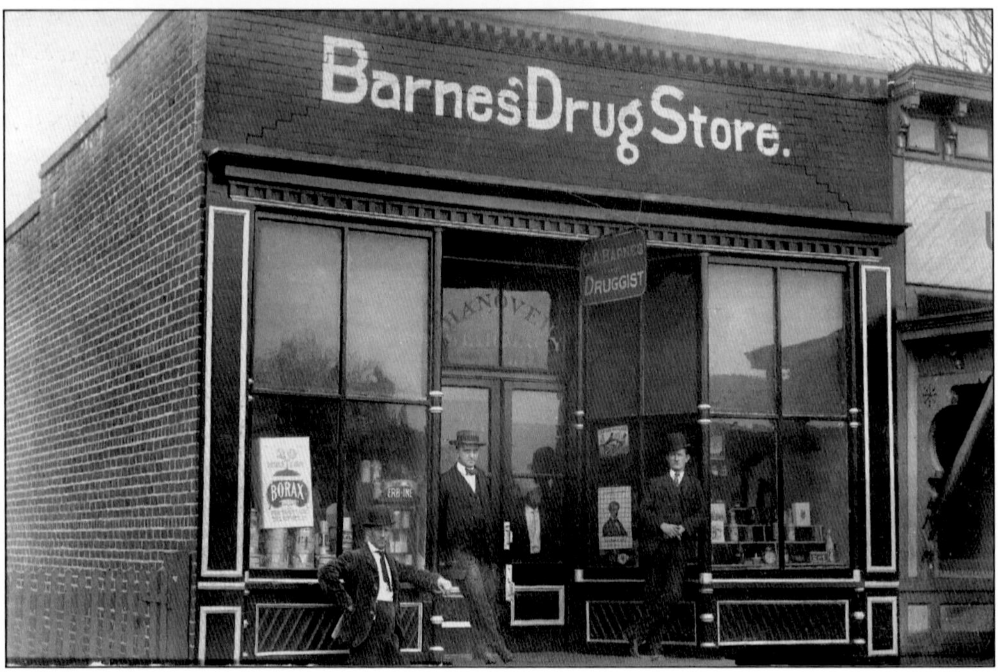

BARNES DRUG. Clyde Barnes opened his drug store sometime around 1899. It was located where Suzanne's Homemades stands today on Railroad Avenue. (Terry Barnes Shaw.)

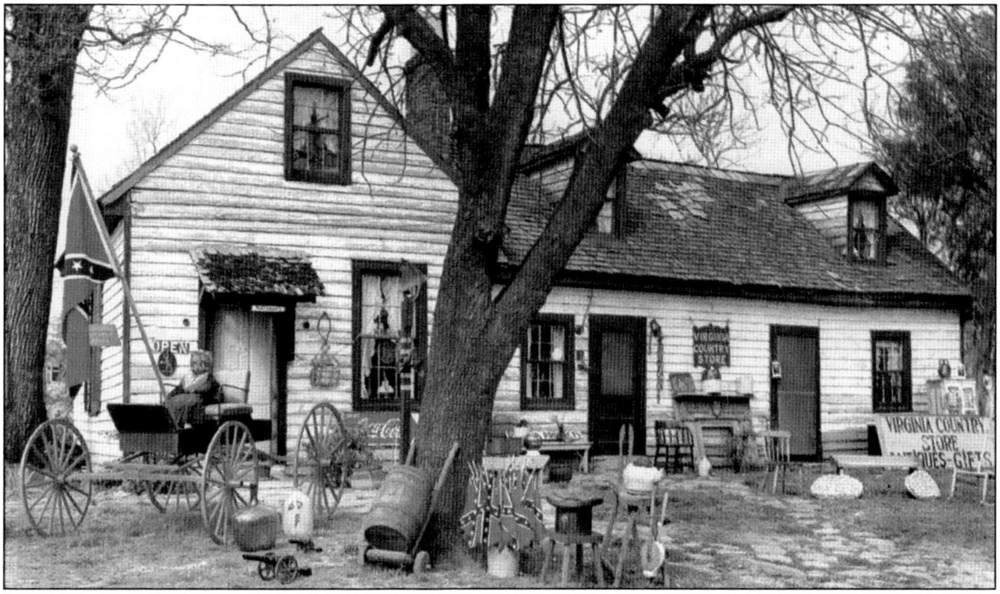

ASHCAKE INN. Gone now, the inn stood on the northeast corner of Ashcake Road and U.S. Route 1. Built in Colonial times, it became a tearoom in the 1920s run by Pearl Woolfolk (Webb) and Emily Carter (DeJarnette). People would travel out from Richmond for the chicken-a-la-king, Nannie Henry's fried chicken, cheese mousse, homemade bread, country ham, peach and strawberry ice cream, and pies. When this photo was taken, the building had become the Virginia Country Store. (*Herald-Progress.*)

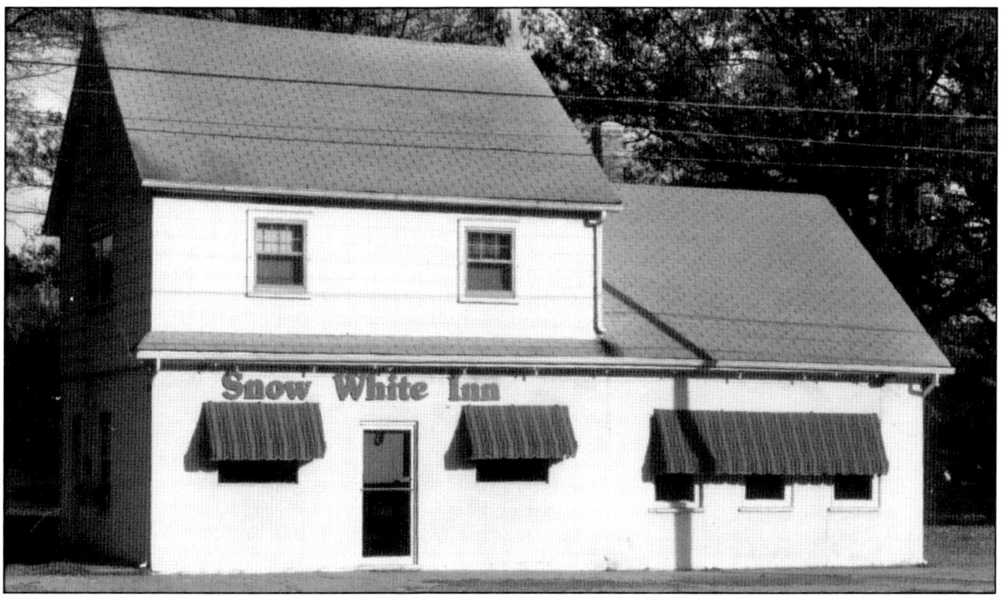

SNOW WHITE INN. Although not strictly in Ashland, this was certainly a part of the community. Who can forget the best barbecue on the planet? Certainly the local and state police who crowded the Snow White Inn on Route 1 for nearly 50 years did not. "Miss Bill" Koch said of her barbecue, "There ain't a thing in this pan but meat. . . . All I can say is that it must be very eatable." The aromas from the soup and barbecue cooking on an old woodstove are still remembered. (Rick Gran.)

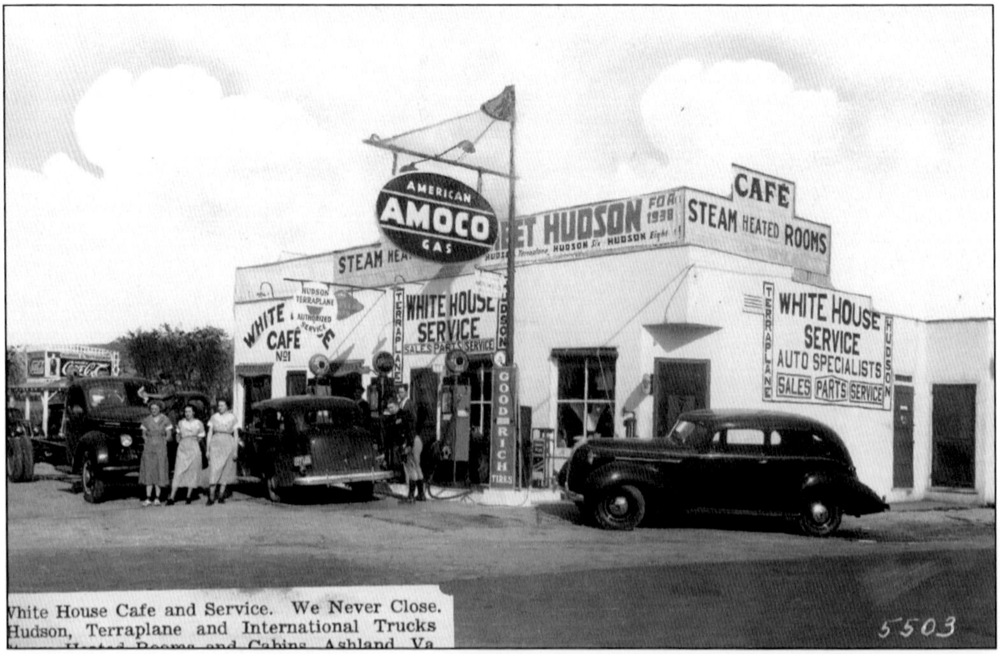

THE WHITE HOUSE CAFÉ. This hot spot for those who wanted to gather and share a beverage in the old days was also called Peregoy's. The Hudson Terraplane automobile advertised on the building was a state-of-the-art car in its day. (Gene Luck.)

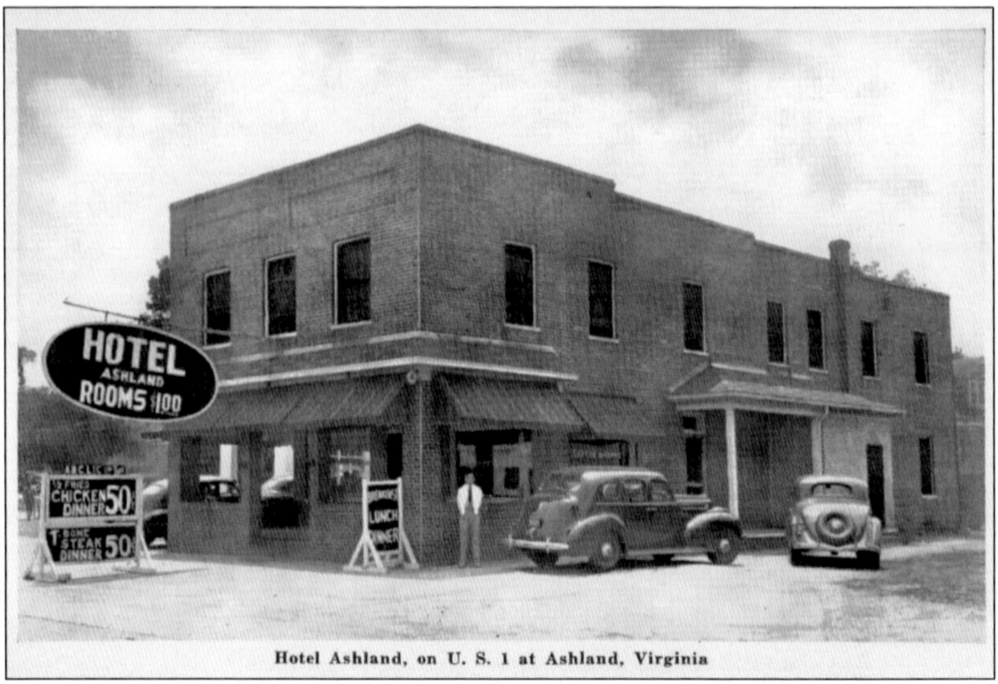

ASHLAND HOTEL. As U.S. Route 1 became the north-south travel route from Maine to Florida, hotels like this one gave motorists an opportunity to rest and refuel. (Rick Gran.)

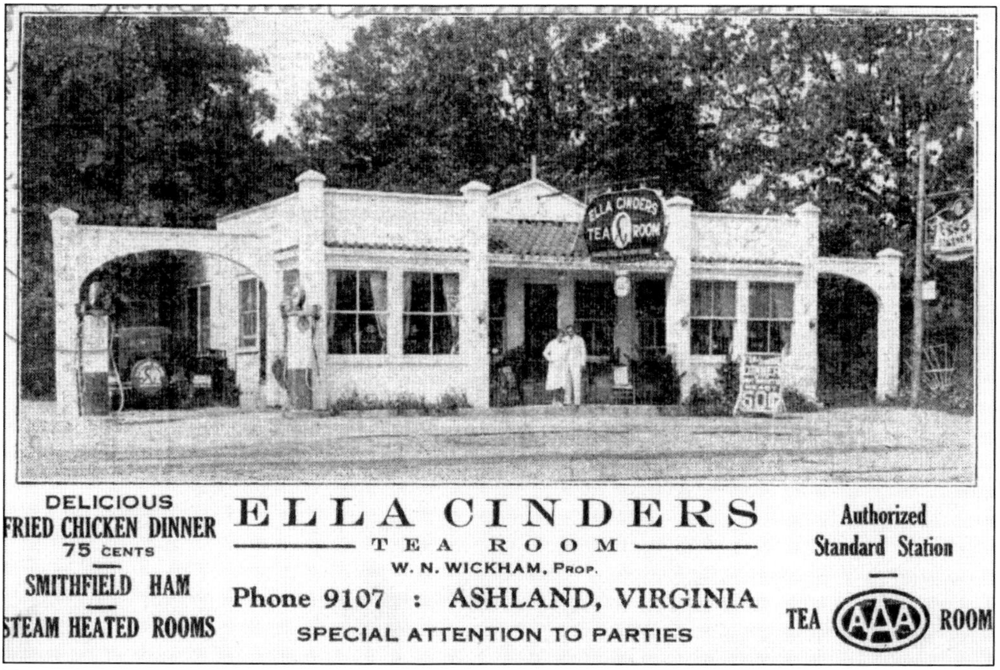

Ella Cinders Restaurant. Established in 1925, Ella Cinders Restaurant advertised itself as "serving wholesome food to wholesome people." It was recommended by AAA and featured ham, chicken, and steak dinners and "an atmosphere of quiet refinement." (Woody and Susan Tucker.)

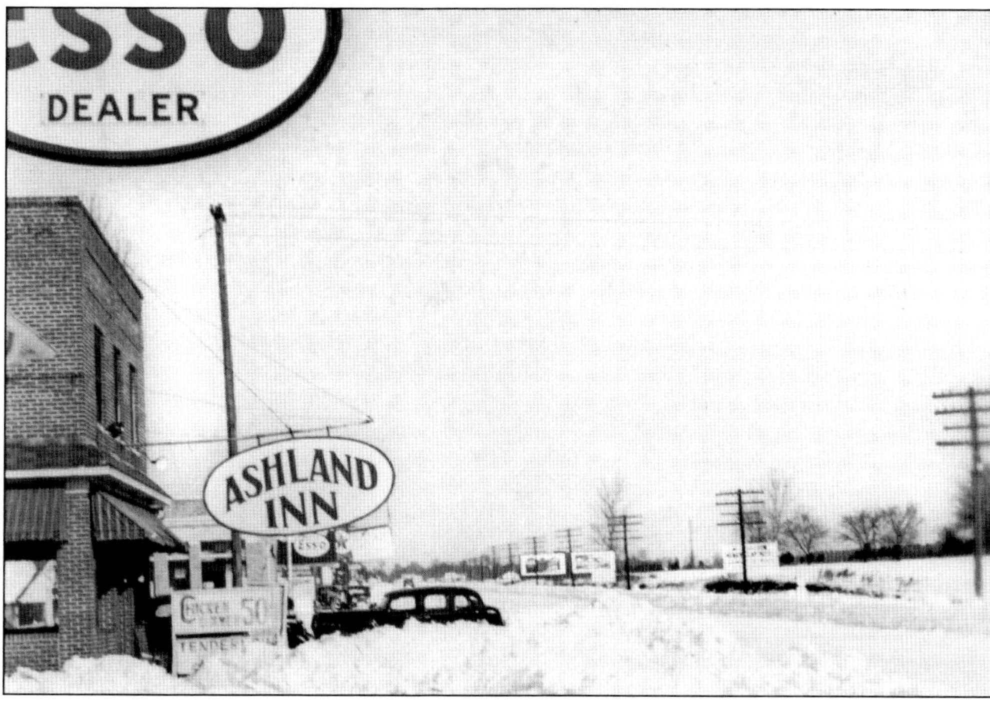

Ashland Inn. On this snowy day, travelers stopped for some Esso gasoline along U.S. Route 1 in Ashland. Of course, Esso later became Exxon. (Terry Barnes Shaw.)

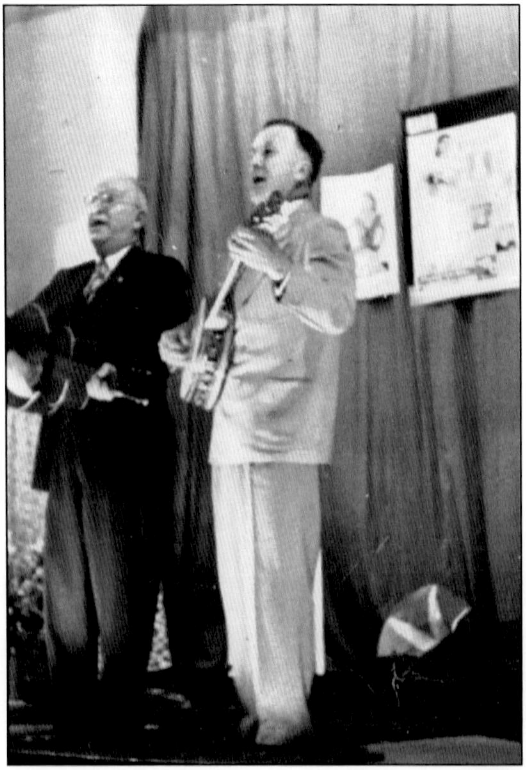

TUCKER AND WIGHTMAN. F.W. Tucker Jr. and John Wightman dedicate the new Ashland Theater in either 1948 or 1949. (Woody and Susan Tucker.)

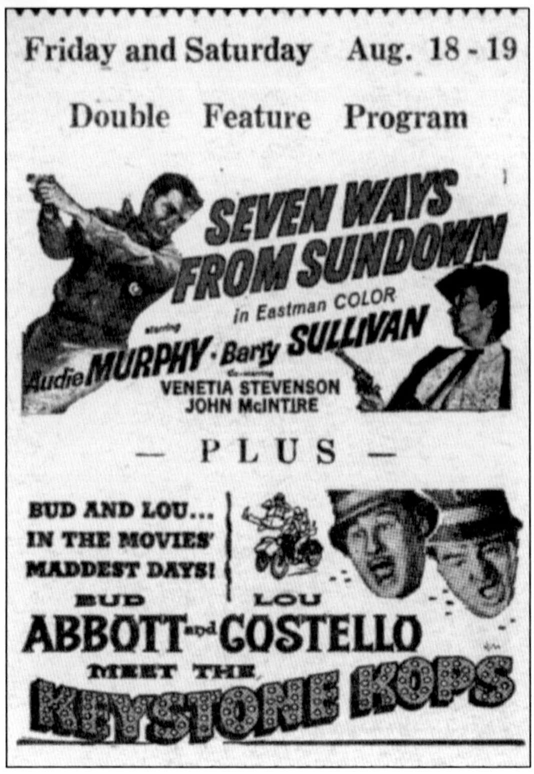

COME TO ASHLAND THEATER. Although the movies may not have always been new, they were new to Ashland when they arrived. (Rick Gran.)

The New Ashland Theater. Change is inevitable, but Marion Herget remembers that Friday or Saturday afternoon was movie time at the old Ashland Theater. "The billing at the theater usually changed twice a week. The flicks were often oldies by the time we got them, but they were fresh to us. It took two years for *Alice in Wonderland* to make it from Richmond's Lowe's Theatre to Ashland, but the wait was worth it. Every Shirley Temple movie packed the house, and *King Kong* practically emptied the theater of its terrified audience." (Rick Gran.)

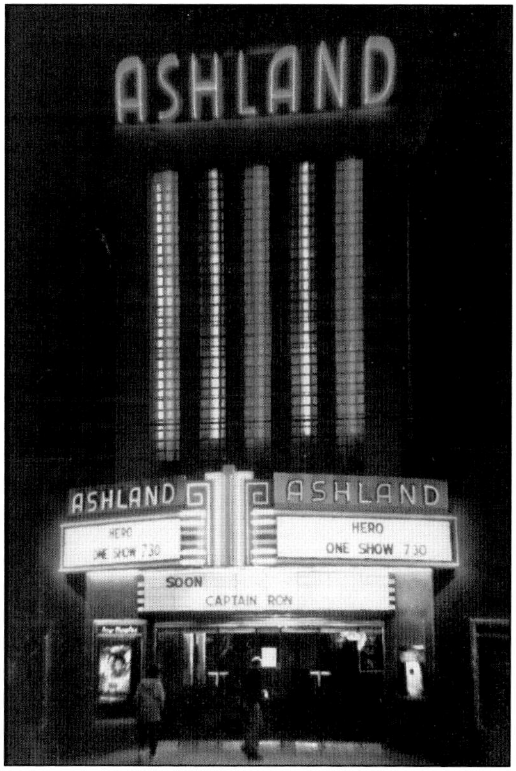

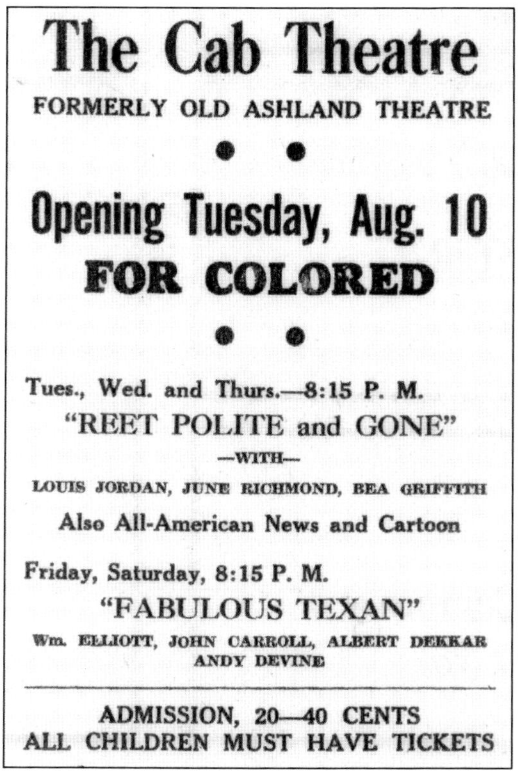

Cab Theatre. From 1927 until 1948, 301 Center Street (site of Work Out Wonder Gym) was home to the segregated Ashland Theatre. The new Ashland Theater was built for whites only in 1948. The old building was renamed the Cab Theatre for "colored" patrons. Film reels were transported by bicycle from theater to theater. This building is within the Ashland Historical District and is listed on the National Register of Historic Places and the Virginia Landmarks Register. (Rick Gran.)

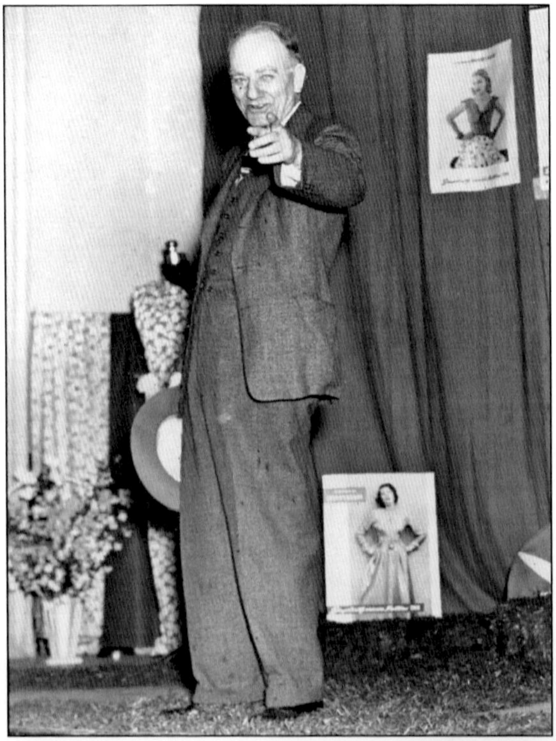

D.B. Cox Store. The department store sold everything, including custom-made millinery and men's and women's clothes. The store had two locations in its time on opposite sides of Center Street. In this photo, James M. Cox teases the photographer in the window of his store. (Liz Stiles.)

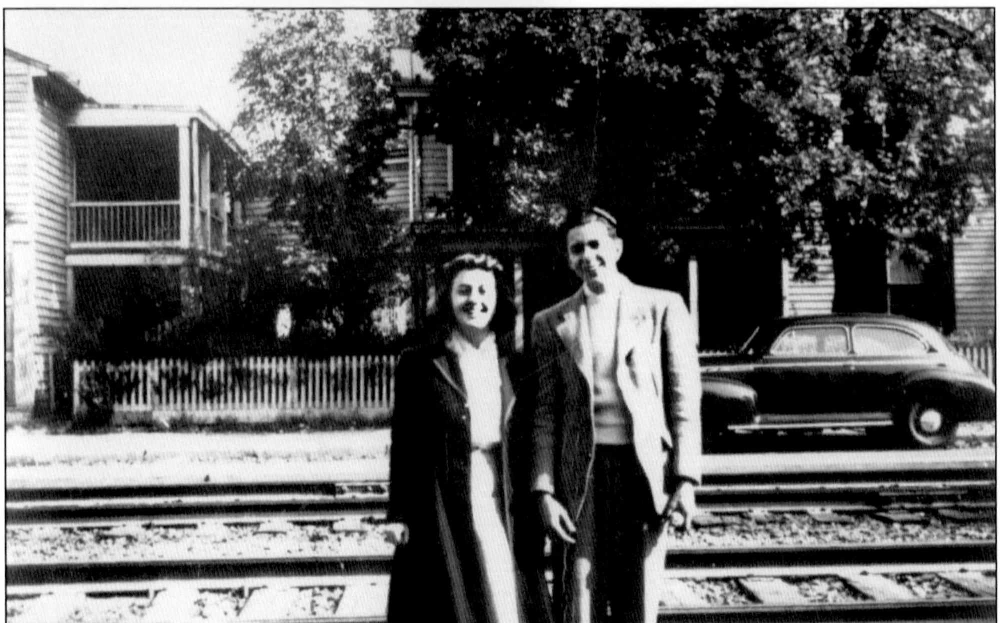

Old Cox Store. This jolly couple is thought to be Lereve Stone and Aubrey Harlow Jr., standing on Railroad Avenue in 1940. This picture shows the house that was the original D.B. Cox Store to the left, on the east side of the tracks. If you look carefully, you can see the walkway that extended from the house to the store. Today the Gillis Library stands in place of the old store. (P.K. Perrin.)

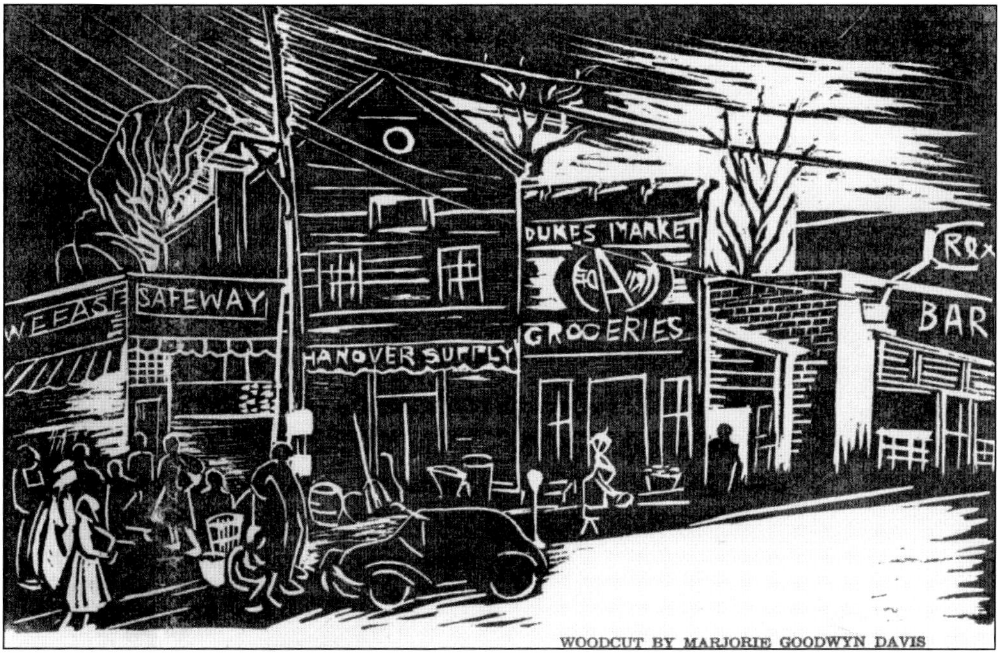

WOODCUT. This woodcut by Marjorie Goodwyn Davis represents the Ashland Business district in days gone by. Barnes Rexall Drug is now Homemade by Suzanne. Duke's Market, home of hand-cut beef; Hanover Supply; and the Safeway are memories. (*Herald-Progress.*)

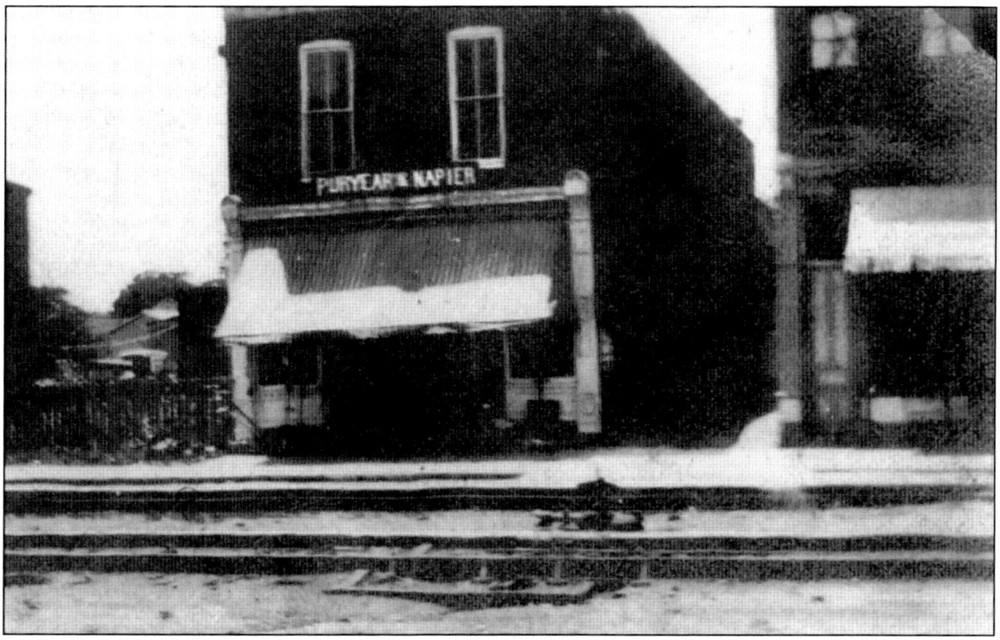

PURYEAR AND NAPIER. This picture is unclear but is an important remembrance of the old store on the west side of Center Street. (*Herald-Progress.*)

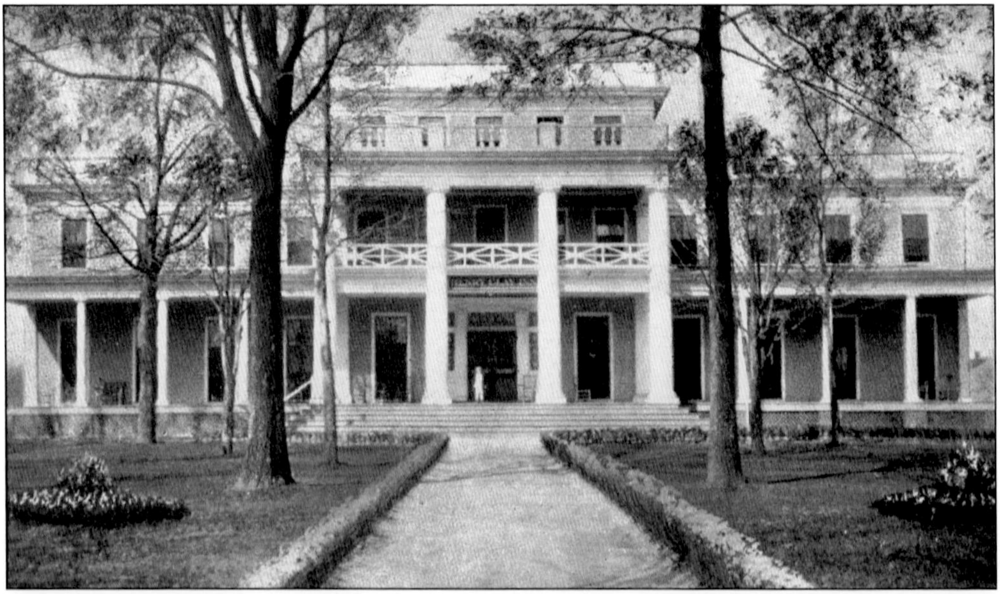

HENRY CLAY INN. Randolph-Macon College owned this property across from the passenger depot on Railroad Avenue in 1946 when the inn caught fire. Marion Herget remembers her first summer in Ashland in 1933, living at the Henry Clay Inn and getting her first experience with Southern hospitality—and the overpowering heat of a Southern summer in a hotel without air conditioning. It is thought that Lewis Blanton (barely visible) is standing on the expansive veranda in this old postcard. (Terry Barnes Shaw.)

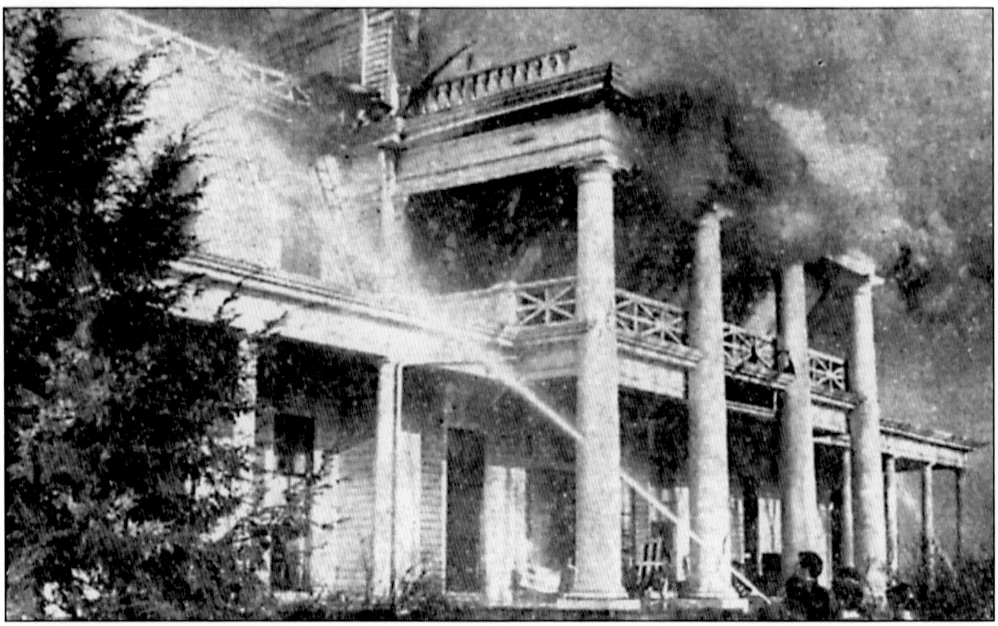

HENRY CLAY INN ON FIRE, 1946. Several times the sparks threatened the adjacent properties of J.G. Hughes and L.F. Blanton, but the fire department kept them under control. For a short period around 8 a.m., residents of Ashland lost water service so that the fire department might have full use of the pressure. Local homes were also without electrical power at the same time. (*Herald-Progress.*)

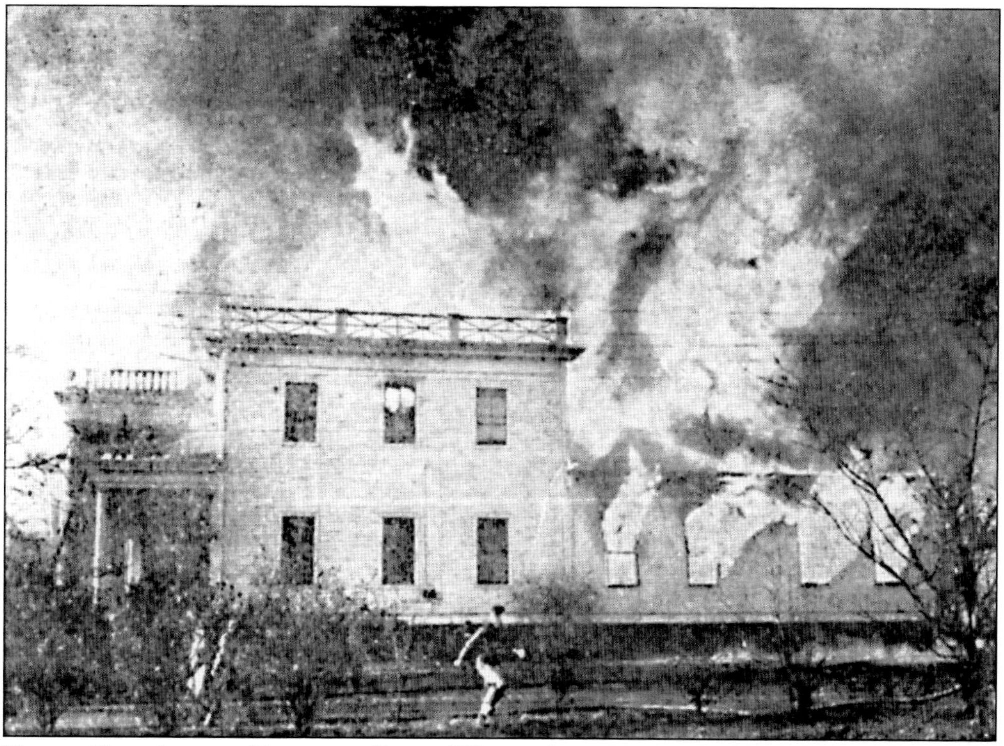

HENRY CLAY INN ON FIRE FROM BACK. When it became apparent that the fire was beyond control, the Richmond Fire Department was called. They responded with two 500-gallon pumpers around 8 a.m. but the water pressure was not sufficient to accommodate two pumpers. By noon, the hotel was completely demolished, with only two chimneys and one of the front-porch pillars standing. A steady breeze from the south pushed the fire along but kept flames from threatening the downtown section of Ashland. (*Herald-Progress.*)

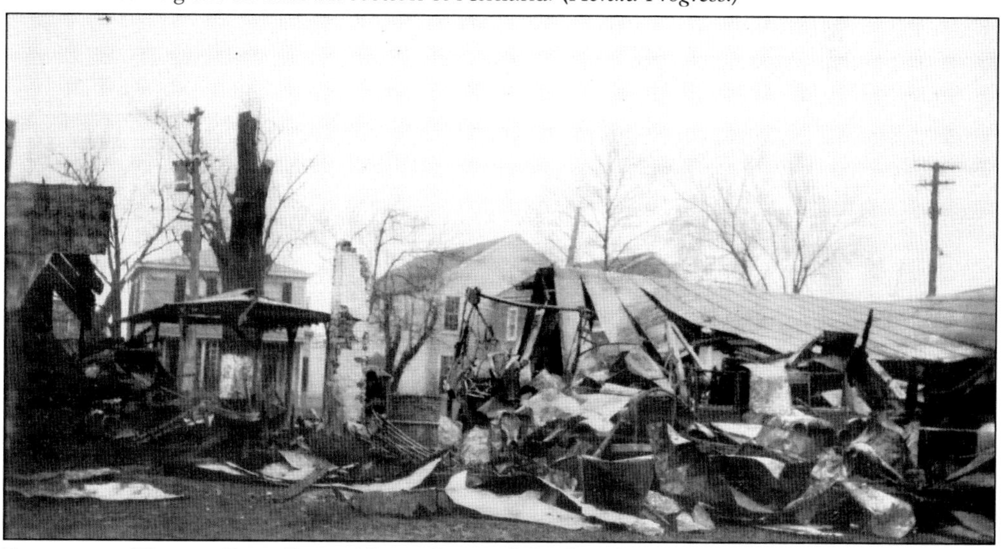

RUBBLE OF HENRY CLAY INN. All residents of the hotel were saved, and although many of them had to descend from the second-floor roof by ladder, there were no serious injuries. (Louis A. Wright Collection.)

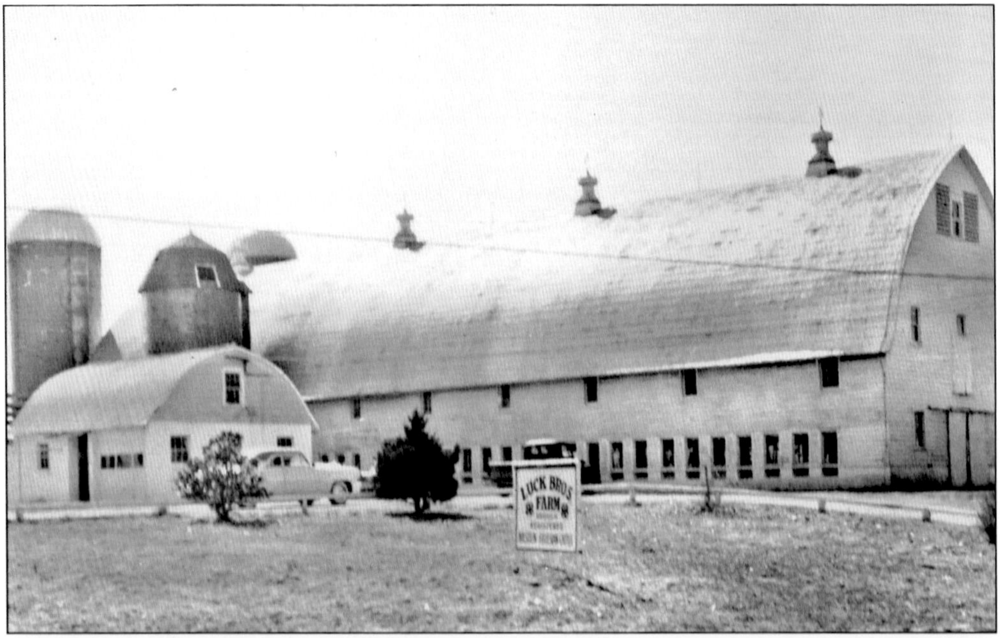

LUCK DAIRY FARM, 1955. Prizewinning registered Holstein cattle were bred, raised, and milked at the farm. Many of the cows were brought from Canada to improve the productivity record of the herd. Cattle were milked there three times per day until about 1956, when a twice-daily schedule was adopted. Barns were constructed in the 1920s and finally destroyed in a storm years later. (Cabell Luck.)

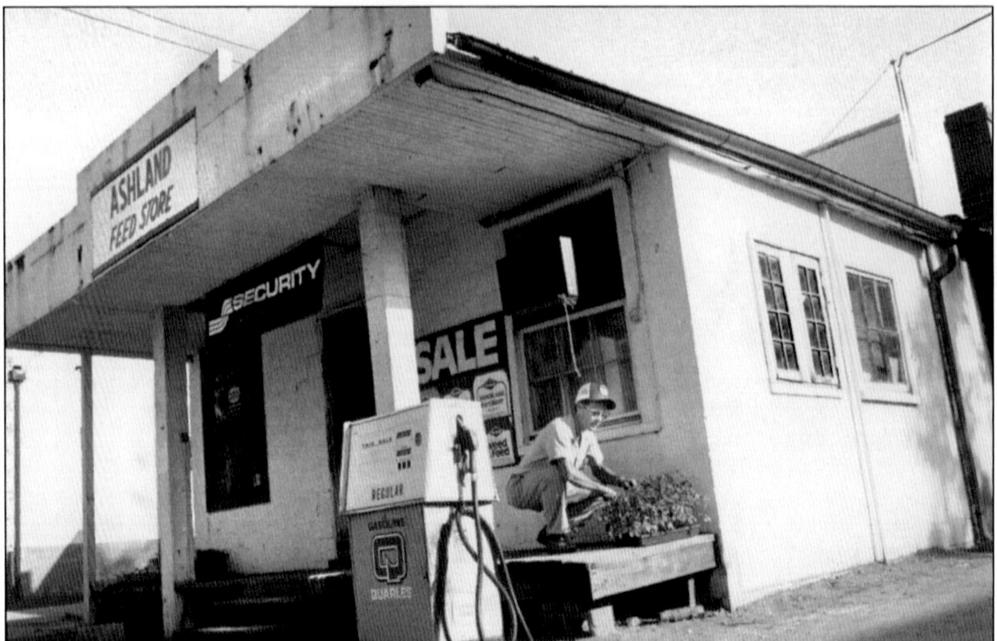

ASHLAND FEED STORE. Still an Ashland landmark, stepping inside takes the visitor back to the 19th century. High-beamed ceilings, smooth wood floors, and the fresh smell of hay speak to another era. (*Herald-Progress*.)

Four

HERALD-PROGRESS

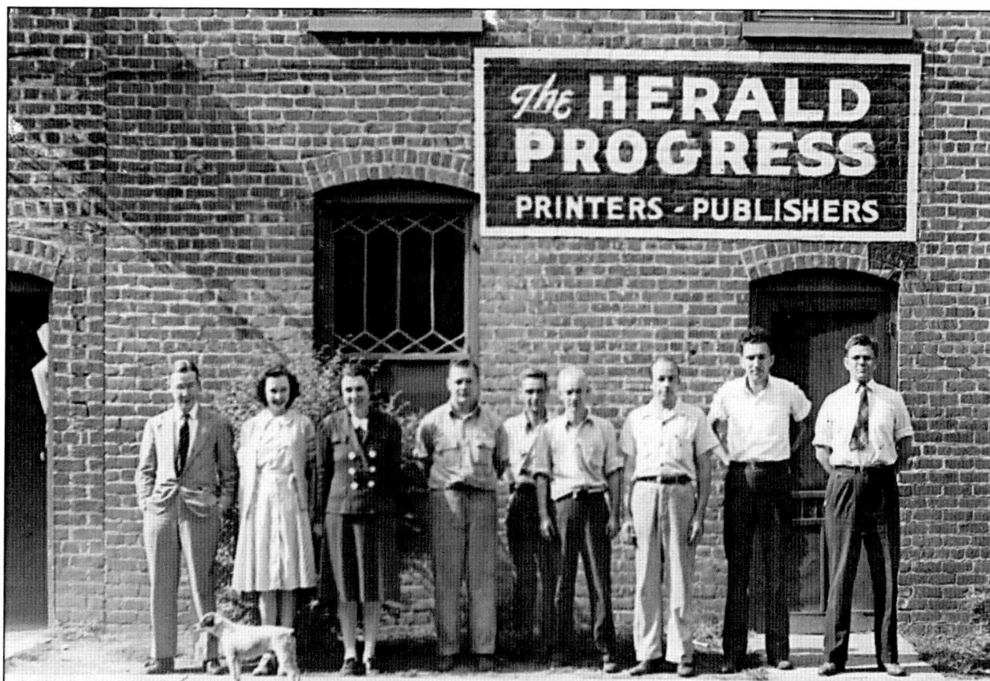

HERALD-PROGRESS IN TOWN BUILDING. Paul Watkins bought the *Herald-Progress* from the Parent family in 1933. The paper was located in the town building. On the left, you can see the opening for the town's firehouse. The newspaper rented the front office. Upstairs was the telephone exchange, the health department, and the town court, and the town lockup was in the rear. From left to right are Paul Watkins, Marion Watkins (Herget), Lois Watkins, Billy Loving, John Carr, Stuart Burruss, Lou Cumbia, Claude Hungate, Dick Gillis, and Skippy the dog. (Marion Herget.)

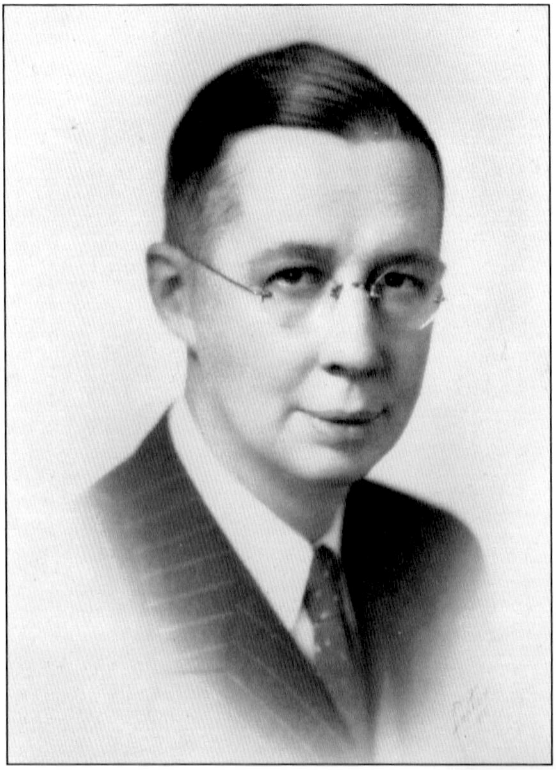

PAUL WATKINS. Watkins left a successful career at the *Chicago Daily News* to scour the South looking for the perfect small town to practice his brand of hands-on journalism. Ashland made the best impression. The small college town near Richmond meant that there would be intellectual life and the opportunity for both culture and growth. Although he would no longer come into daily contact with the likes of Carl Sandburg, Clarence Darrow, John Gunther, Babe Deidrickson, Amos and Andy, and the like, he thought the Ashland citizenry a fair trade. (Marion Herget.)

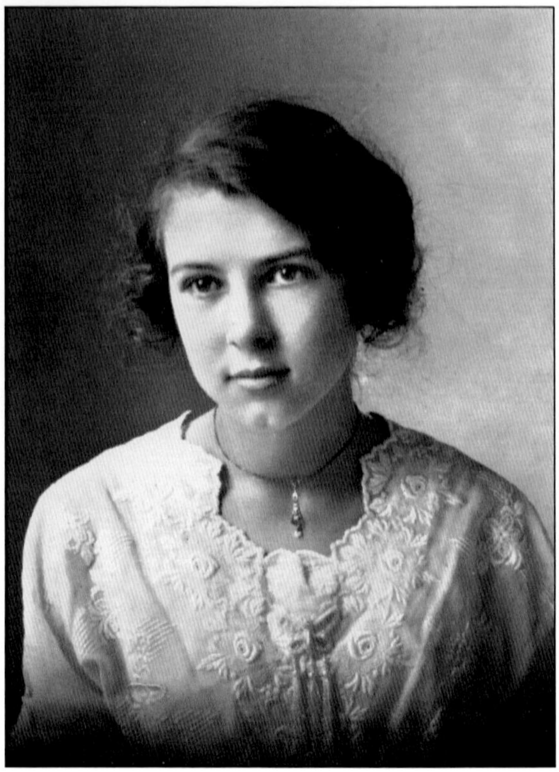

LOIS WATKINS. This photo was taken at Illinois College between 1914 and 1918. A true partner in marriage and business, Lois married Paul Watkins when he came back from Europe after World War I. When Paul died in 1951, Lois continued to publish the *Herald-Progress.* In 1974, the Virginia Press Association named her Press Woman of the Year, and in 1976, the National Federation of Press Women gave her the National Woman of Achievement Award. Mrs. Watkins lived to be 100 years old. (Marion Herget.)

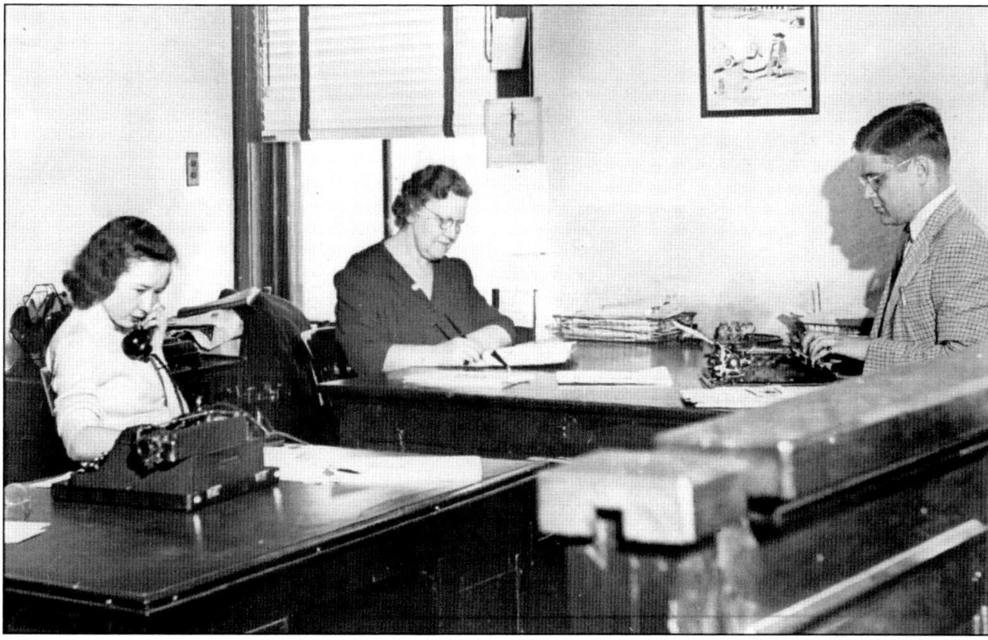

MRS. PAGE HARTSOOK. Marion Herget said, "Mrs. Page used to say that my father, when he purchased the *HP*, bought three old desks and one large secretary." She was the one large secretary with curly red hair, blue-green eyes, and a smile that melted butter. Mrs. Hartsook was the society editor of the paper and wrote the material that was most important to everyone. News was a wedding, a birth, a funeral, a party, a trip, a vacation—the things people were really interested in. Shown here are, from left to right, Marion Watkins, Mrs. Page Hartsook, and Dick Gillis. (Marion Herget.)

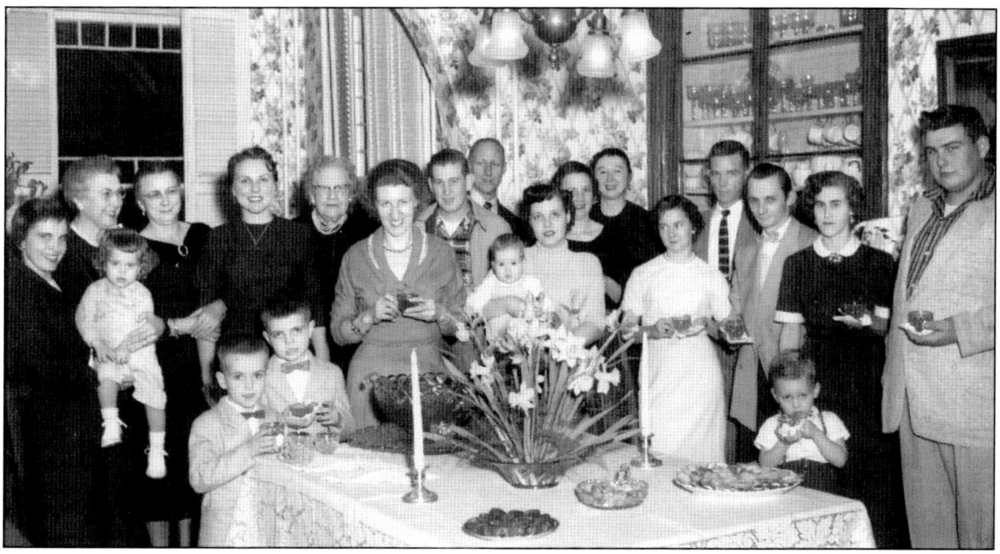

***HERALD-PROGRESS* PARTY.** Everyone threw a going-away party for Helene Walch. From left to right are Lucille Cleaton holding Janie, with Donnie and Allen in the foreground, Lois Watkins, Mrs. T.G. Jerome, Tafi Yourtee, Page Hartsook, Helene Walch, Alvin and Irma Adams with son Dennis, Rev. Harris Kesler, Mrs. ? Kesler, Marion Herget, Delane and Sanford Edwards, and Ronnie and Nell Fontaine with Wayne and Douglas Tate. (Marion Herget.)

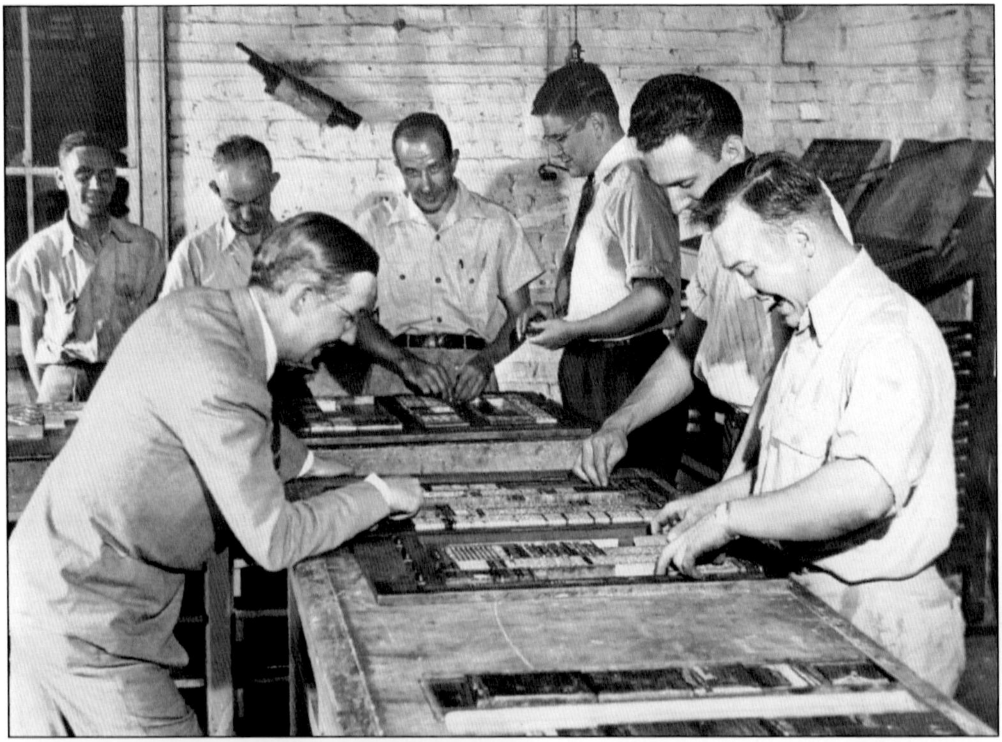

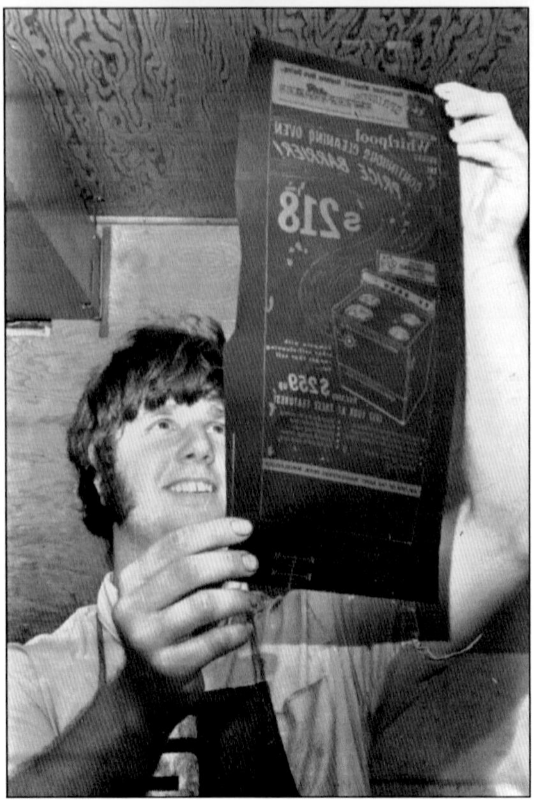

PAUL WATKINS CHECKS A PROOF. In the production room at the *Herald-Progress*, Paul checks pages for letterpress printing. From left to right are John Carr, Stuart Burruss, Lou Cumbia, Dick Gillis, Claude Hungate, and Billy Loving. (Marion Herget.)

READING A PROOF. Pat Snoddy holds a *Herald-Progress* offset negative. (Marion Herget.)

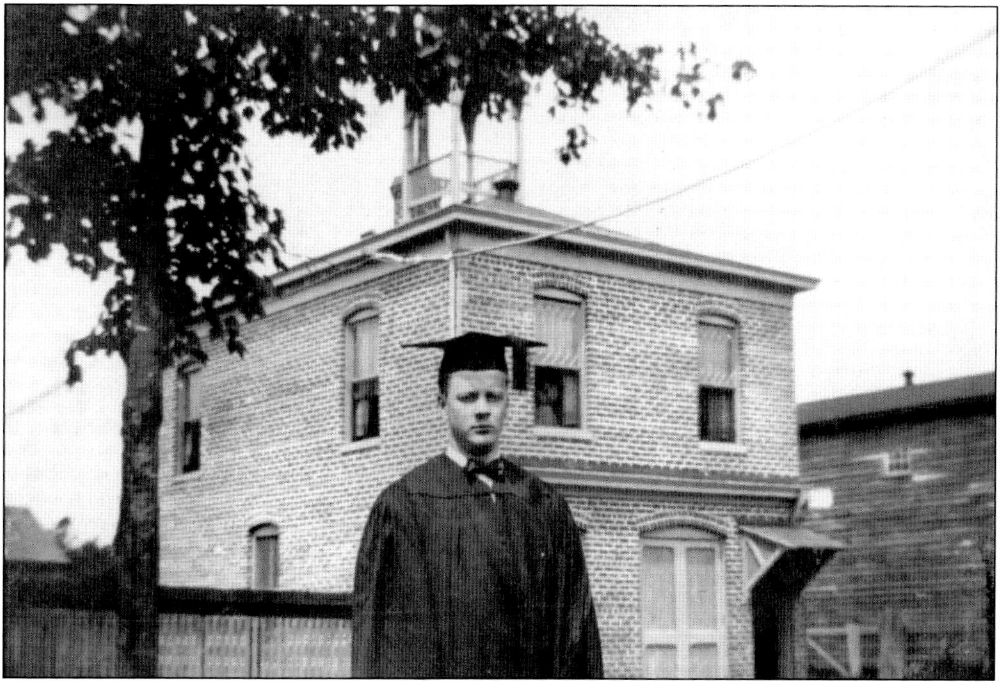

THE ORIGINAL *HERALD-PROGRESS* LOCATION. This building was also the original fire department, as evidenced by the fire bell on top of the building. (Woody and Susan Tucker.)

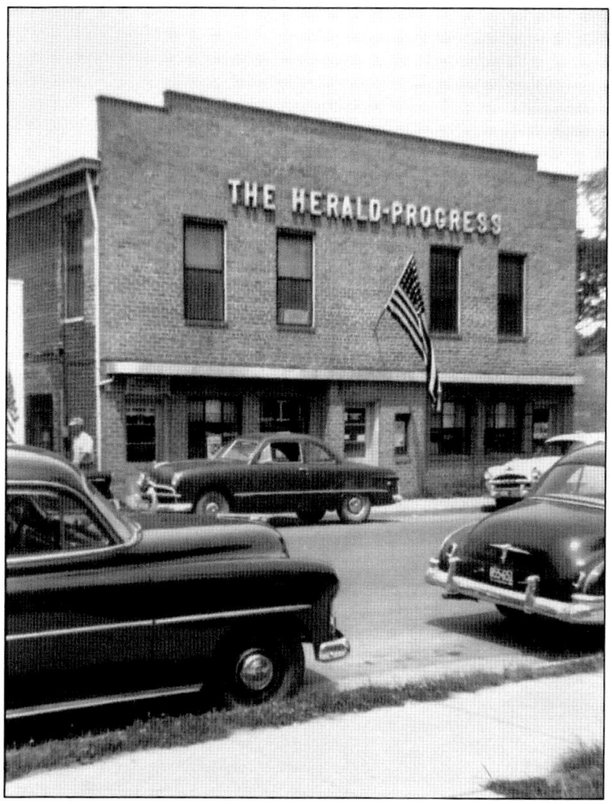

***THE HERALD-PROGRESS* EXPANDS.** When the town building went up for public auction in the 1950s, Lois Watkins bought the property, which was expanded gradually, even annexing the old town jail to the rear. The building is still on Thompson Street, and although used for other purposes, it still bears the name of *The Herald-Progress* on its front, as if it had to remind everyone what a rich heritage the building has had. (Marion Herget.)

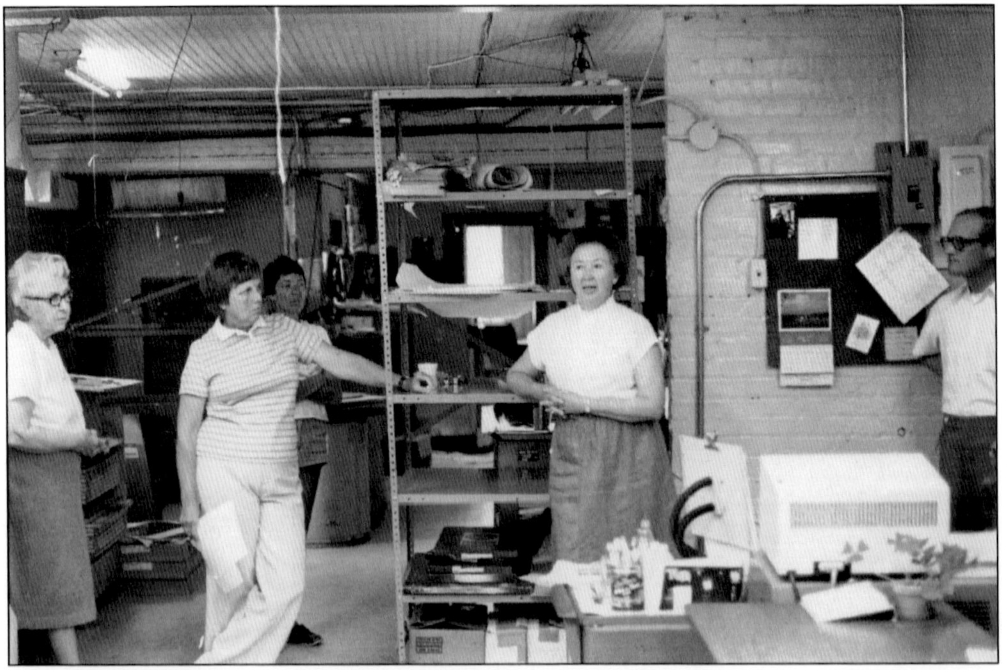

ON HERGET'S WATCH. Marion Watkins Herget (center), the daughter of publisher-emeritus Lois D. Watkins and the late editor and publisher Paul F. Watkins, wrote *The Watkins Years*. After a career in New York as a television and radio writer, she returned to Ashland in 1954 to join her mother at the weekly newspaper. Later, she became editor, winning a number of Virginia Press Association awards for news and editorial writing. (*Herald-Progress*.)

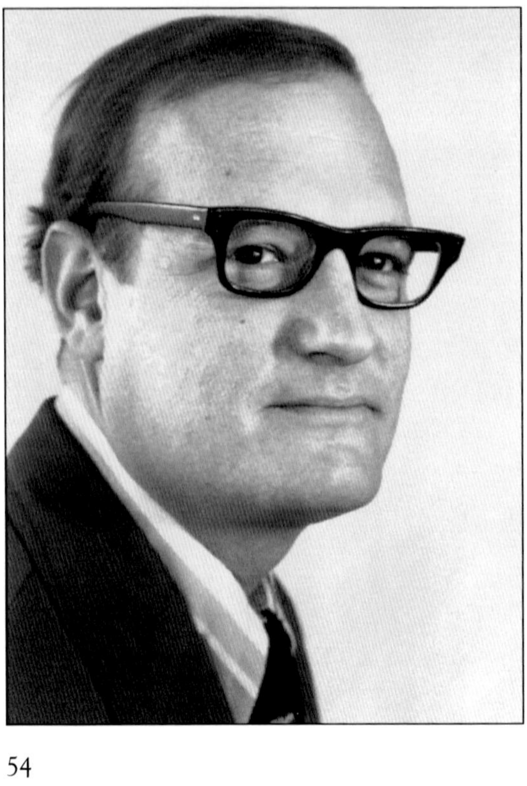

J. MALCOLM PACE III. Married to Patricia Lewars Pace, Jay had been (says Marion Herget) the "*Yellow Jacket* editor whose talents, strength and disposition made such an impression on all of us at the *HP* that we managed eventually to lure him away from a promising secure career with Life of Virgina to become the first *HP* editor outside the Watkins family in over 40 years." (*Herald-Progress*.)

Five

KIDS

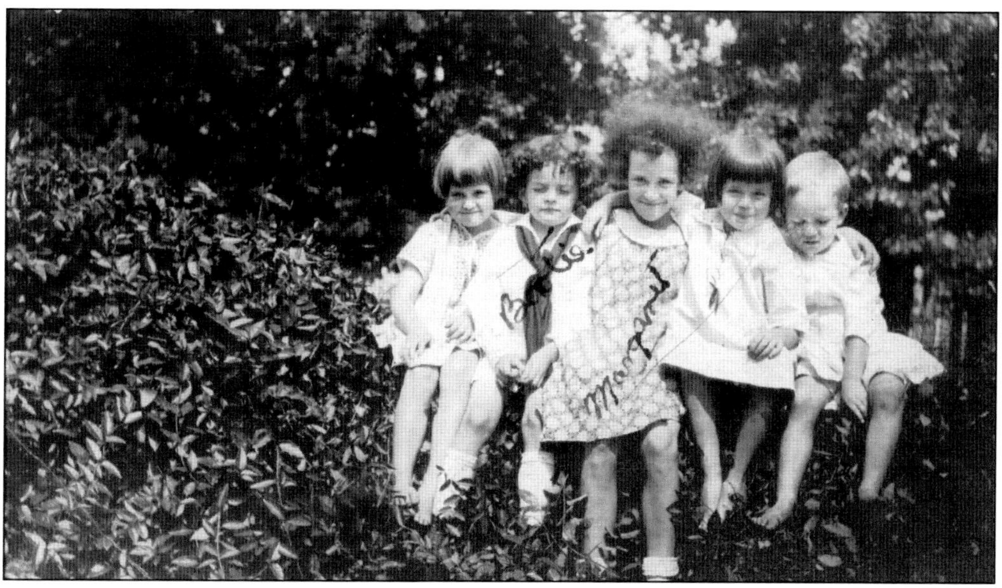

KIDS WERE PARAMOUNT. Ashland must have been idyllic for children with so many families clustered together, sharing the notion that all the children were everyone's responsibility. Mothers put them all down for naps at 1:00 in the afternoon and strolled to the center of town for some conversation and a "co-cola." Everyone knew not to telephone anyone or try to conduct business during afternoon naps. Second from left is Bootie Tucker. Next to him is Margaret Gilman. (Woody and Susan Tucker.)

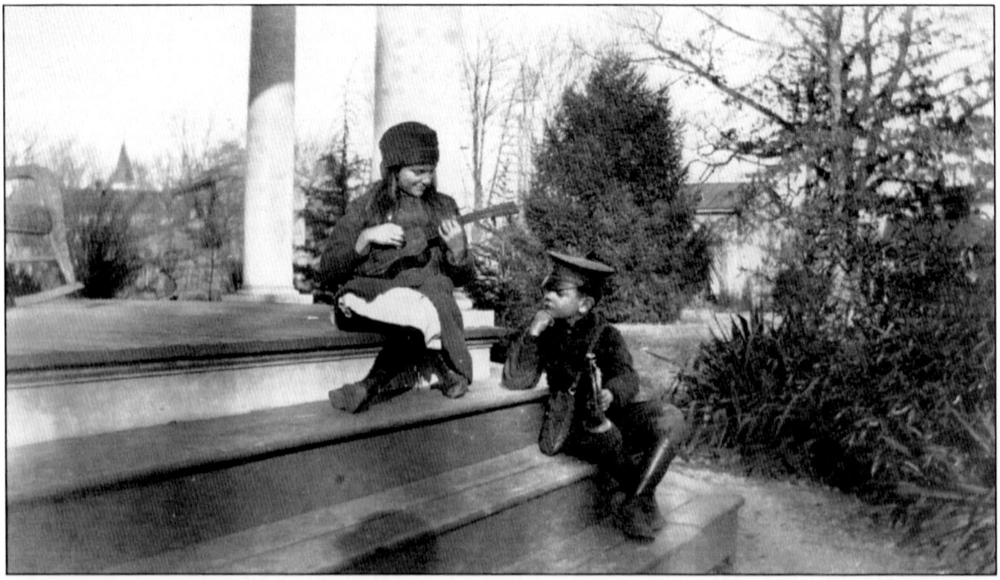

LITTLE SOLDIER BOY. Elizabeth Pendleton Cox serenades Kimbrough "Kimmie" Cox in his Great War uniform. (Pen and Betty Carol Stevenson.)

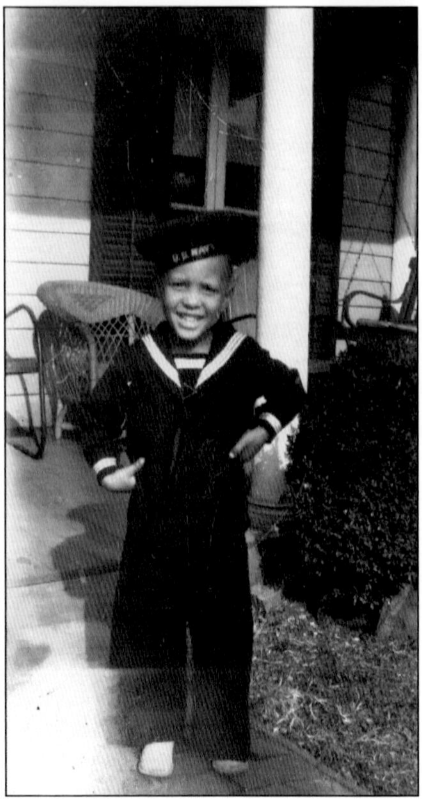

LITTLE SAILOR BOY. Leroy Carrington Jr. was George Gray's nephew and the son of Ida Carrington, who lived in Berkleytown. (Inez Gray.)

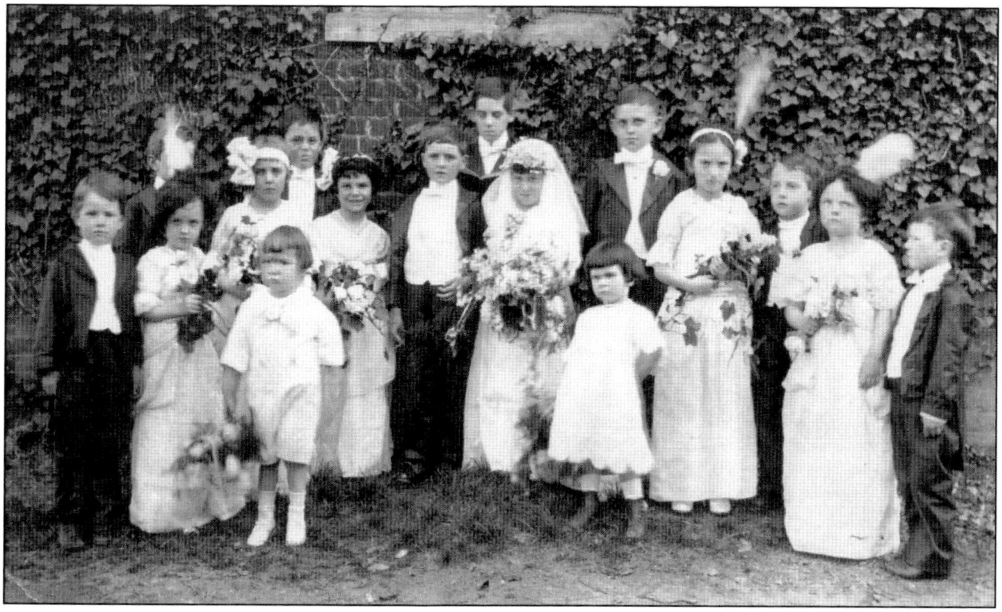

LILLIPUTIAN WEDDING. Elizabeth Pendleton Cox was director of this community event held at Ashland High School during the 1920s. Not all of the children could be identified, but the picture is charming enough to engage anyone for a few minutes. The small girl next to the "bride" is Elizabeth Pendleton Cox Stevenson. (Pen and Betty Carol Stevenson.)

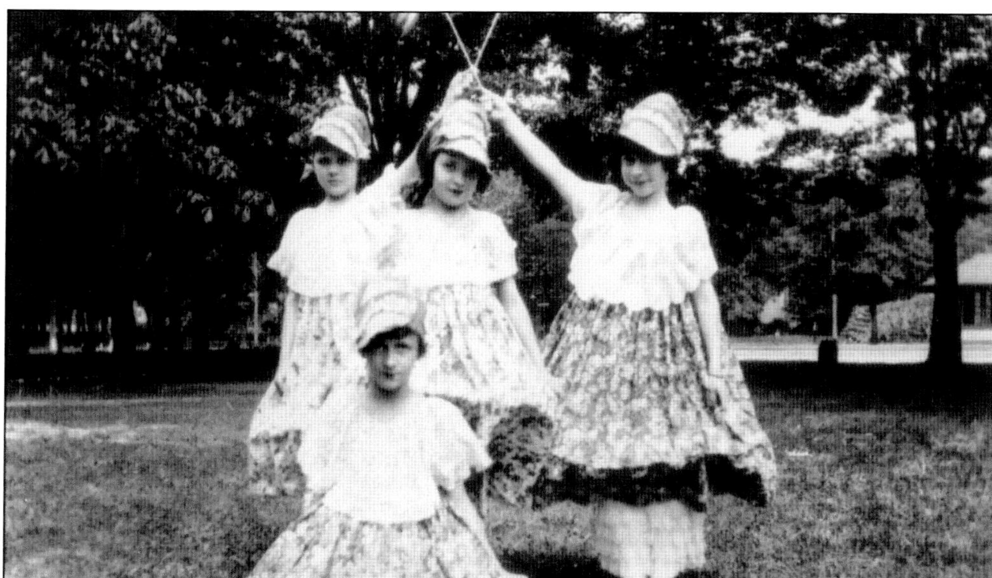

LET'S PUT ON A SHOW! From left to right, Conde Booth, Virginia Sydnor, Anne Duggan, and Polly Bridges put on a pageant of their own, perhaps in the fourth grade. (Lelia Palmore Weyman.)

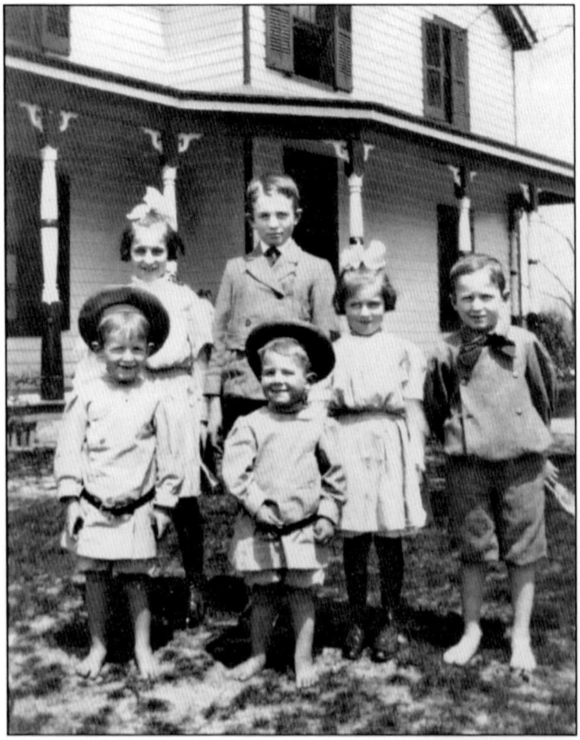

AT LAKEVIEW DAIRY, 1907. The children of Mr. and Mrs. Charles Samuel Luck pose in front of the house at Lakeview Dairy. The Luck children are, from left to right, (front row) Cabell and Betty Chandler; (back row) Anne Josephine, Charles Merle, Cecile Terrell, and Charles Samuel Jr. (Cabell Luck.)

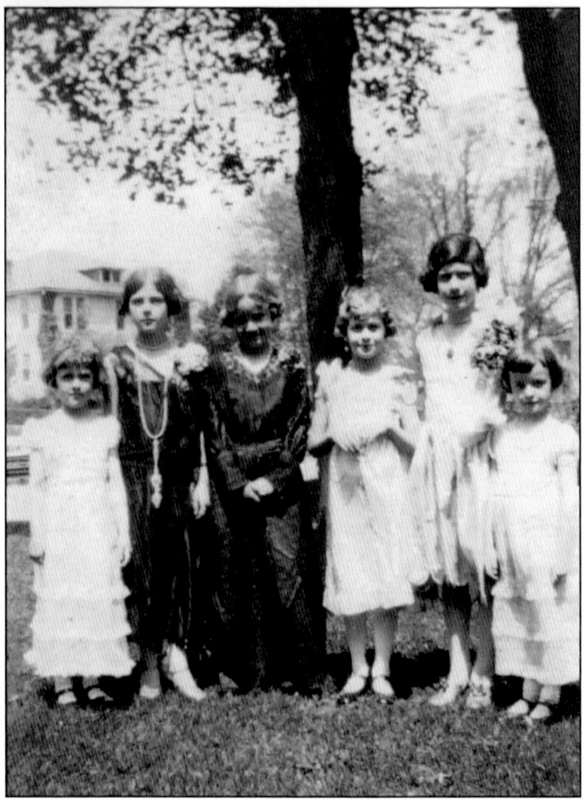

DRESS UP. The little girl on the far left is Mary Byrd Tucker. The tall "belle" is Virginia Sydnor. Everyone seems very proud of their attempt to look like their mothers. (Woody and Susan Tucker.)

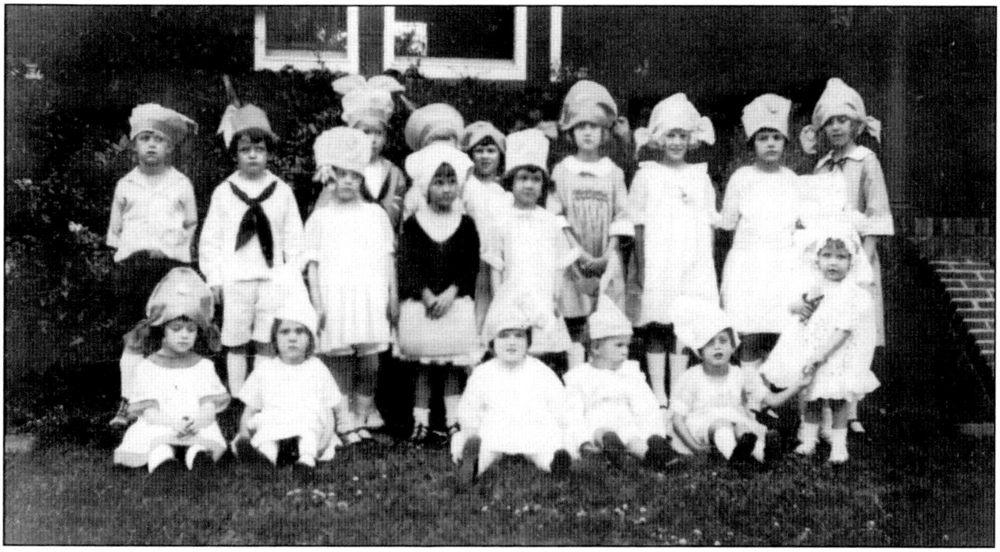

ELLEN MORRIS JONES'S FIFTH BIRTHDAY. Although the majority of the children remain unidentified in this wonderful photo of Ellen Morris's party in the 1920s, the second from the right on the bottom row is Sarah Newman Jones (Wright). In the top row at far right is Dorothy Jones. (Sarah Jones Wright.)

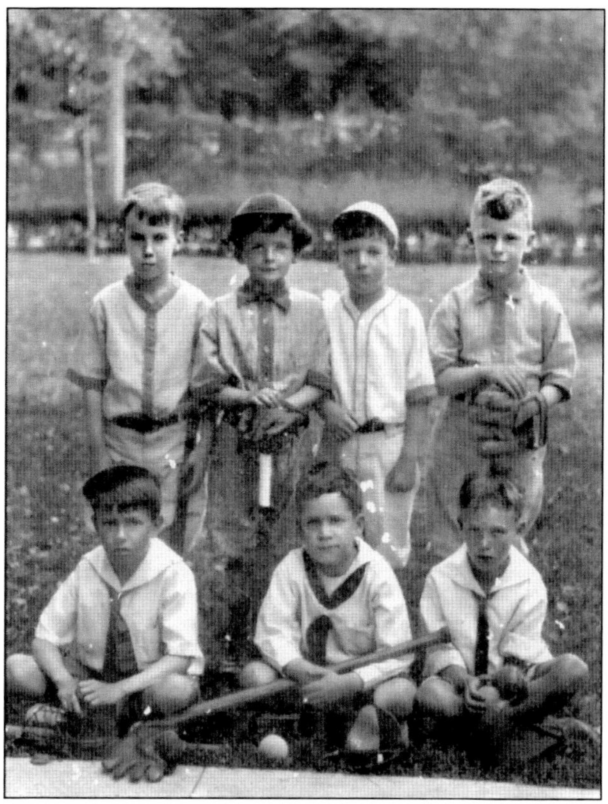

FLOYD TUCKER'S SIXTH BIRTHDAY PARTY. Standing second from left is Floyd Woodruff Tucker III. His buddy Drewry Kerr is seated on the far left. It is apparent that the boys did not go for hats, but they did for bats. (Woody and Susan Tucker.)

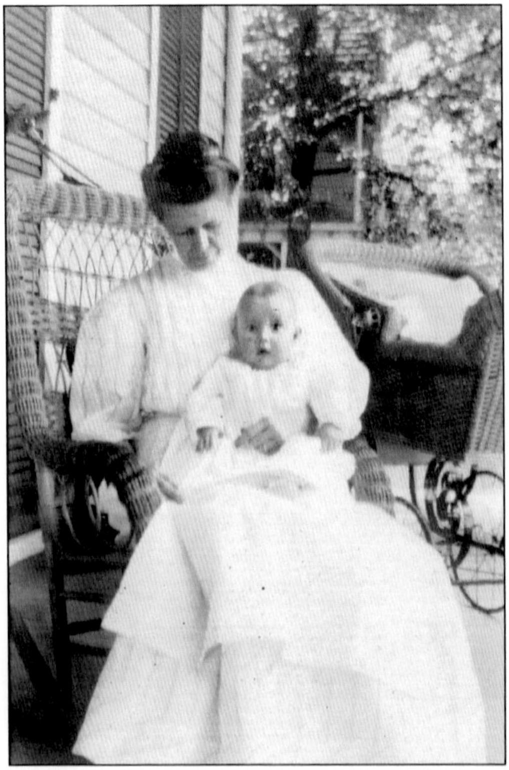

Mother and Child. Louise Ladew Kerr sits on the porch at her home on Howard Street holding her daughter, Rebecca Robbins Kerr, in 1909. Mrs. Kerr gave dancing lessons at her home. She also worked at Hughes Drug Store. (Harvey "Todie" Grattan.)

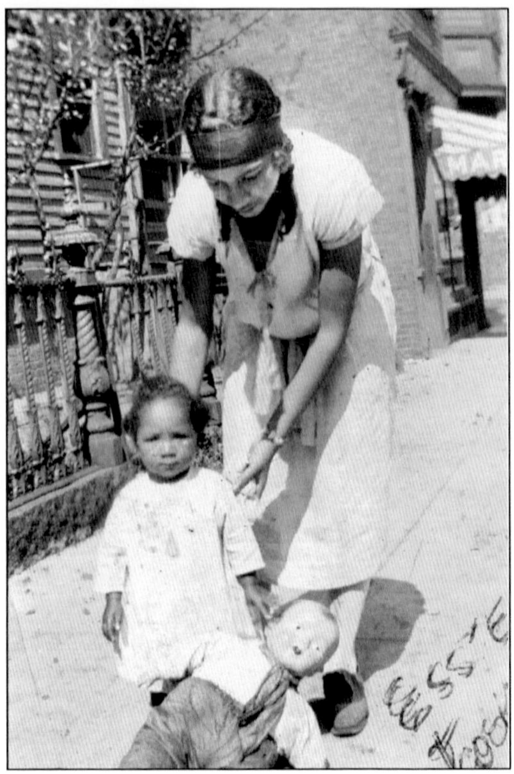

Essie Ford Coleman. Coleman was the granddaughter of Rev. William Ford, who preached the gospel throughout Hanover County. She is tending to her little daughter Cookie. The family lived in Ashland. (Inez Gray.)

MOTHER AND CHILDREN. Elizabeth Pendleton Cox is seen in an idyllic pose with her children, Elizabeth Pendleton Cox (Stevenson) and Kimbrough Cox. (Pen and Betty Carol Stevenson.)

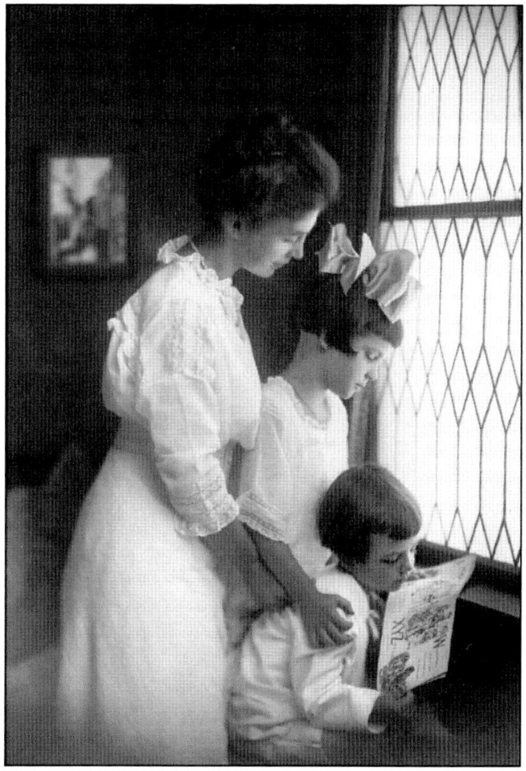

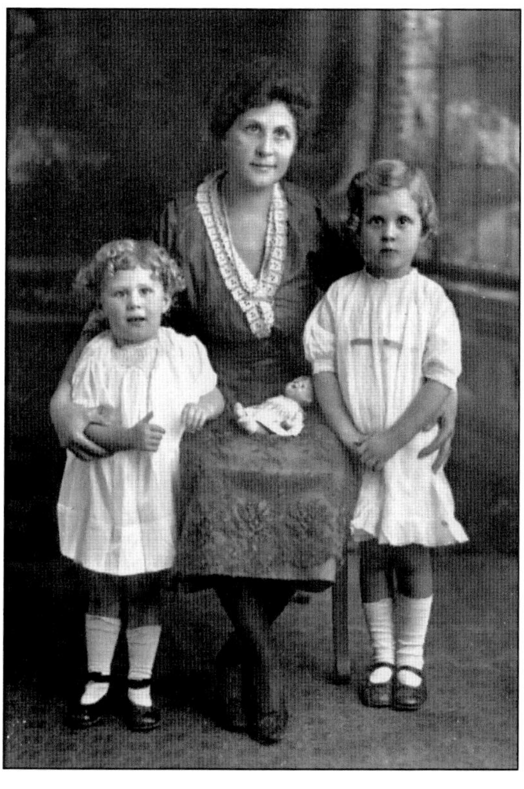

CONDE BRIDGES BOOTH. Mrs. Booth finds time to sit for a portrait with her daughters, Clifford Booth (Pierce) at left and Conde Booth (Palmore) at right. (Lelia Palmore Weyman.)

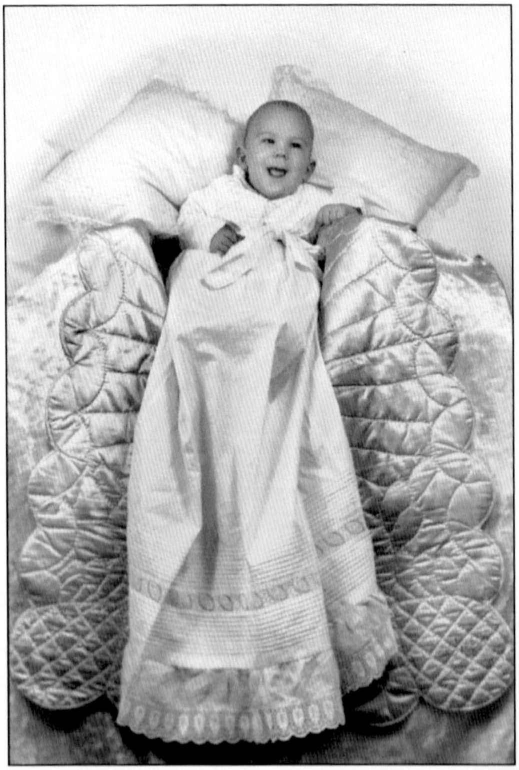

Baby Cabell Luck, 1945. Cabell Luck Jr. poses in a family baptismal gown. (Cabell Luck.)

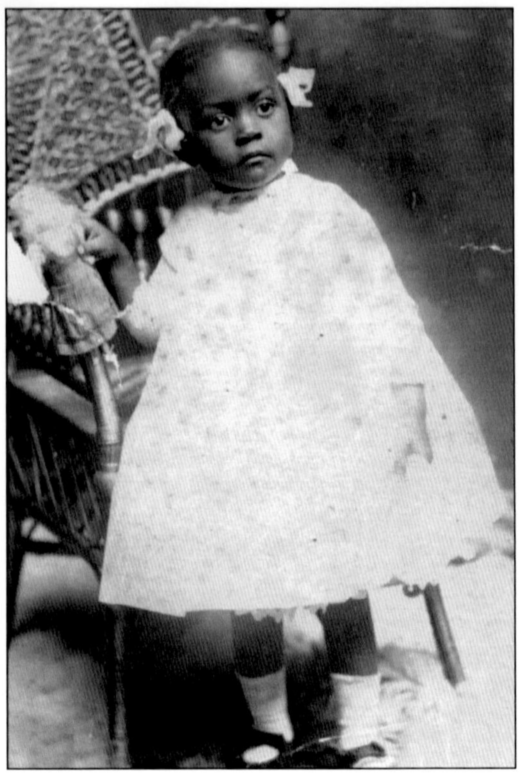

Baby Elaine Winston. Johnnie Clinton Winston's niece became a teacher and taught at Bethany School in Montpelier. (Inez Gray.)

REBECCA ROBBINS KERR GRATTAN, 1913. A dramatic flair helped make Rebecca a mainstay in the Tucker and Wightman Minstrel Show. She also became a featured player in the local production of *Mr. Patrick Henry*, along with New York actor James Bell. She was a longtime member of the Ashland Village Theater. Perhaps she will be best remembered as a teacher of second grade and the first woman member of the Town Council of Ashland. (Harvey "Todie" Grattan.)

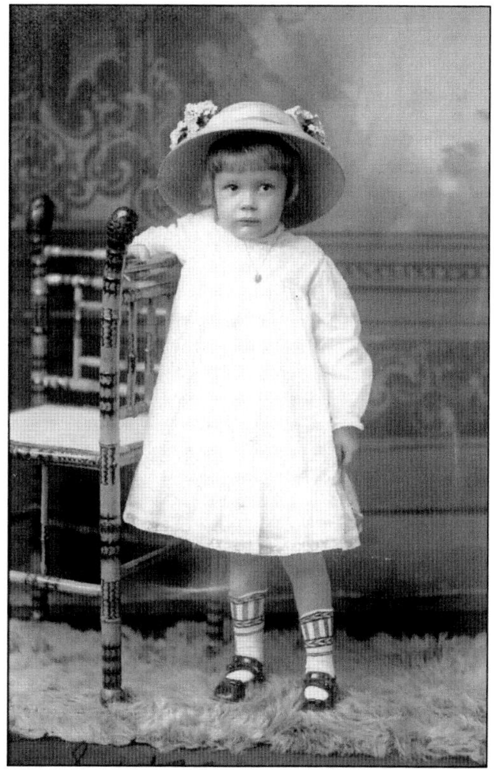

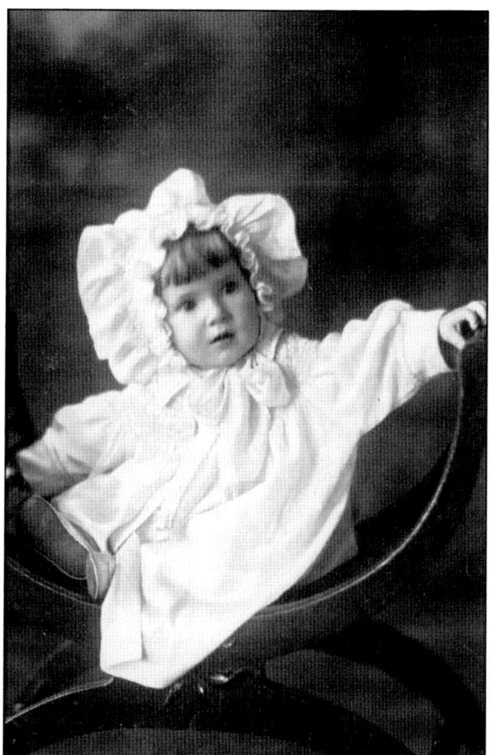

ELOISE GODDIN (PICCOLO). In this photo, it seems the hat is bigger than the baby. Eloise is still just as cute, though. Eloise earned a degree in biology from Randolph-Macon, where she was a cheerleader. She and her husband Robert "Pic" Piccolo raised four children while running their own business, The Hanover Pharmacy on England Street. Eloise remains active in the Ashland Woman's Club.(Eloise Piccolo.)

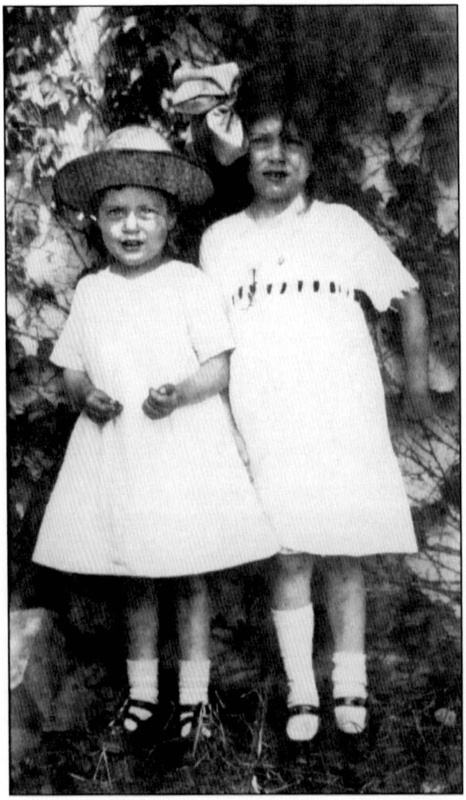

THE JONES SISTERS. Sarah Newnan Jones (left) and Ellen Morris Jones (right) stop to have their picture taken at their home on Duncan Street sometime in the 1920s. (Sarah Jones Wright.)

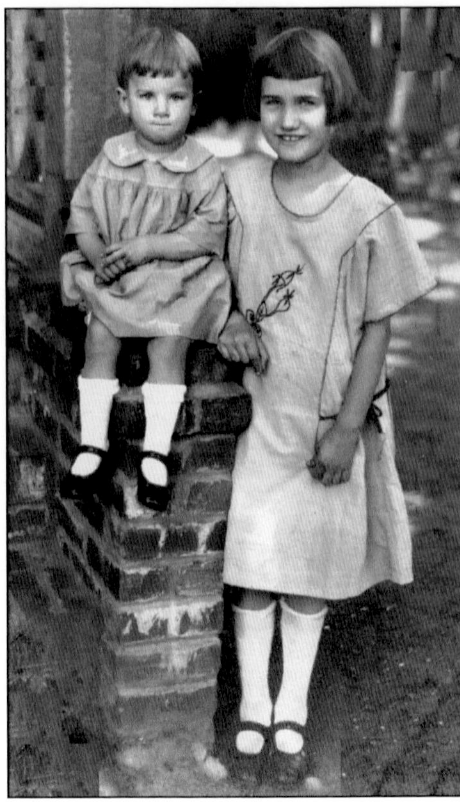

THE SMEEMAN SISTERS. Mildred (sitting on the wall) married Wilson Davis. Many Ashland children will remember her as "Auntie," as so many of them attended Auntie's Day Care. Dorothy married Clyde Barnes Jr. (Mildred Smeeman Davis.)

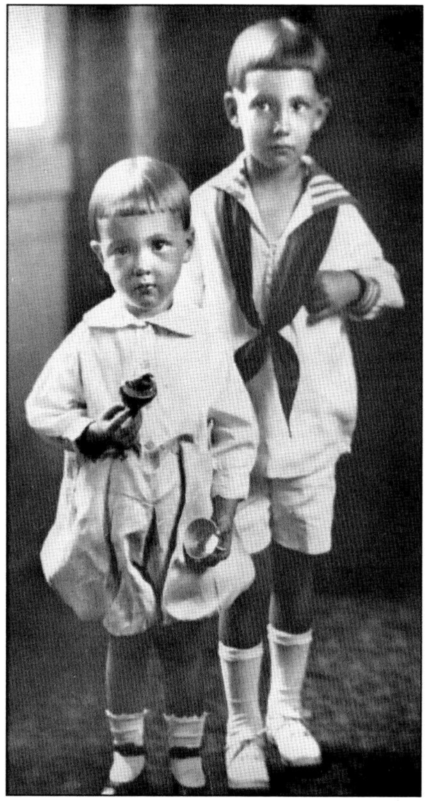

The Palmore Boys. Russell Vaughan and Fred Wharton Palmore are pictured here. Fred married Betty Keith Taylor. Vaughan married Conde Booth. (Ann Curtis Palmore.)

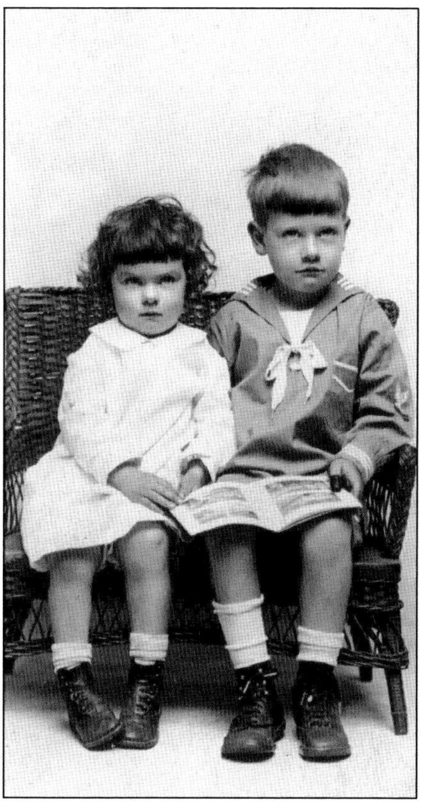

Juliana and Park Hartsook. Who can resist the charm of this brother and sister duo? (Woody and Susan Tucker.)

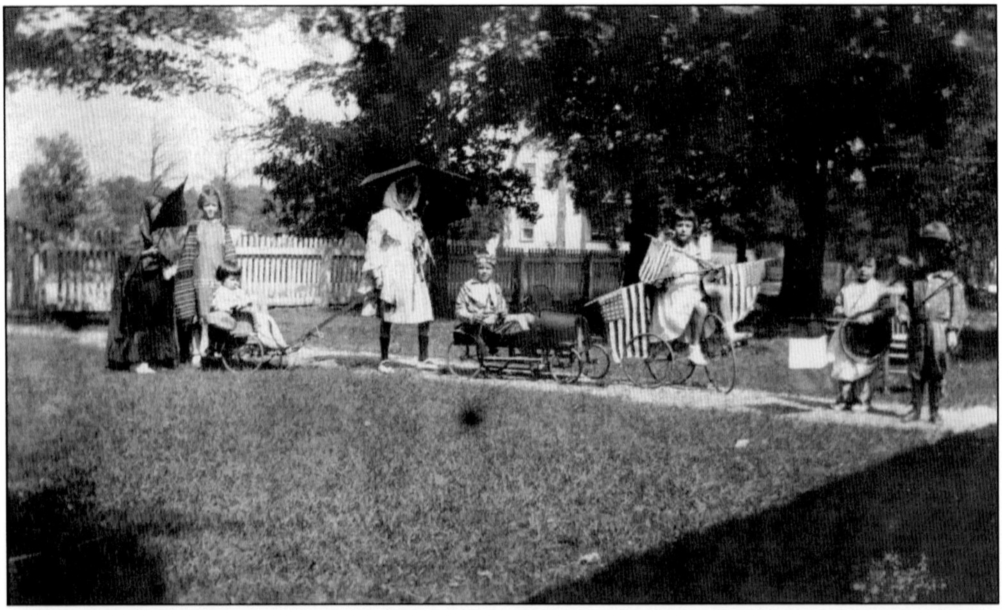

KIDS ON PARADE. Summers were long and lots of fun for children who had endless friends and time to parade and dress up and pretend. Although not all of the children can be identified, it is clear that this parade is on the lawn at the Robert Lancaster house on Howard Street. (Woody and Susan Tucker.)

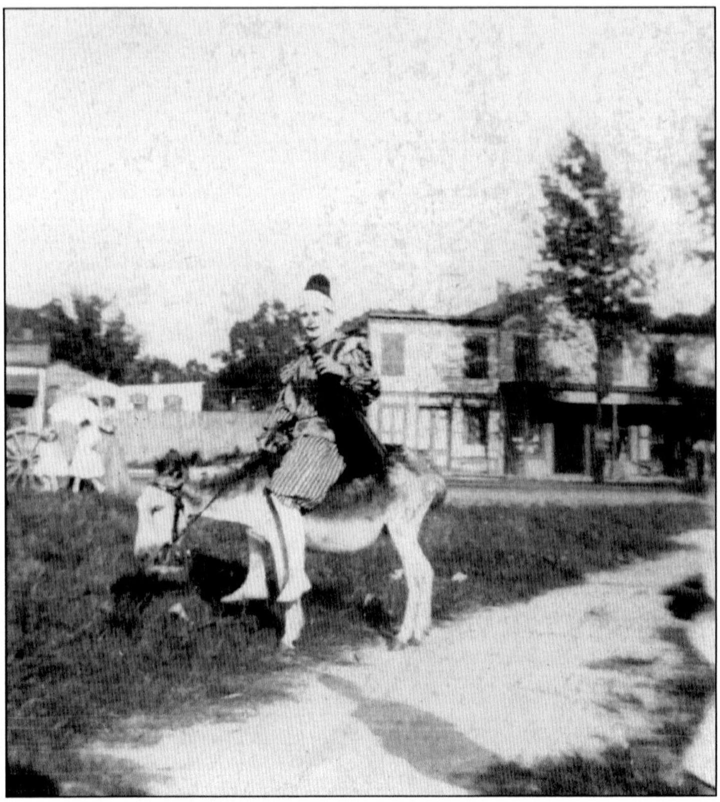

CLOWN ON TOWN SQUARE. No one who has seen this picture can identify the location in town, but the tracks are clearly visible in the background. The theory is that traveling carnivals often came and put on a show in the ballfield that faced the tracks on the west side. Sometime in the early 1920s, someone posed as Pagliacci on a donkey. We can just imagine the kids crowded around to giggle at the odd sight. (Woody and Susan Tucker.)

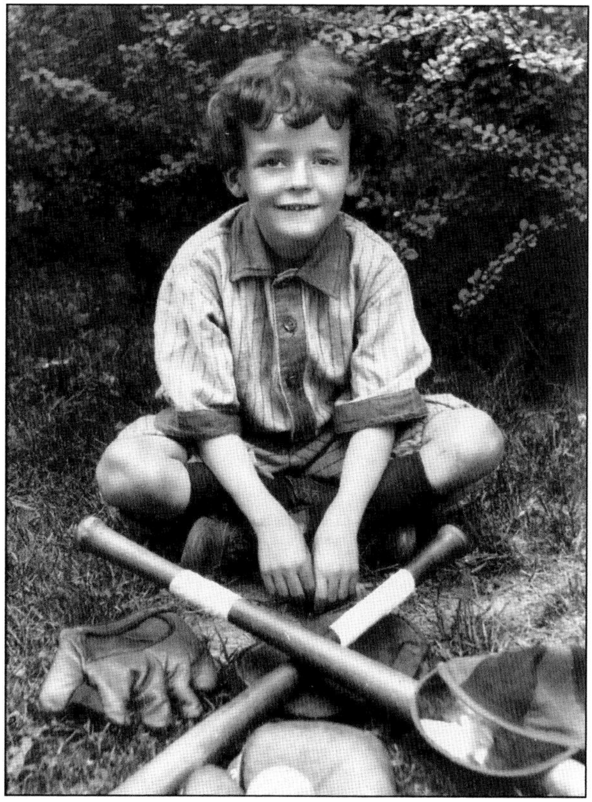

BOOTIE TUCKER. This is Bootie's sixth birthday. Baseball was a passion with this child (and perhaps the man as well). Sarah Wright remembers all the kids playing baseball in her backyard on Duncan Street when stray balls would often land on the roof. "All you had to do was call 169J and Bootie would come over and climb onto the roof to get the ball for you." (Woody and Susan Tucker.)

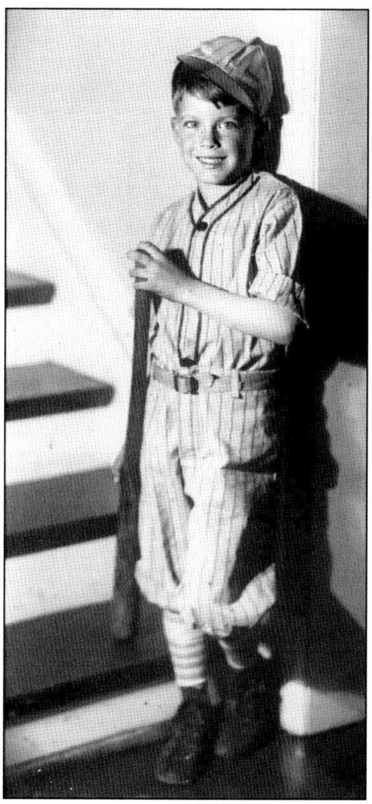

WALTER KIDD "BROTHER" JONES. This photograph was professionally done sometime in the early 1930s. Perhaps inspired by Norman Rockwell, this professional photographer captured Sarah Wright's little brother in the front hallway of the house on Duncan Street. (Sarah Jones Wright.)

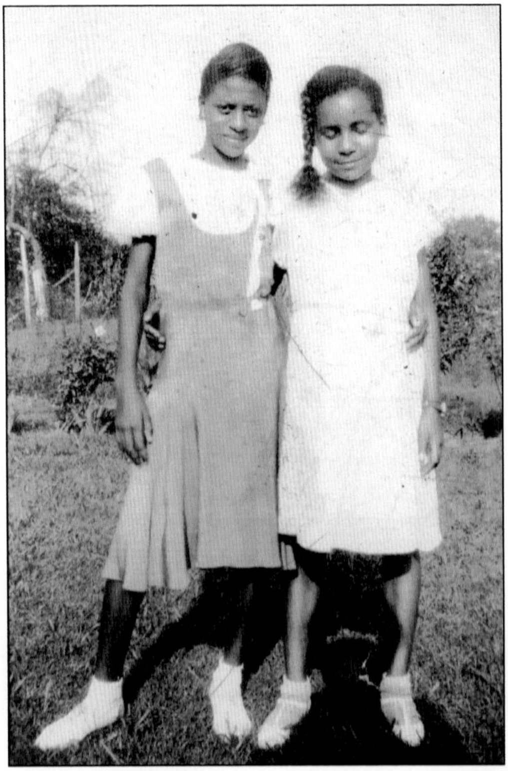

Inez Winston and Camilla Melton. Camilla (right) was the daughter of Herman and Julie Melton and the niece of Annie Laura Winston. Camilla became a nurse at Medical College of Virginia. Inez (left) had a long career in the medical examiner's office in Richmond. (Inez Gray.)

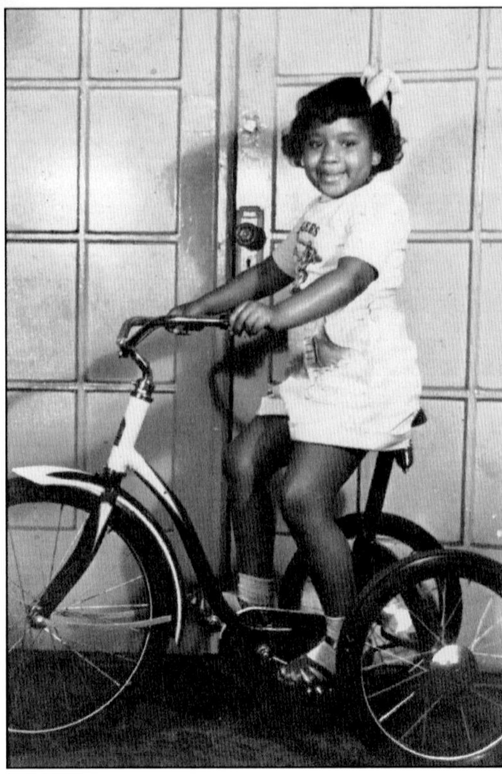

Johnetta Gilliam Spurlock. Johnetta rides her favorite bike. She was the only daughter of Hattie Winston. (Inez Gray.)

Six

SCHOOLS

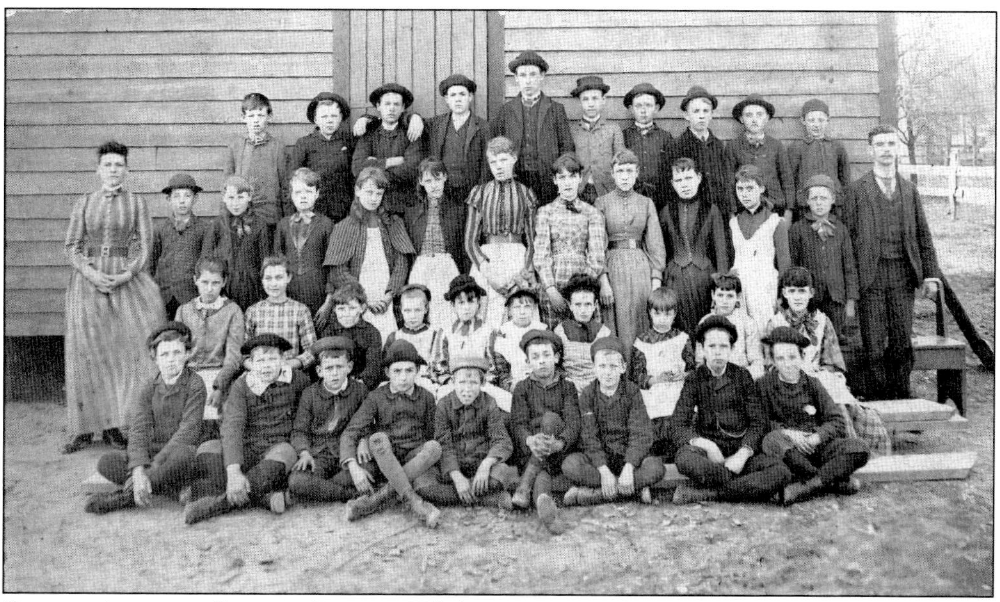

OLDEST ASHLAND SCHOOL PHOTO. While we cannot identify the students in this picture taken in the late 1800s, it is included because it serves to demonstrate that the intellectual life and education of children in the community has always been paramount. It also seems to show that several grades were contained in one ascending class. (P.K. Perrin.)

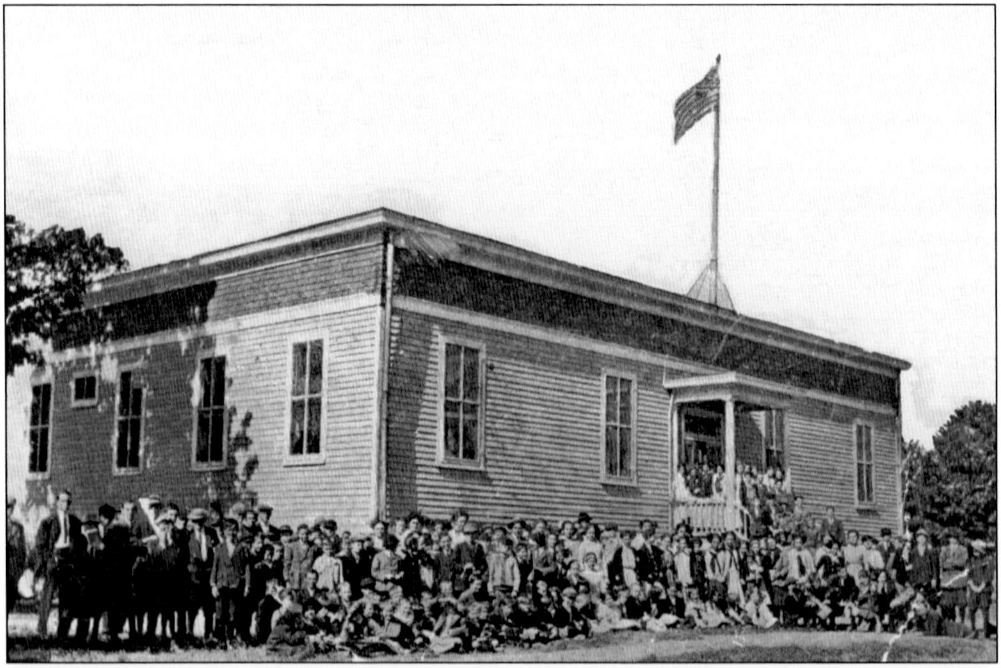

EARLY SCHOOLHOUSE, AROUND 1912. This frame structure was built on James Street for white children after an earlier structure burned down. It is generally thought that black students attended classes at Shiloh Baptist Church. When Ashland High School was built around 1915, this school was moved to the site of the Hanover Training School for black students. (Sarah Jones Wright.)

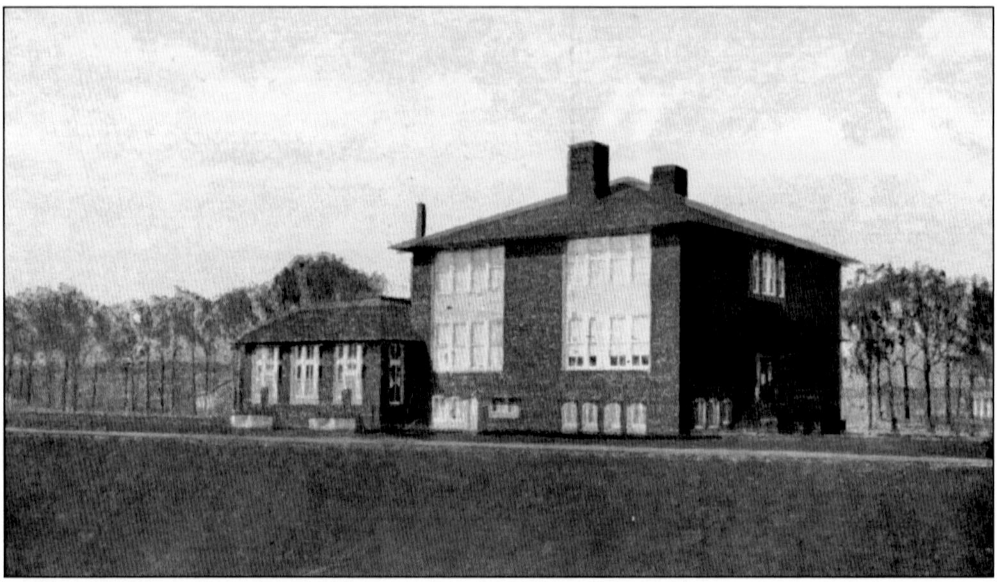

ASHLAND HIGH SCHOOL BUILDING. The school was built in 1915 on James Street. It was a segregated white school that boasted an auditorium for 500, a library, science laboratory, six classrooms, electricity, and steam heat. The structure would fill the town's need for roughly 55 years. It was demolished in the 1970s, and local students moved their activities west on Route 54 to the new and integrated Patrick Henry High School. (Gene Luck.)

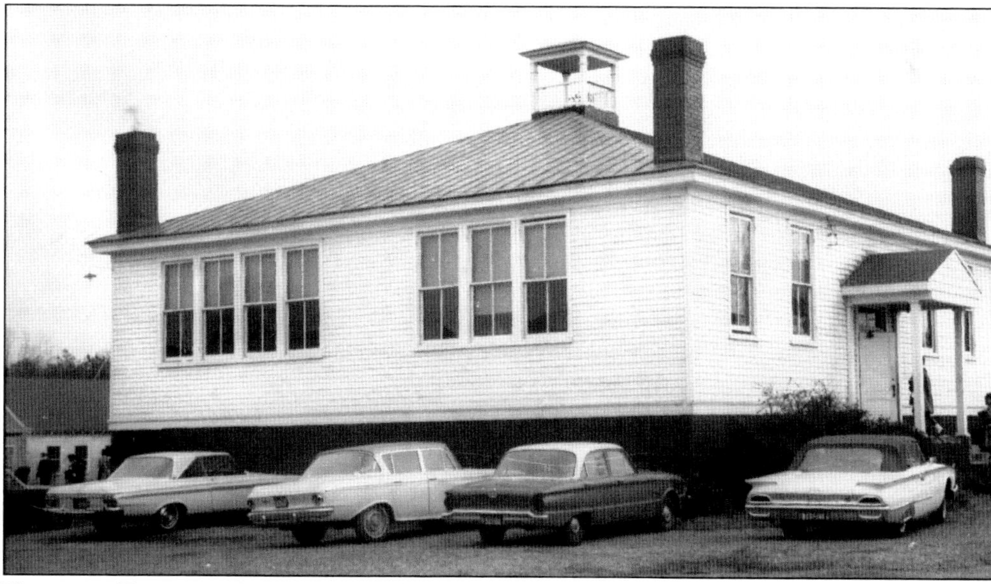

HANOVER TRAINING SCHOOL. According to Inez Gray, the school "was on the site where Gandy stands today. There were four large rooms. All of the classes from kindergarten to 11th grade were in that one large building with three grades per room except 10th and 11th which were together. Boys studied woodwork; girls were taught sewing and cooking along with academic subjects. It was segregated." (*Herald-Progress.*)

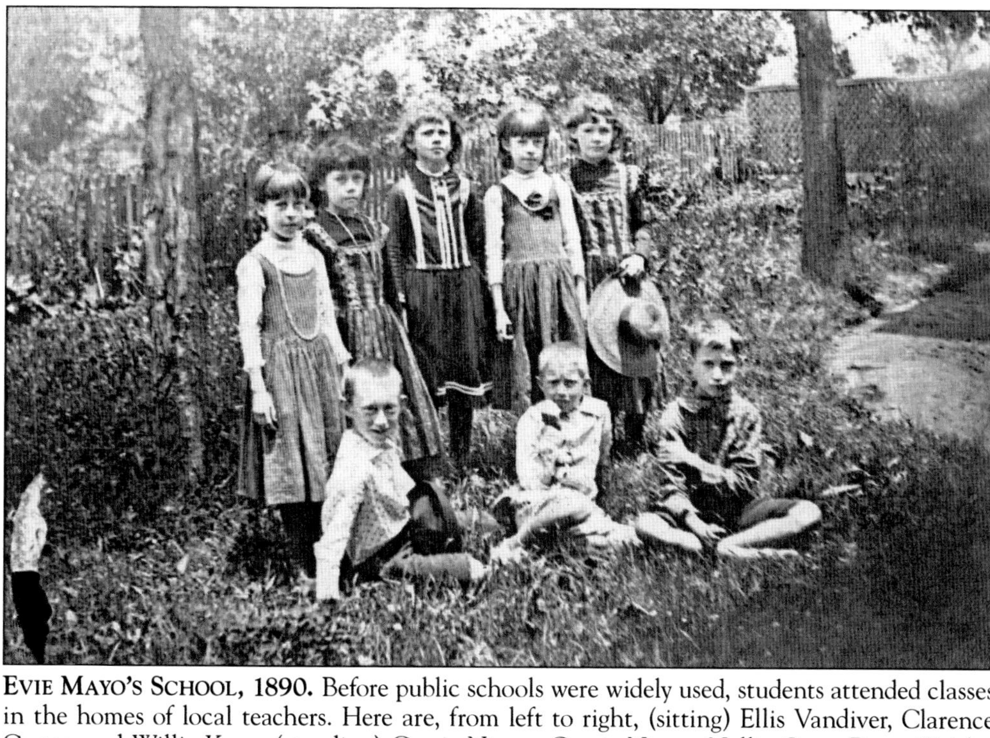

EVIE MAYO'S SCHOOL, 1890. Before public schools were widely used, students attended classes in the homes of local teachers. Here are, from left to right, (sitting) Ellis Vandiver, Clarence Carter, and Willie Kean; (standing) Carrie Nixon, Gussie Nixon, Nellie Crew, Berta Wright, and Marguerite Wright. Another popular school of this type was Miss Herndon's School. (Sarah Jones Wright.)

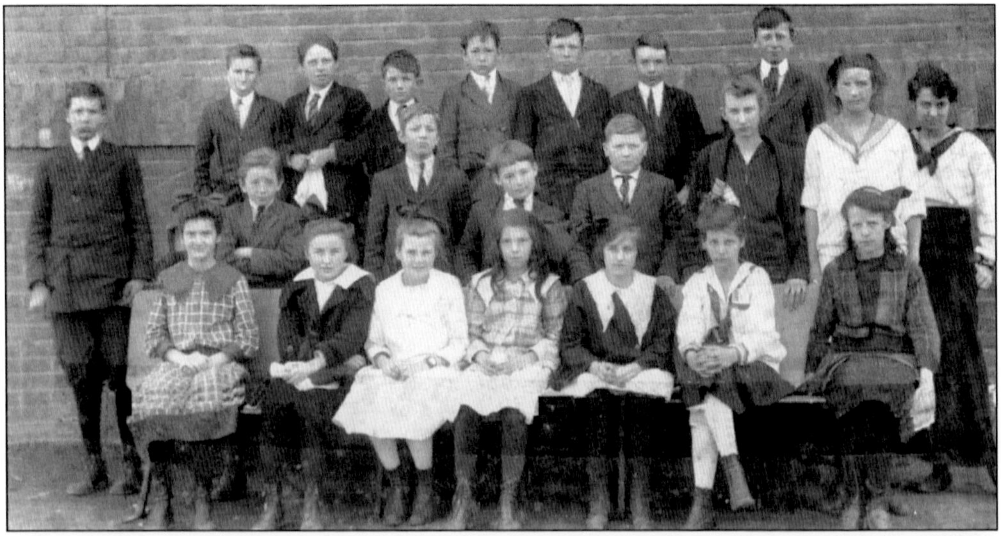

Ashland Graded School, 1916. Shown here from left to right are (front row) Sallie Pollard, ? Cross, Pauline Doswell, Daphne Dugdale, ? Hatcher, Martha Carlton, and Marion Fox; (middle row) Russell Luck, Watkins Hughes, Herbert Griffin, Bobbie Grisham, Roy Sutton, ? Mallory, and two unidentified; (back row) Lewis Cross (expressing an opinion), Atlee Richardson, Arthur Dugdale, Earl Slaughter, Bruce Perrin, Charles Walton, and William Luck. (P.K. Perrin.)

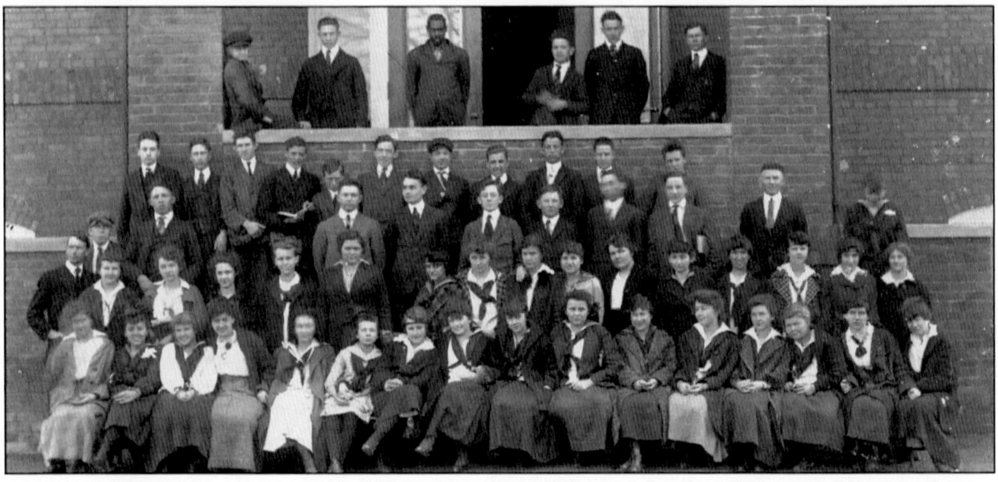

Ashland High School, 1915. Shown here from left to right are (first row) Winnie Carter, Virginia Blasingame, Florine Guilbert, ? Waits, Virginia Bass, Mary Carter, Mary Terrell, Sarah Hughes, Anna Hart, Lyda Gilman, Susan Cross, Elizabeth Blount, Delzelle Puryear, Eleanor Perrin, Juliet Fox, and Lucille Stone; (second row) Mr. ? Garnett (principal), Sallie Morris, Helen Skillmon, Ruth Griffin, Ella Jinkins, Irene Vass, Helen Stone, Gladys Taylor, Janice Thomas, Dorothy Jenkins, Virginia Bagby, Mary Bailey Ragland, Ruth Brinkley, Katherine Ellis, Julia Guilbert, and Rita Wicks; (third row) Carlton Fox, Otto Meyberg, Ernest Luck, Winston Woolfolk, Richard Chenery, Garland Quarles, Chastine Coleman, Lee Hunt, William Thompson, and Sue Carter; (fourth row) Hampton Jesse, Andrew Burton, Mosby Hilliard, Alex Fleet, Maylon Hutcheson, Jack Roberts, William Blincoe, Philip Brinkley, Archie Priddy, Nat Lancaster Jr., and Joseph Stone; (fifth row) Clarence Woodfin, Claiborne Carter, William ? (janitor), Woodson Mills, Wendell Skillmon, and Richard Cardwell. (Sarah Jones Wright.)

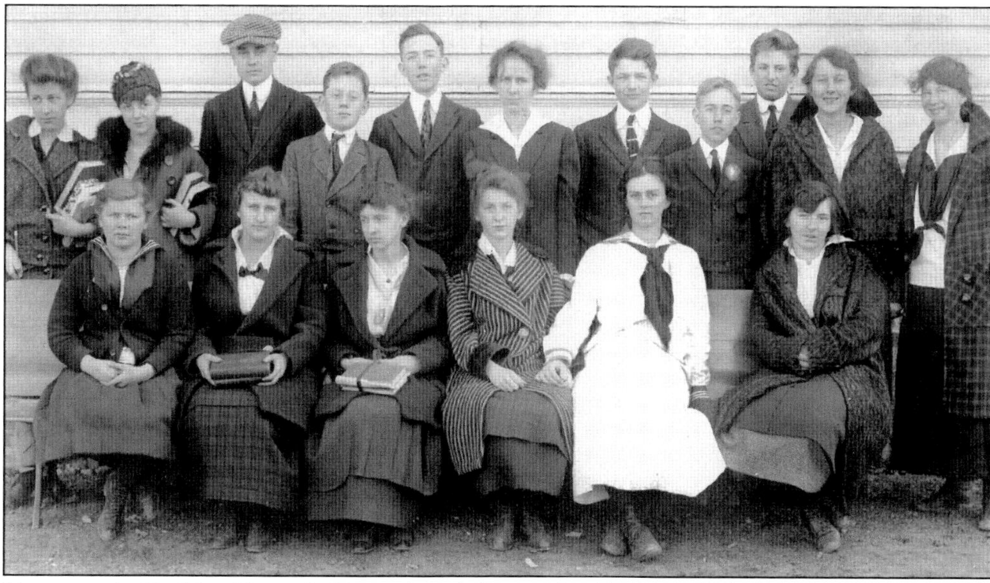

CLASS OF 1918. The Class of 1918 is, from left to right, (front row) Eleanor Perrin, Sallie Penn Morris, Helen Skillmon, Delzelle Puryear, Janice Thomas, and Juliet Fox; (back row) Byrd Sydnor, Anna Hart, Winston Woolfolk, Dick Chenery, Jack Roberts, Miss Mary Cocke, Bill Blincoe, Jim Roberts, ? Carneal, Elizabeth Blunt, and Lucille Stone. (Sarah Jones Wright.)

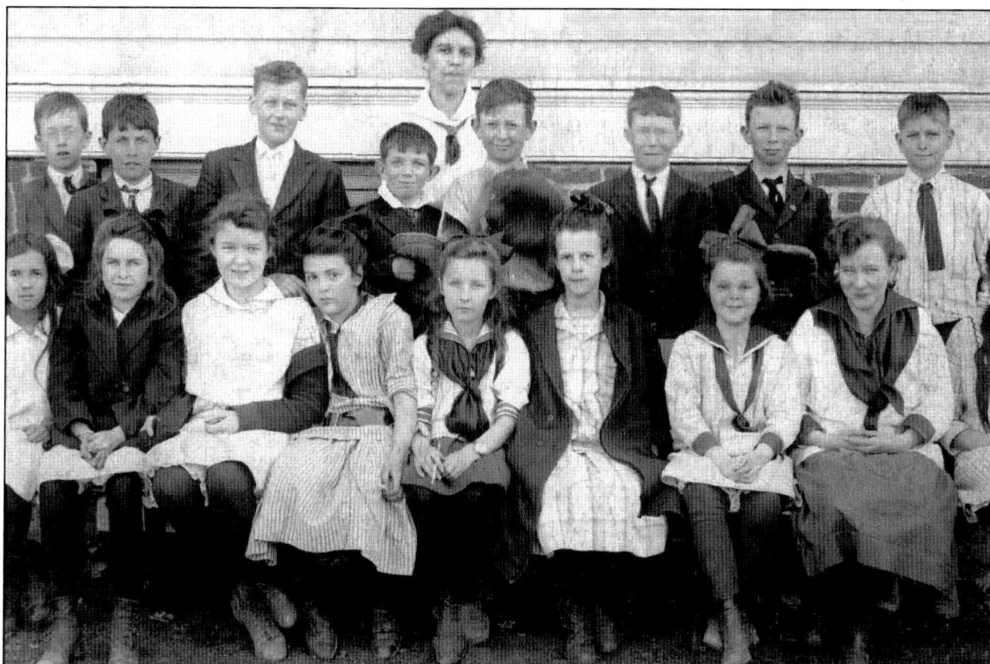

ASHLAND SCHOOL FIFTH GRADE, 1915. Miss Spain (middle of last row) taught these Ashland youngsters. From left to right are as follows: (front row) Zara Dugdale, Dorothy Cardwell, Katherine Tucker, Eloise Blasingame, Mary Lydia Quarles, Marion Fox, Grace Martin, Inez Slaughter, and Sofia Stone; (back row) Hatcher Wells, Oswell Headley, Alfred ?, Troy Sutton, Buck Dugdale, Willie Luck, unidentified, Bruce Perrin, and two unidentified. (P.K. Perrin.)

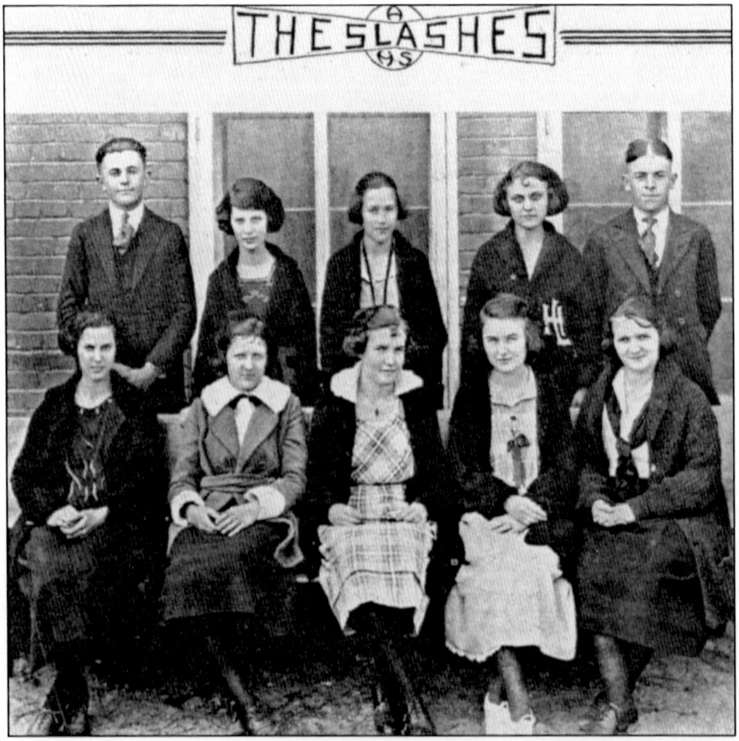

THE SLASHES YEARBOOK, 1920. Sadly, yearbooks of this vintage did not provide a key to locate the students in the picture. However, it is known that the ten students are, in no particular order, Gladys Boschen, Martha Carlton, Noland Donahoe, Margaret Upshaw, Elizabeth Cross, Pauline Doswell, Hatcher Wells, Louise Wells, Gertrude Saunders, and Dorothy Luck. These were the junior members of the class. (*Herald-Progress*.)

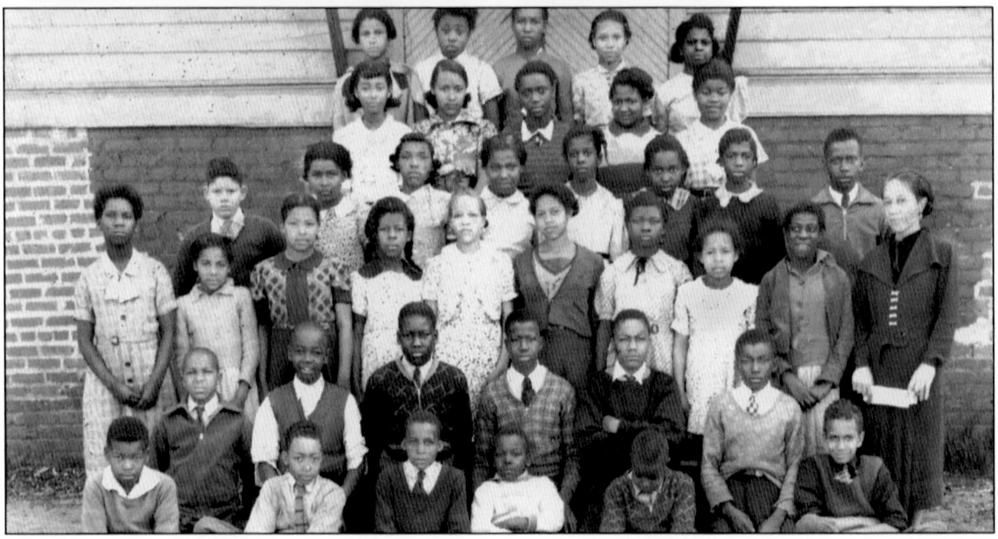

FIFTH AND SIXTH GRADES, HANOVER TRAINING SCHOOL, 1938. The students are, from left to right, (first row) unidentified, Alton Robinson, unidentified, Pillsbury Shelton, two unidentified, and ? Lewis; (second row) unidentified, Marshall Morton, unidentified, Howard Abrams, "Dee" Carter, and unidentified; (third row) Ruth Bowles, Florine Hughes, unidentified, Ann Sue Thompson, Jeanette Hunter, Juanita Robinson, two unidentified, "Doll Baby" Robinson, and Miss Alexander; (fourth row) unidentified, Gladys Shelton, unidentified, Frances Tinsley, Ruby Robinson, unidentified, Odessa Robinson, and unidentified; (fifth row) Dorothy ?, Rose Dabney, ? Lewis, Addie Bernice Winston, and unidentified. The sixth row remains unidentified. (Inez Gray.)

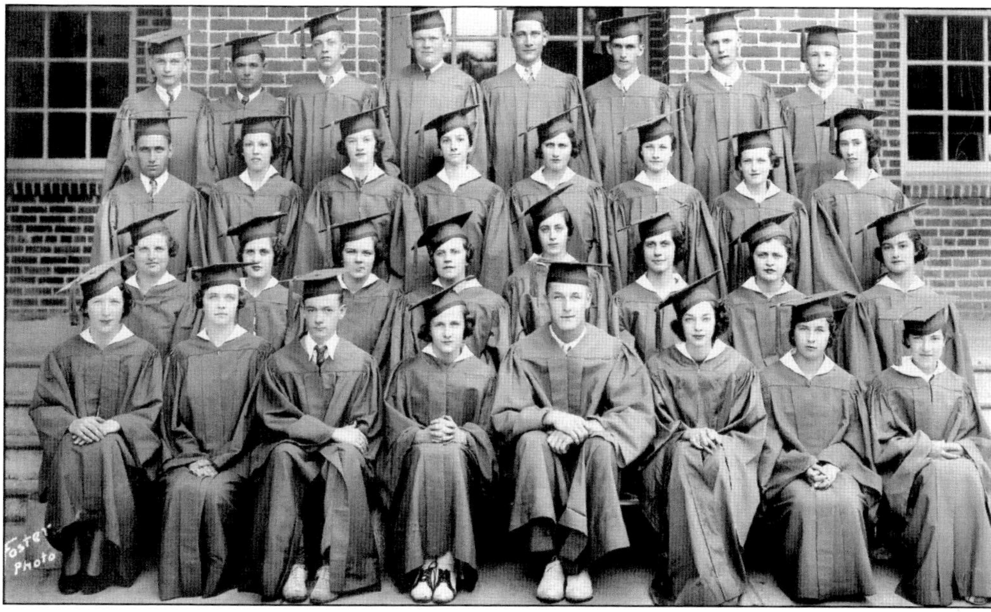

ASHLAND HIGH SCHOOL, 1935. Shown here from left to right are the following: (first row) Katie Corkley, Ruth Lane, Fritz Palmore (treasurer), Polly Bridges, Ray Taylor (president), Julia Gray Saunders (vice-president), Louise Loving, and Virginia Miller; (second row) Ellen Lumsden, Conde Booth, Dorothy Raper, Josephine Thrower, Sarah Jones, Virginia Sydnor, Bec Campbell, and Linda Lavin; (third row) Oneil Strother, Elizabeth Carter, Betty Taylor, Anne Taylor, Annie Good, Roberta Gilman, Jane Pollard, and Virginia Fox; (fourth row) Rose William Jenkins, Arthur Lee Davis, Hunter Jones, James Armstrong, Sparlan Hedrick, James Haley, Harold Starke, and William Gilman. (Ann Curtis Palmore.)

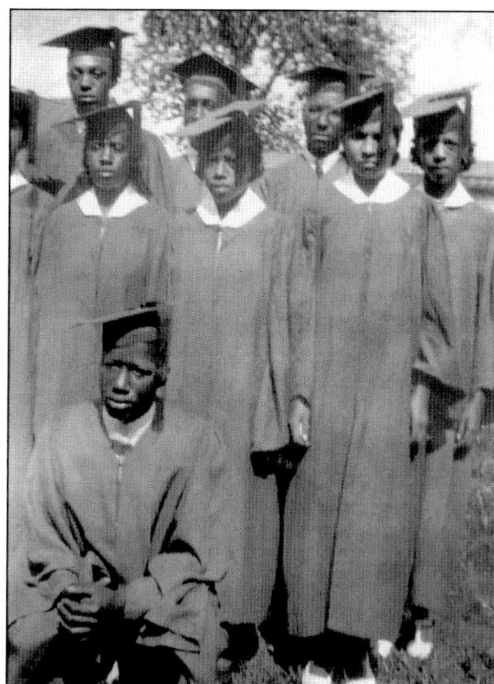

ELEANOR AND ROBERT WINSTON'S GRADUATING CLASS. Graduating from Hanover County Training School in 1933 were, from left to right, (seated) Douglas Burruss; (standing) Eleanor Winston (partially obscured), Frances Miller Davenport, Edna Carter, Thelma Carter Peterson, Marie Goodloe Jackson, Leroy Carrington, Robert Winston, and Bruce Carter. (Inez Gray.)

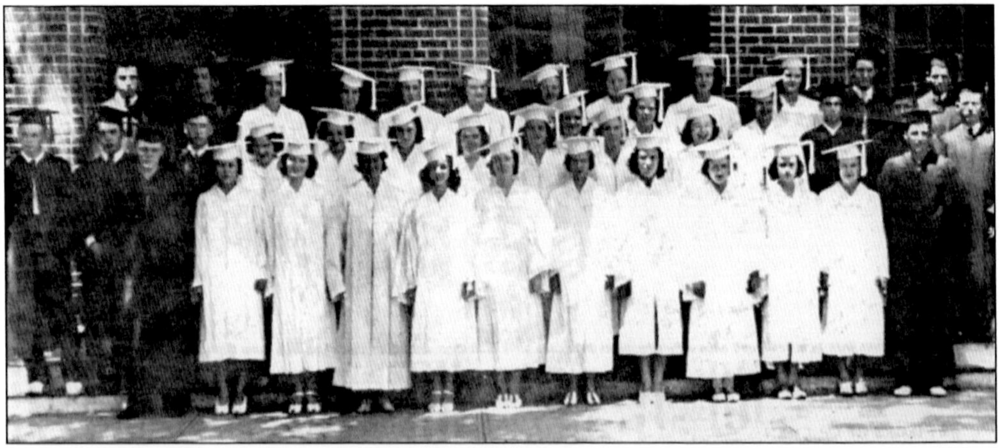

HENRY CLAY HIGH SCHOOL GRADUATES, 1939. Shown here from left to right are (front row) Joe Stiles, Frances Mallory, Virginia Vellines, Boo Yarbrough, Virginia Burruss, Margaret Cannon, Myrtle Clark, Marian Jacobs, Mary Jackson, Mildred Trevett, Grace Hale, and Ashton Taylor; (middle row) Charles Dowdy, Billy Broach, Ballard Jewell, Nan Dowdy, Lillian Boettcher, Elizabeth Jones, Ethel Mason, Evelyn Waggoner, Clara DePanicis, Sally Hamilton, Florence Moore, Marion Watkins, Margaret Shelton, Howard Smith, Edward James, and Robert Pemberton; (back row) Gray Gilman, Charles Vaughan, Sarah Harris, Virginia Broyles, Effie Boettcher, Nell Houston, Norine Campbell, Barbara Granger, Helen Raper, Nell Luck, Raymond Lawhead, and Charles Johnson. Not pictured is David Melton. (*Herald-Progress.*)

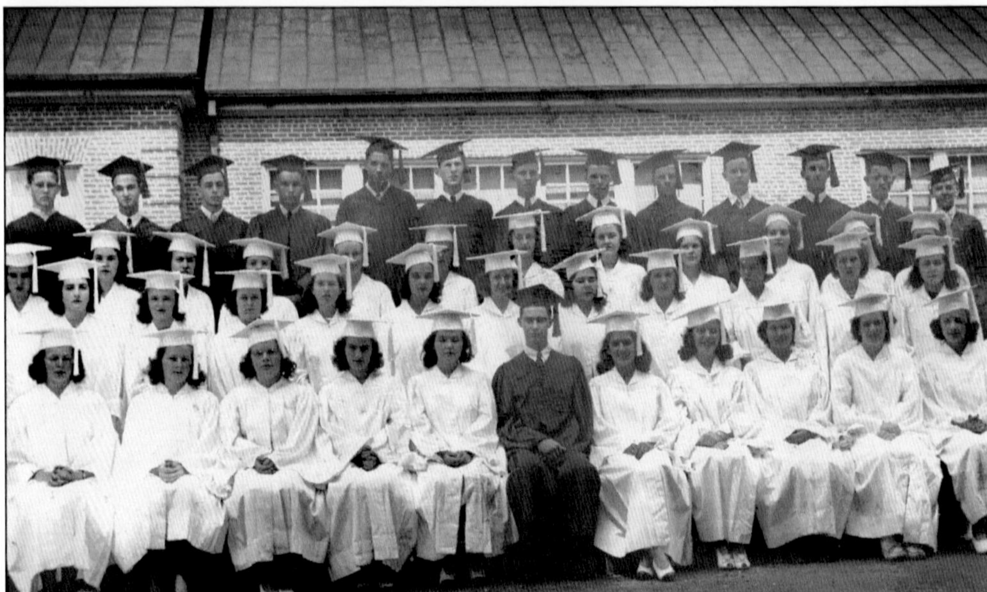

HENRY CLAY HIGH SCHOOL, 1942. Pictured are, from left to right, (first row) Mary Stuart Mason, Gladys Coulter, Doris Harlow Quarles, Betty Louise Priddy Kendrick, Rowena Asher, Norvell Scott, Eloise Goddin, Jane Moreland, Jane Beck, Adina Allen, and Douglas Jerome Zeno; (second row) Eleanor Skinner, Frances Loving Hale, and Marguerite Davis; (third row) four unidentified students, Laura Yancey Jones, and seven unidentified students; (fourth row) Leslie Campbell, James Pine, Lawrence Jacobs, Gordon Witbeck, unidentified, Billy Johnson, and seven unidentified students. (Eloise Piccolo.)

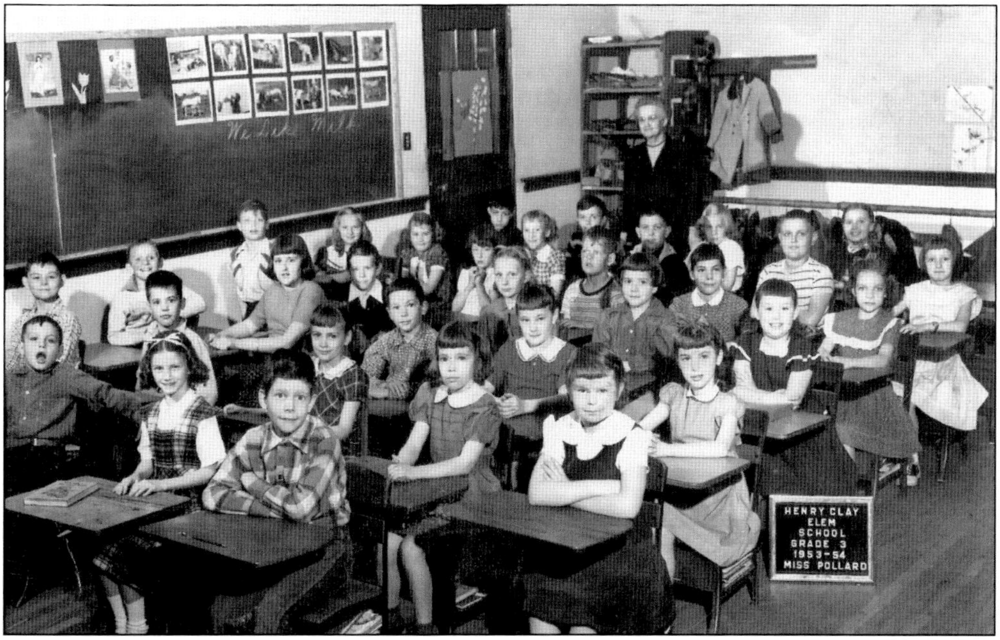

HENRY CLAY ELEMENTARY SCHOOL, 1953. Miss Eva Pollard is standing at the rear. Pictured here from left to right are (first row) Barbara Luck, Beverly Loving, Margaret Knight, Carolyn Lane, and Patricia Kelly; (second row) Berkley Hall, Lyn Letson, Carolyn Keyes, Barbara ?, Beth Anne Moses, Edward Leslie, and Shirley Harper; (third row) Dorothy Toombs, Judy Christian, Fred Palmore, Shirley Noel, Tommy King, Cabell Luck, and unidentified; (fourth row) Richard Lloyd, Ronald Grubbs, Frances Hall, Edwin Jones, unidentified, Bertie Crawley, and Earl Luck; (fifth row) Randy Lloyd, Benny Holloway, Kenneth Mallory, two unidentified, and David Hubbard. (Cabell Luck.)

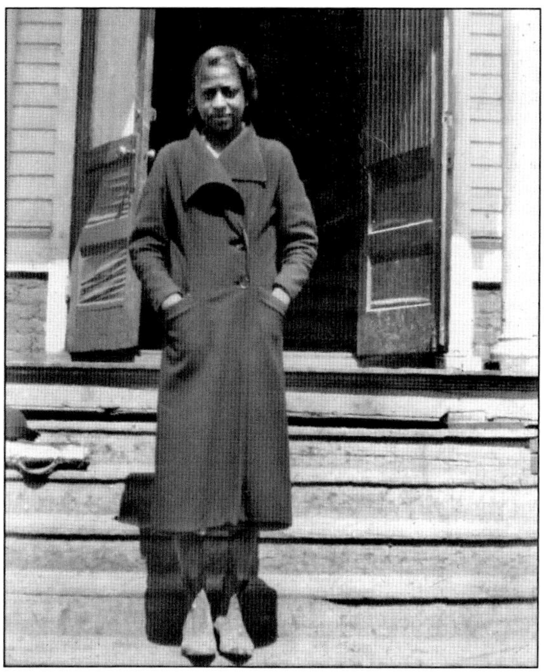

INEZ GRAY IN FRONT OF HANOVER COUNTY TRAINING SCHOOL. Inez Gray studied here and went on to work at Medical College of Virginia, learning histology under a German immigrant named Dr. Walter Riesse. In 1952, she began work at the medical examiner's office in Richmond and stayed until 1979. (Inez Gray.)

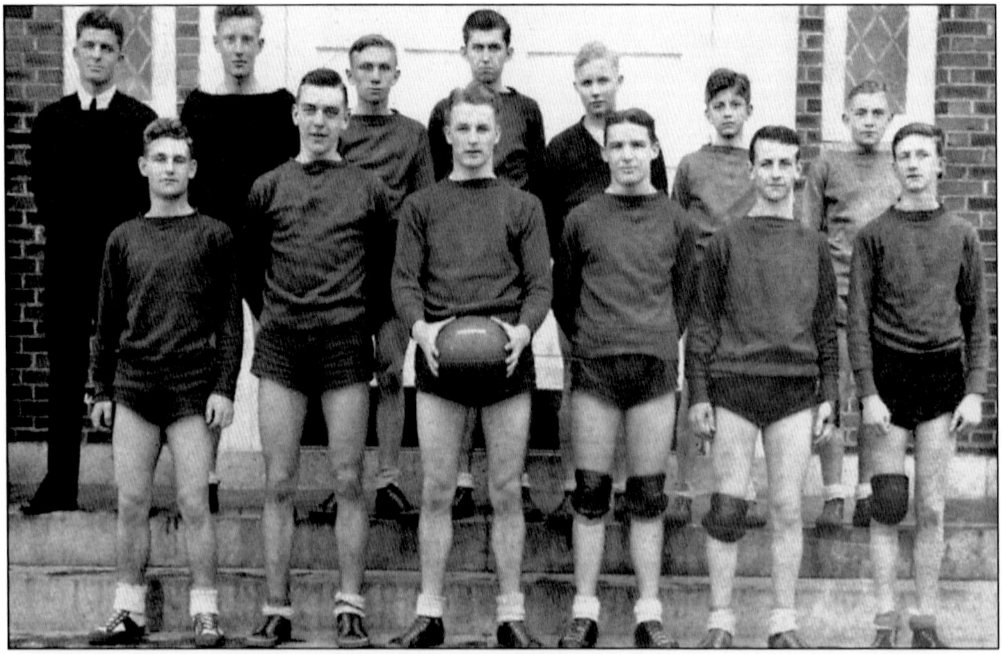

Basketball at Henry Clay High School, 1934. The players are, from left to right, (front row) George West, William Ray, captain Ray Taylor, Lewis "Doc" Taylor, and William Fox; (back row) Robert Smith, Cecil Saunders, Carter Ellis, Joseph Jones, Harold Starke, Hunter Jones, and James Via. This was one of the most successful high-school teams in Ashland history. The team stands in front of the Alumni Gymnasium. (*Herald-Progress.*)

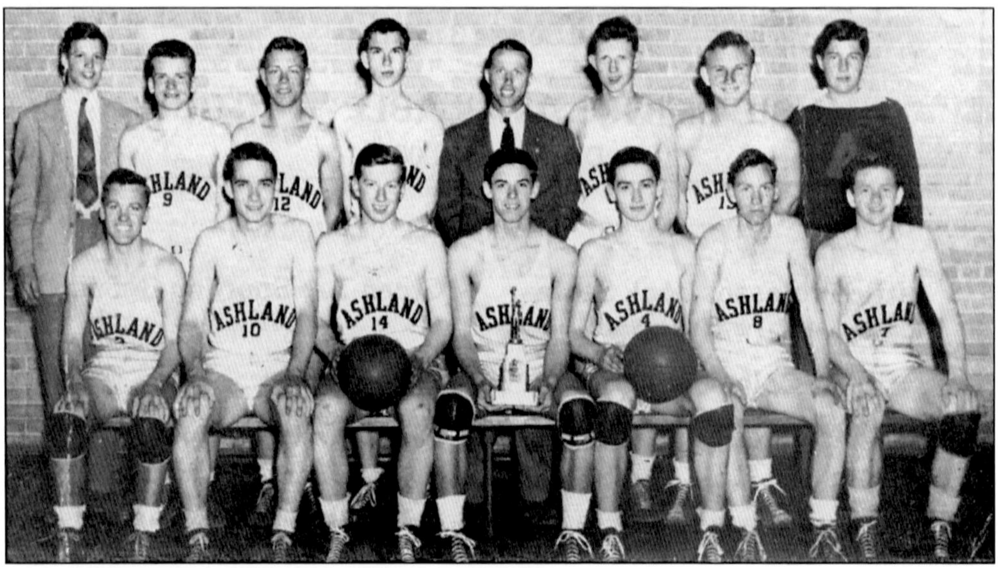

Basketball at Henry Clay High School, 1945–1946. Shown here are, from left to right, (front row) "Twig" Mallory, Shelburn Smithson, Jim Pollard, Bill Buchanan, Christian Compton, Archie Cannon, and Jimmy Taylor; (back row) manager Dan Simpson, Leitch Wright, Tommy Mills, Bobby Wall, coach Lyle McFall, P.K. Perrin, Chastine Mallory, and Gordon Hammond. The school completed the season under two coaches. George Compton coached the first two games, and Lyle McFall took it from there. (*Herald-Progress.*)

Seven

CARS

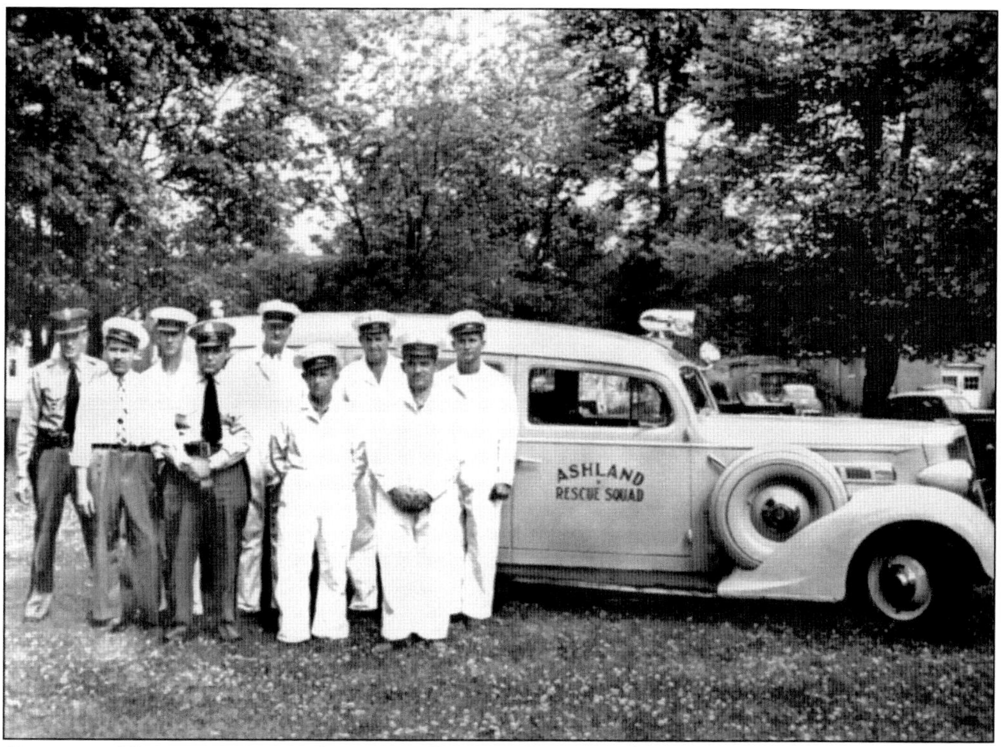

CHARTER MEMBERS OF THE ASHLAND RESCUE SQUAD. This picture was taken in the spring of 1951 on the town lot before the Municipal Building was constructed. The former Crew and Clayton Funeral Home donated this 1937 Packard Hearse. It was Ashland Rescue Squad's first ambulance. From left to right are Police Officer Shook, Joseph Long, John Billingsley, Police Officer John A. Houchins, Hunter Lane, Lewis Bryant, Joseph Jones, Edward Stanley, and Herbert Sledge. All of these were charter members of the organization except Joe Long, who served for 25 years. A charter member not pictured here was Russell Lowry. Ashland Volunteer Rescue Squad was first established in May of 1950. (Ashland Rescue Squad.)

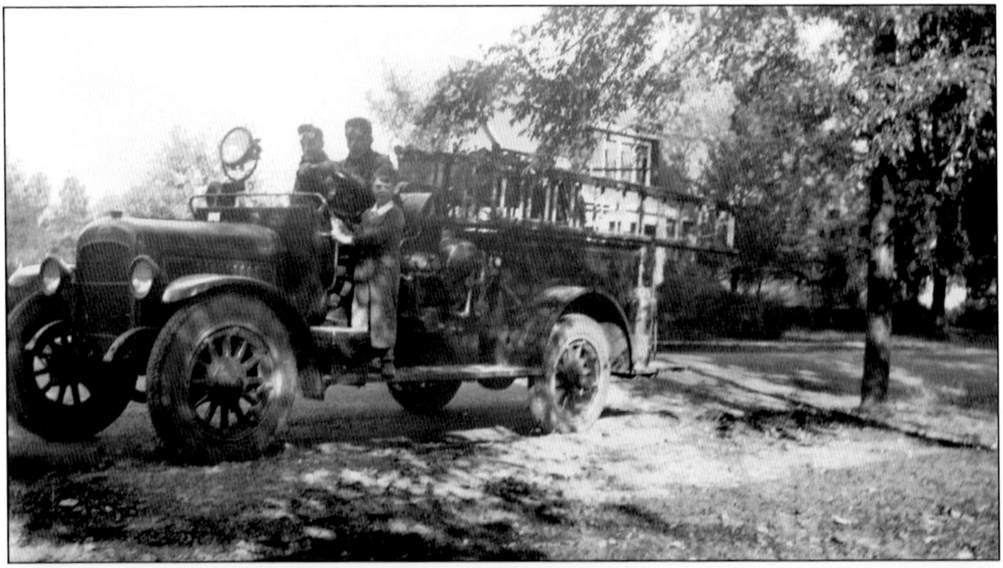

Where's the Fire? This fire truck seems prescient as it parks for a photo in front of the Henry Clay Inn, which later burned to the ground in 1946. (Lelia Palmore Weyman.)

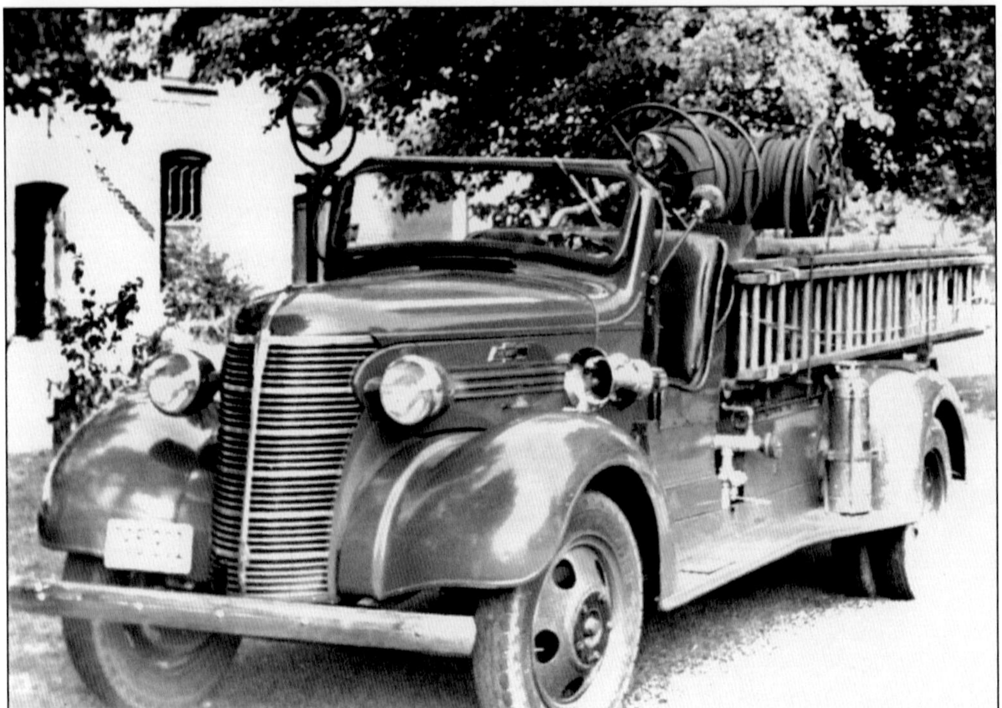

Vintage Fire Truck. Marion Herget remembered: "I sometimes pinch hit for missing volunteer firemen and went out with the trucks on calls, working the pumper while the men (people like Ed Stanley and Bootie Tucker, whoever was available and willing to) manned the hoses. I had my eyebrows singed off and my hair frizzed by a woods fire and thereby lost some of my enthusiasm, but still answered the call whenever they were desperate enough to need me." (Lelia Palmore Weyman.)

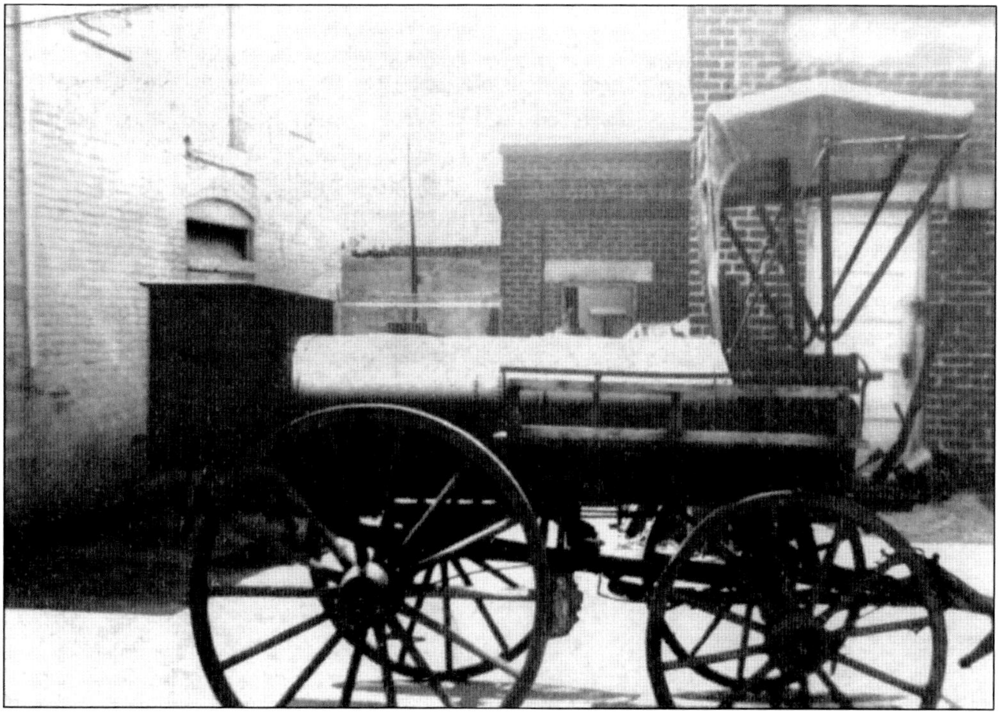

ESSO WAGON. This was one of the first wagons used to deliver fuel to Ashland. J.M. Pollard and Sons of Maple Street in Ashland most likely used this vehicle. (*Herald-Progress.*)

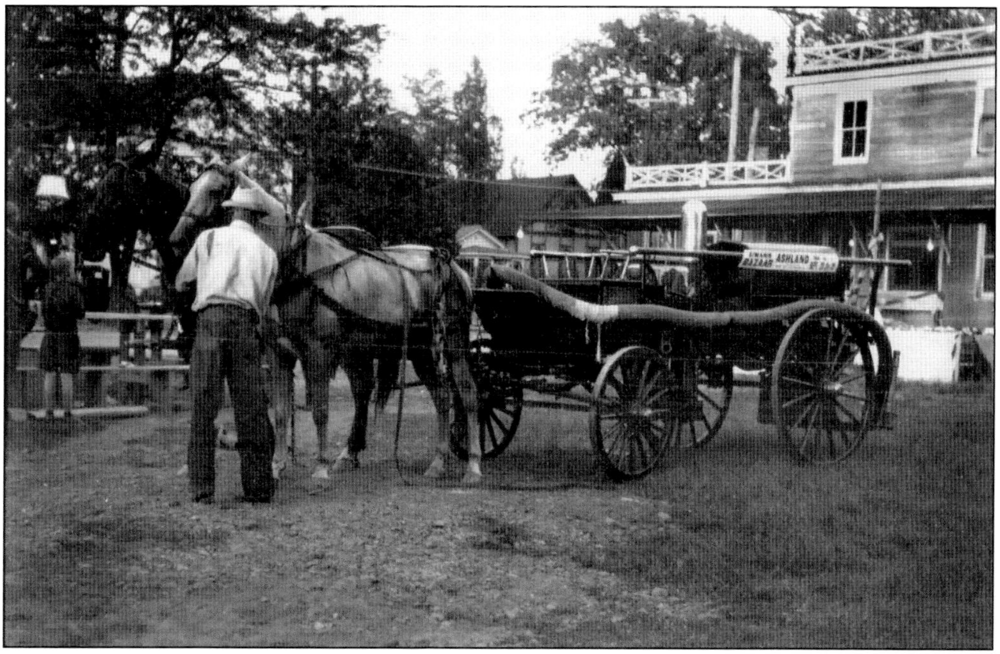

KIWANIS WAGON. Fire was always a danger in Ashland. In 1893, almost the entire business block on the west side of Railroad Avenue burned to the ground. Horse-drawn wagons like this were an improvement over the bucket brigades that had sufficed for fire protection. (Terry Barnes Shaw.)

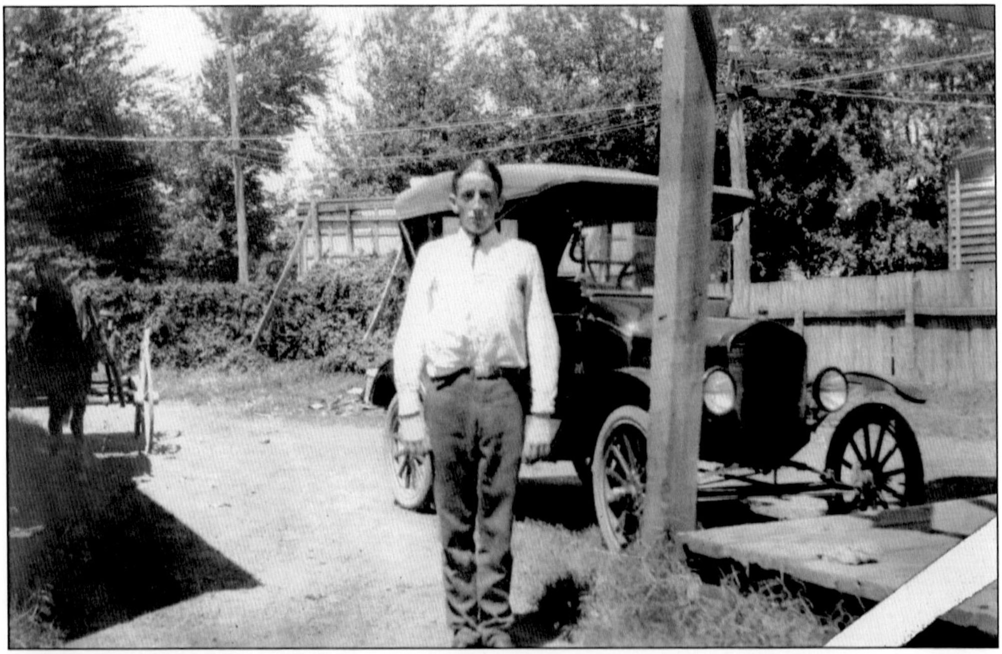

"DOT" HUGHES. Although many in Ashland called T.W.L. Hughes "Doc"—a logical reference since he became a pharmacist—in his high-school annual, he was called "Dot." No one knows when or how the shift was made or whether it was a typo in the annual. (Hughes family.)

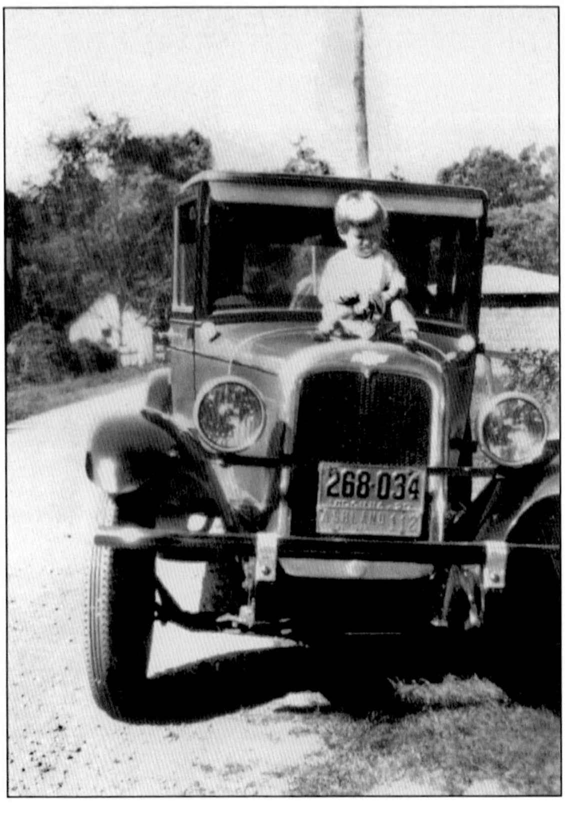

ELOISE GODDIN. Sitting on top of the family's first Chevrolet, Eloise seems perfectly content to smile at the Brownie camera. (Eloise Piccolo.)

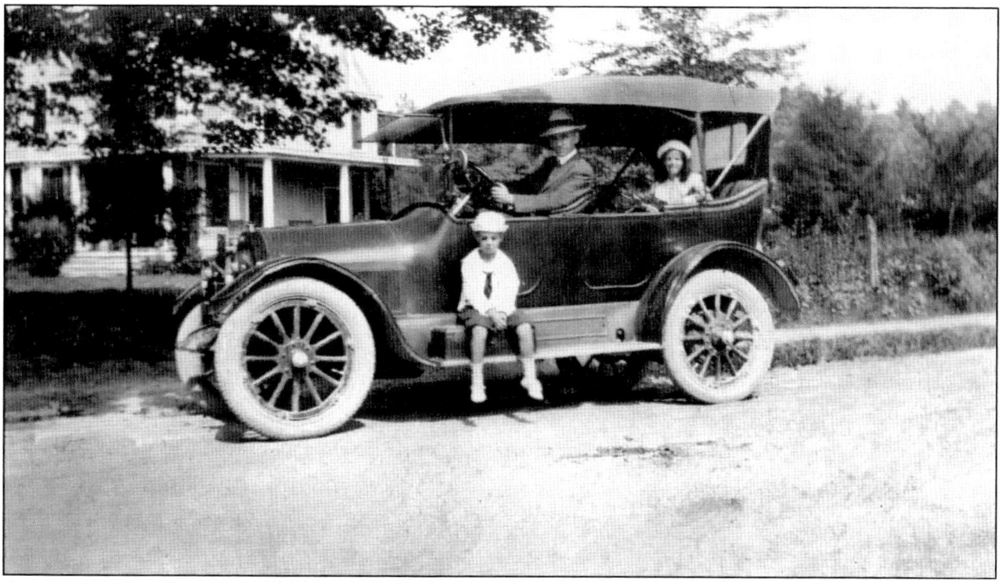

CHALMERS. James Marcellus Cox, Elizabeth Pendleton Cox, and James Kimbrough Cox sit in their new Chalmers. This image is thought to be sometime in 1918. (Pen and Betty Carol Stevenson.)

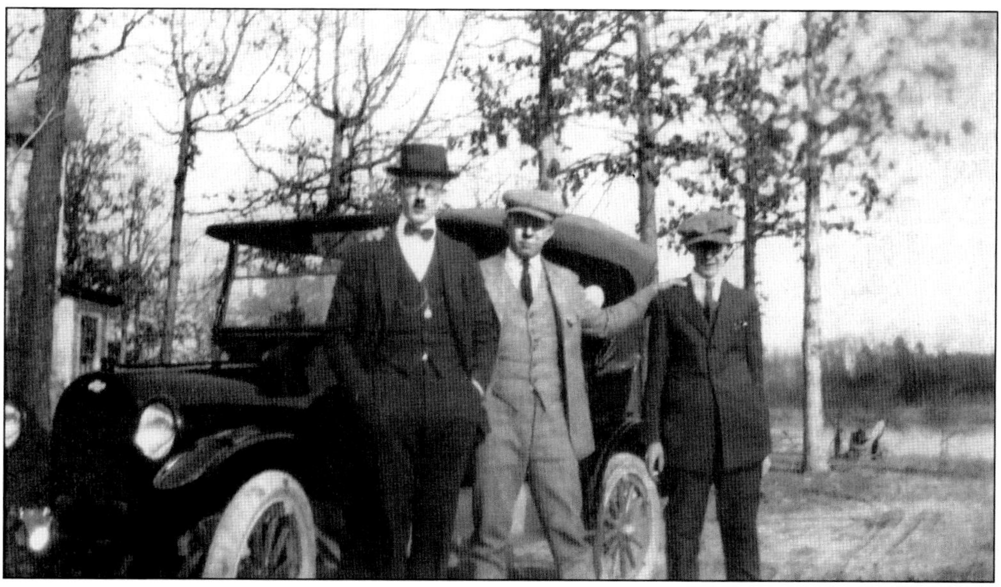

FIRST FORD. This was allegedly the first Ford to arrive on flatbed train in Ashland. (P.K. Perrin.)

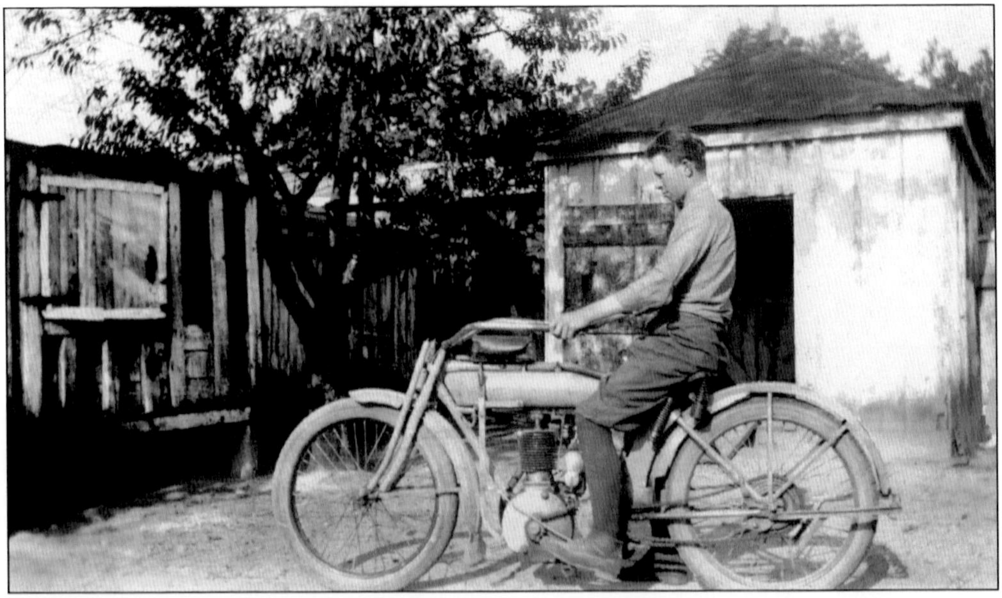

Bruce Perrin on Motorcycle. Showing off his new motorcycle, Perrin comes to rest in front of a garage on England Street. (P.K. Perrin.)

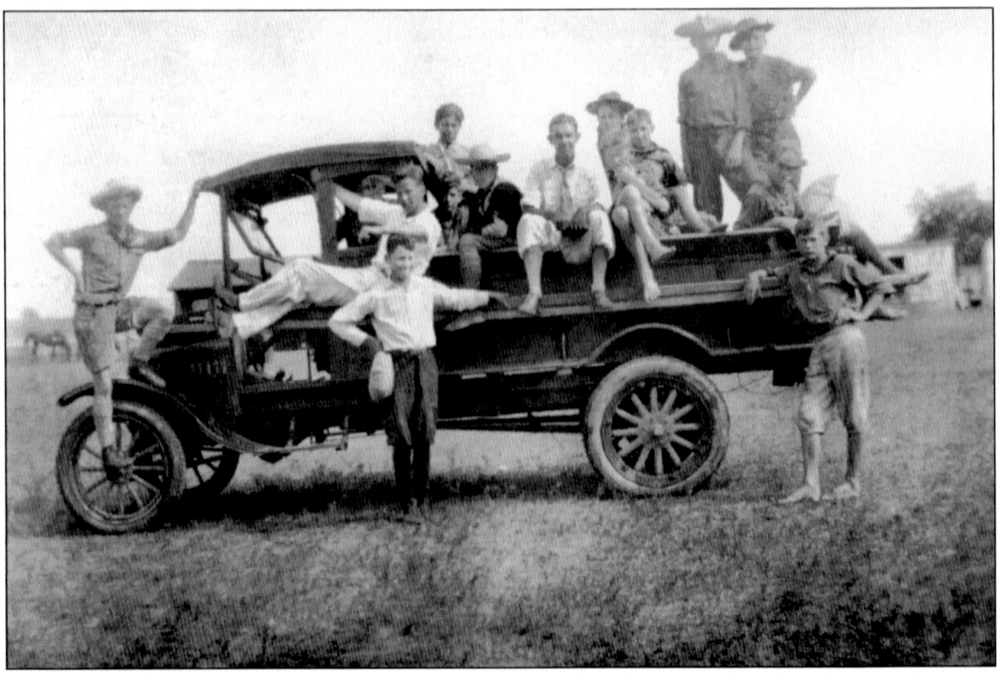

Boys on Trucks. Sadly, we do not know who any of these boys are, but the photograph seems to evoke a sense of the camaraderie of old Ashland. (P.K. Perrin.)

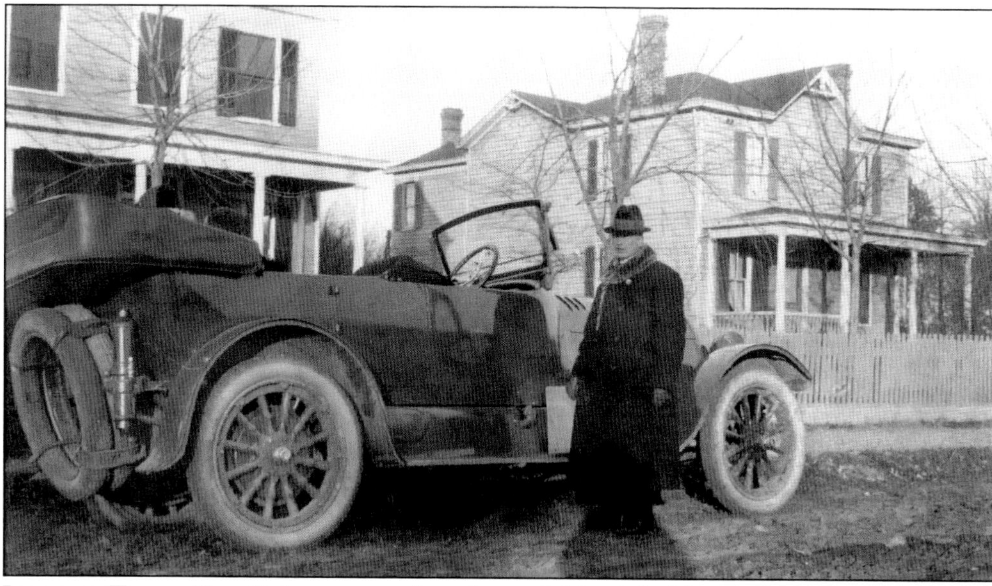

LEAVING TOWN. Tom Oakes gets ready to leave Ashland for New Jersey in his Fiat. (Sarah Jones Wright)

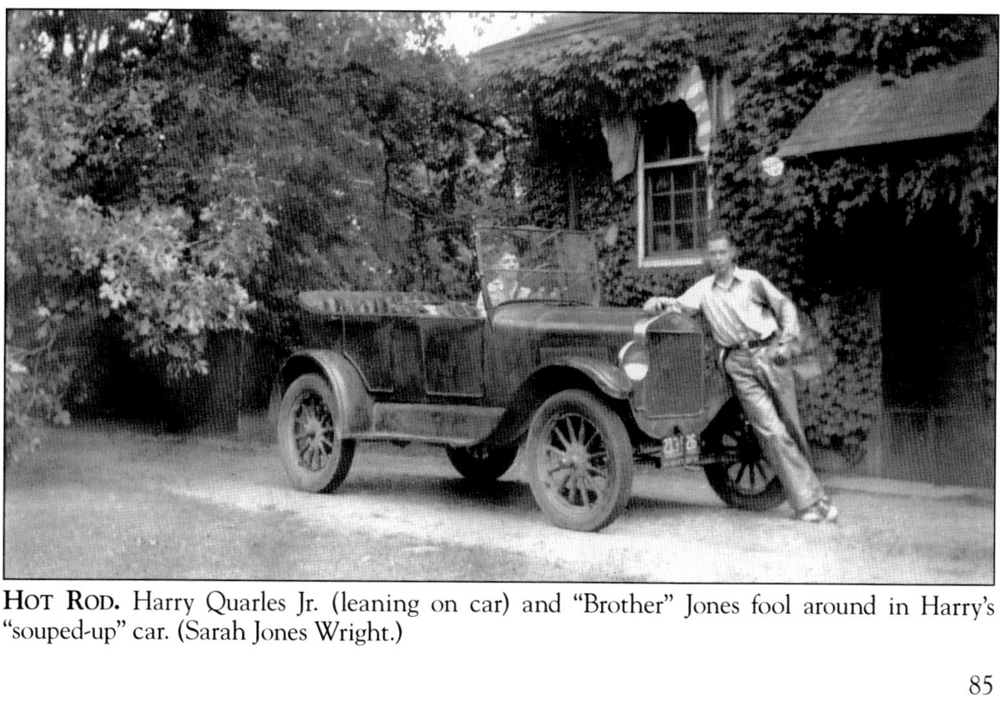

HOT ROD. Harry Quarles Jr. (leaning on car) and "Brother" Jones fool around in Harry's "souped-up" car. (Sarah Jones Wright.)

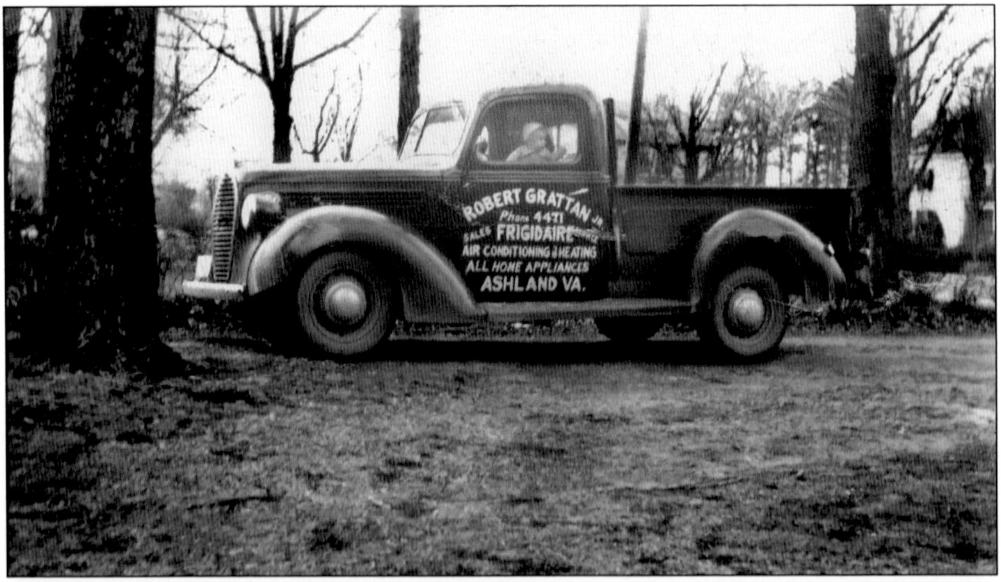

TODIE GRATTAN. Robert Grattan's store delivered in this now-vintage truck. In the 1950s, his son Todie waived from the driver's window. (Harvey "Todie" Grattan.)

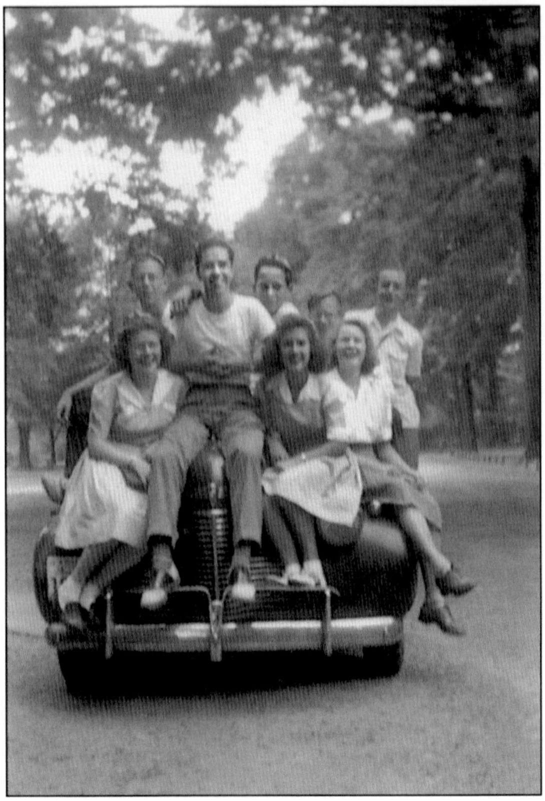

FRESHMAN SPREE. On a balmy day in 1942, these Randolph-Macon students, wearing their "rat caps," piled on top of Doris Harlow's car. From left to right are (front row) Doris Harlow (Quarles), Roy Jarrett, Eloise Goddin (Piccolo), and Gladys Coulter; (back row) A.B. Vaughan, Leslie D. Campbell, Curtis A. Palmore, and Adolphus Shepherd. (Eloise Piccolo.)

Eight

CLUBS

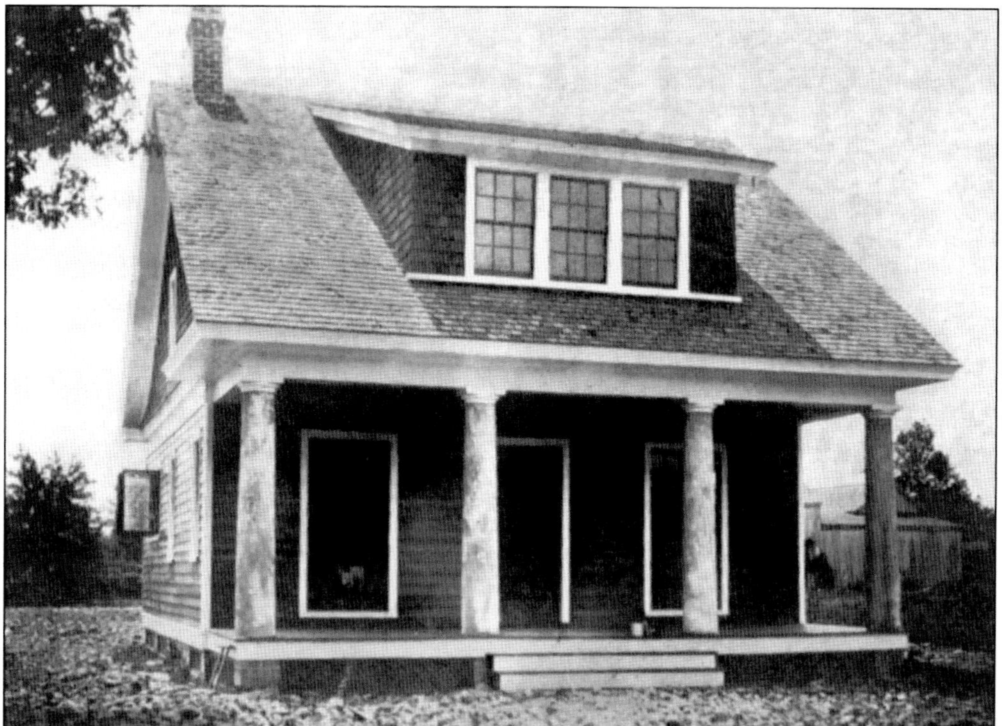

HANOVER CLUB. Chartered in Ashland in 1905, the Hanover Club is the second-oldest men's social club in the state. The Hanover Club had 20 original members, including C.E. Potts (president), E.A. Evans (vice-president), and S.J. "Stoney" Doswell (secretary-treasurer). Even before the charter, they met for several years in rooms over Hughes Drug Store. The club bought a lot facing Henry Clay Road behind the Henry Clay Inn and built a clubhouse in 1906 and 1907. The house was sold to the Kappa Sigma fraternity in 1920. The men continued meeting in rented rooms above D.B. Cox's store and later above the *Herald-Progress*. In 1943, the club bought back its old house from the fraternity. (Woody and Susan Tucker.)

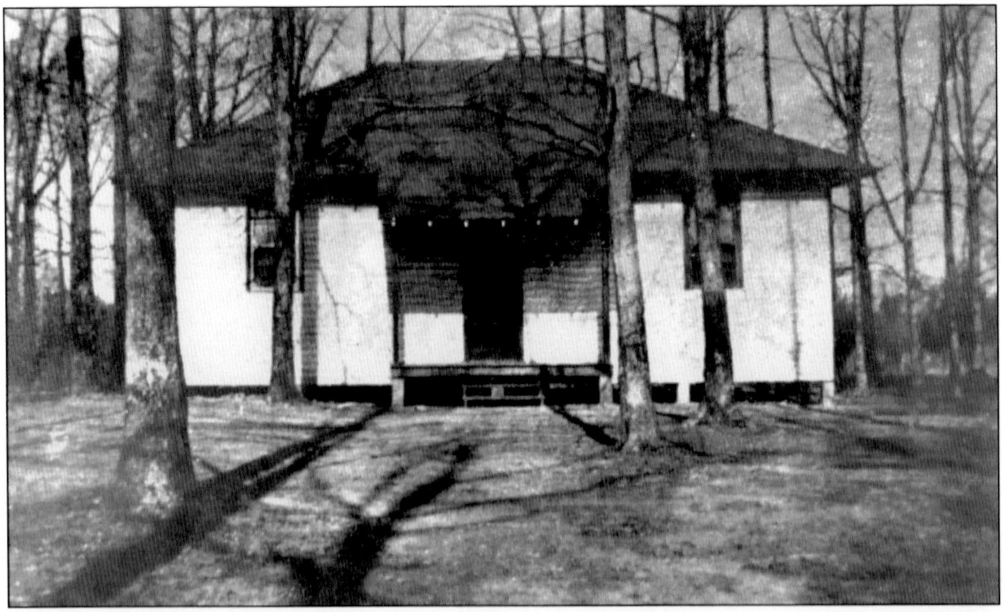

Boy Scout House. This clubhouse stood behind what is today the Henry Clay School on James Street. (Harvey "Todie" Grattan.)

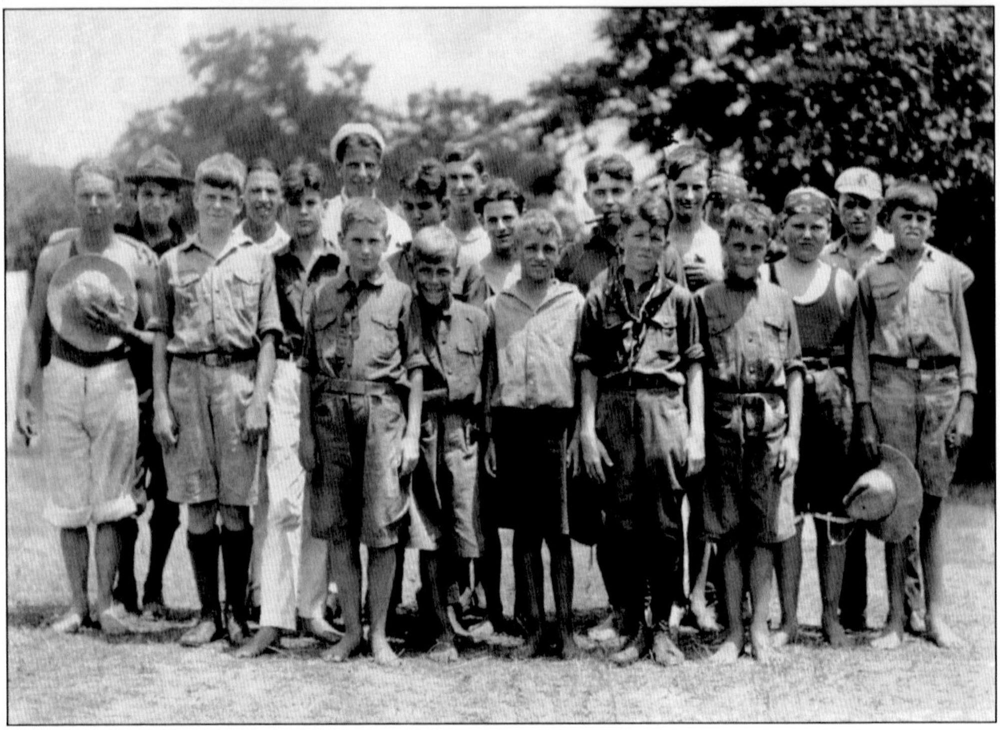

Scouts in 1924. Shown here from left to right are Leslie Lumsden, Arthur Dugdale, W.C. Blanton Jr., Reginald Dunn, Ben Chisholm, S.L. Blanton, Monroe Bennett, Calloway Brown, J.K. Cox, Hill Carter, Overton Sale, James L.W. West, Dick Cross, Tom Lancaster, Jack Fisher, Tom Wells, Clyde Barnes, Edwin Davis, Murdock Chisholm, and Willard Wells. (*Herald-Progress.*)

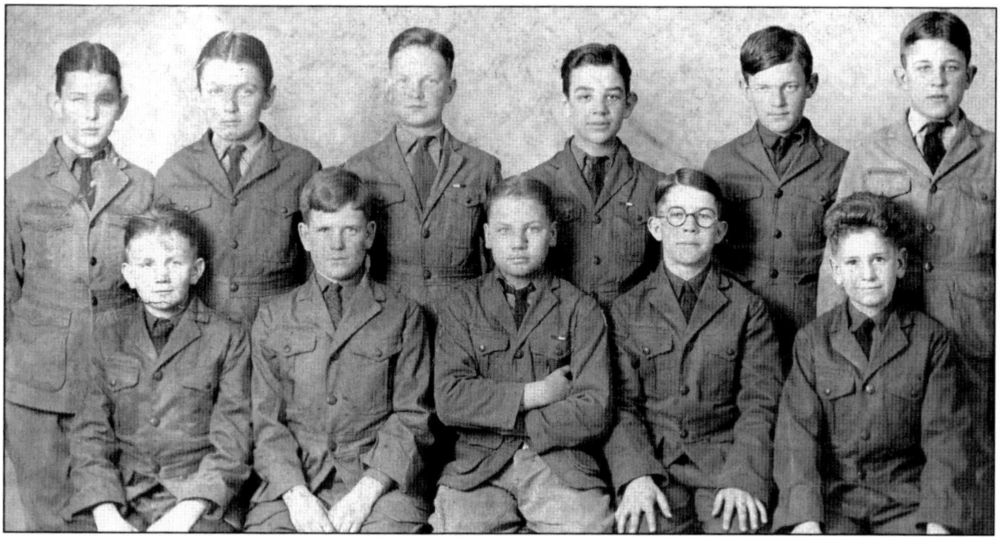

BOY SCOUT TROOP NO. 1. Chartered in 1912, this is the oldest Boy Scout troop in Virginia. Shown above from left to right are (front row) Charlie Boy Stone, Mutt Blanton, Edward Ballard, Tom Lancaster, and Jeff Blanton; (back row) Richard Beirne, Robert Grattan Jr., Bill Puryear, Kimmie Cox, Robert Miller, and Steve Luck. Foster Studios took this photo in the early 1920s. (Harvey "Todie" Grattan.)

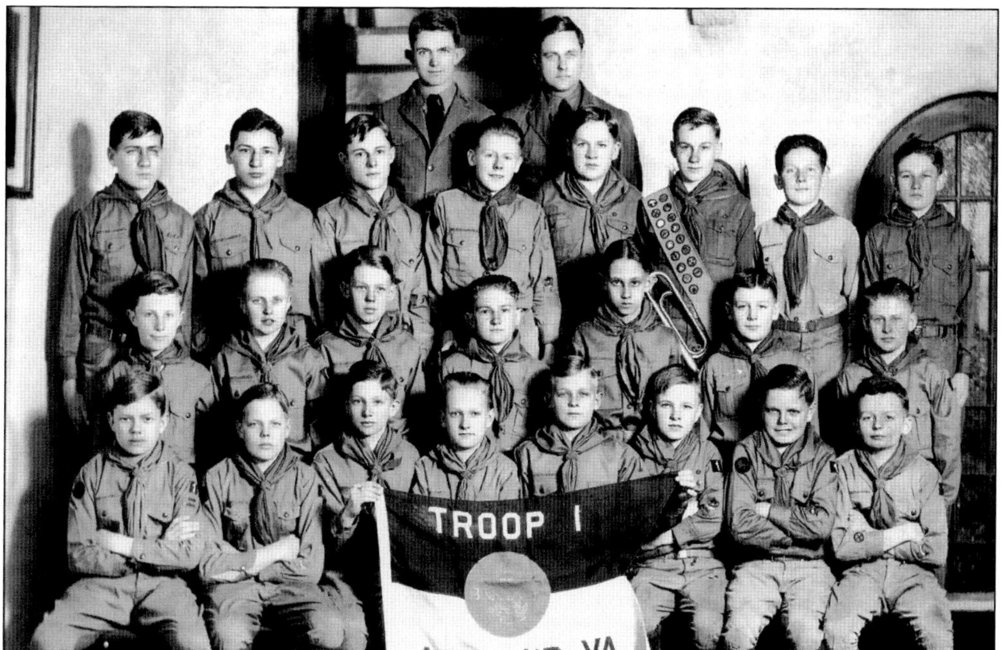

THE TROOP EXPANDED. The scouts are, from left to right, (first row) Drewry Kerr, Merriwether Lewis, Vaughan Palmore, John Moncure, Frank Perkins, Ed Gilman, Mickey Lewis, and Bootie Tucker; (second row) William Gilman, Dougie Boschen, Jimmy Gordon, Lewis Fuqua, Jimmy Peregoy, Spottswood Keene, and Victor Yowell; (third row) Bobby Stone, Sam Tyler, Clyde Barnes, Walton Hall, Buell Weems, Virginius Vaughan, Bill Blanford, and Watson Fuqua; (fourth row) Buck Dugdale and Monk Wightman. (Woody and Susan Tucker.)

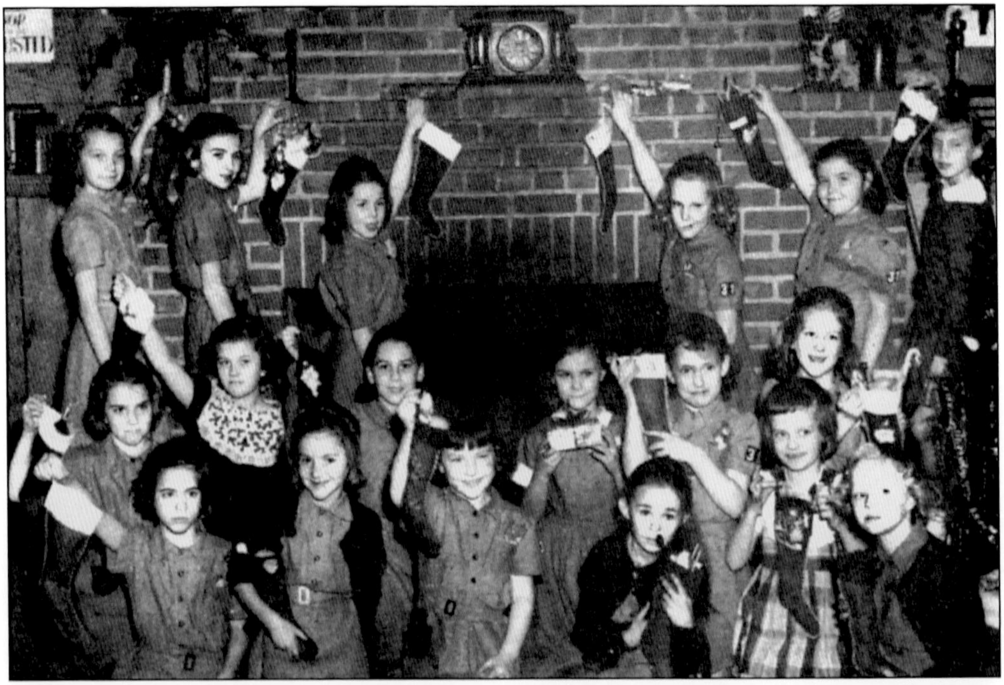

Brownies. Troop 31 hangs stocking in 1952. From left to right are (front row) Sue Miller, Patty Babcock, Lorraine Brown, Barbara Marr, Brenda Mills, and Evelyn Coates; (middle row) Louse Roberts, Linda Goard, Carol Anne Britton, Emily Spurlock, Gail Bryant, and Sandra Jones; (back row) Beverly Rae Howard, Carolyn Doggett, Dottie Lewis, Martha Shaw, Diane Coates, and Judy Starke. (*Herald-Progress.*)

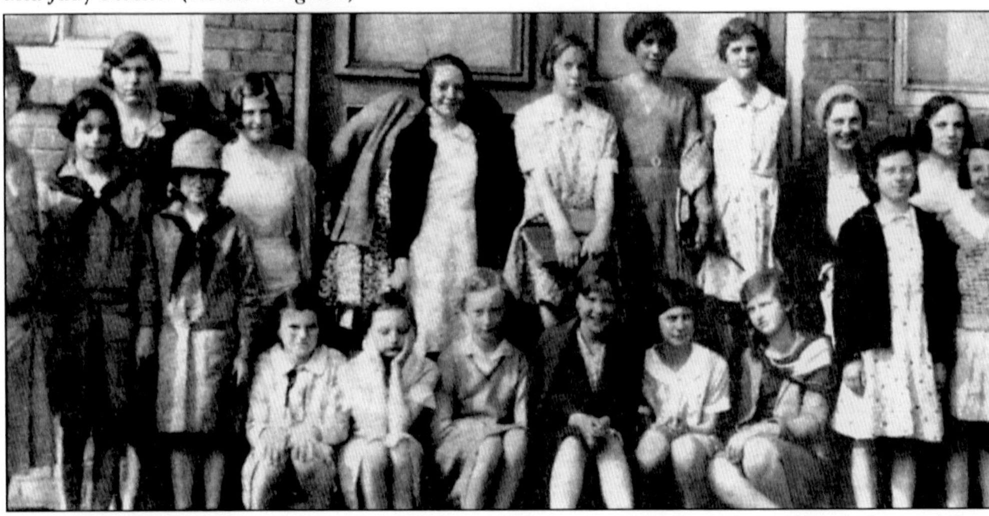

Ashland's First Girl Scout Troop. This photo was taken in 1930 and includes members of Ashland's first Girl Scout troop. Pictured are, from left to right, (front row) Mrs. ? Moncure, Sarah Newman Jones, Mary Moncure, Frances Taylor, Louise Vaughan, Nell Starke, Dorothy Boschen, Virginia Sydnor, Ellen Kent Lumsden, Virginia Gordon Hall, and Julia Gray Saunders; (back row) Virginia Reed, Margaret Gray, Julianna Hartsook (hiding), Ann Dugger, Katherine "Sis" Cross, Polly Bridges, Conde Booth, Dorothy Jones, and Mac Stiles. (*Herald-Progress.*)

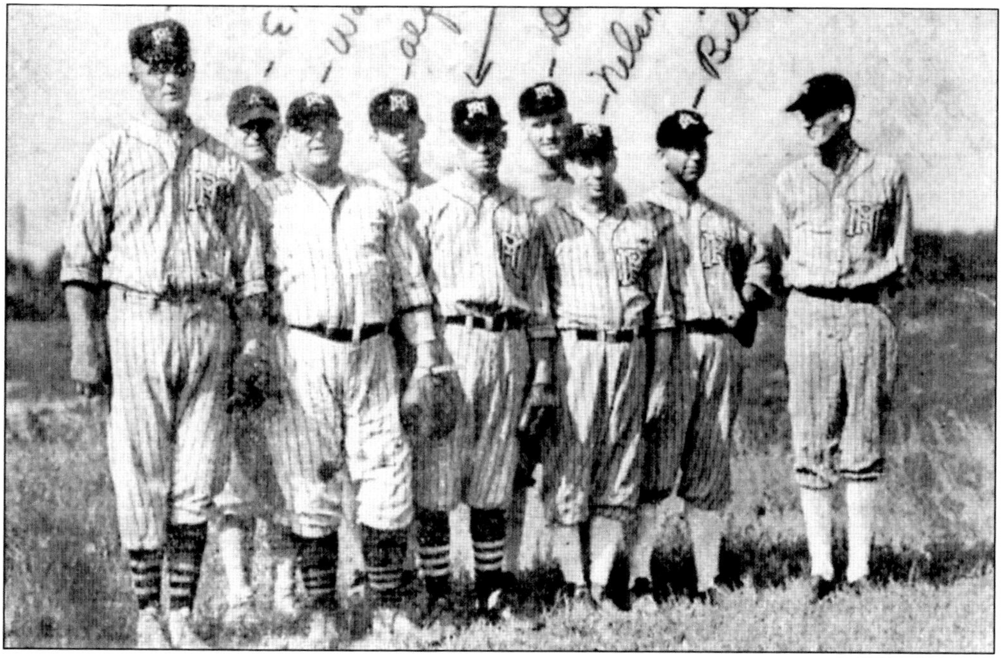

"WE REALLY PLAYED BALL." Although the team is wearing Randolph-Macon College uniforms, there is no connection. "The letters R-MC made us look big, therefore, half of the game was won," a team spokesman said. From left to right are J.C. Stiles Sr., E.T. DeJarnette, Walton Hall, Alfred Turner Sr., B.P. Loving, Dick Bryant, Nelson Vaughan, Billy Hammond, and an unidentified player. (*Herald-Progress.*)

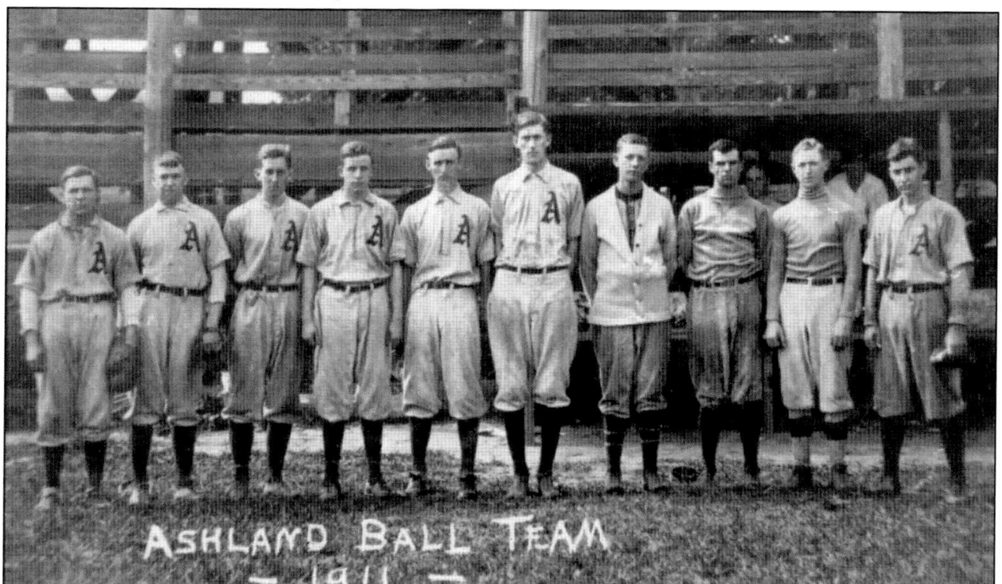

ASHLAND BALL TEAM, 1911. Included in this image from 1911 are Joe Bonitz, Scott Swift, Billy Midyette, Shirt Blanton, Sleepy Harlan, Billy Blakey, G. Hulcher, Snooks Trevillian, Jack Collins, Webb Midyette, and a fellow identified as Mulie. No one is certain in what order these names are listed, but several felt strongly that the fourth from the right is Shirt Blanton. (P.K. Perrin.)

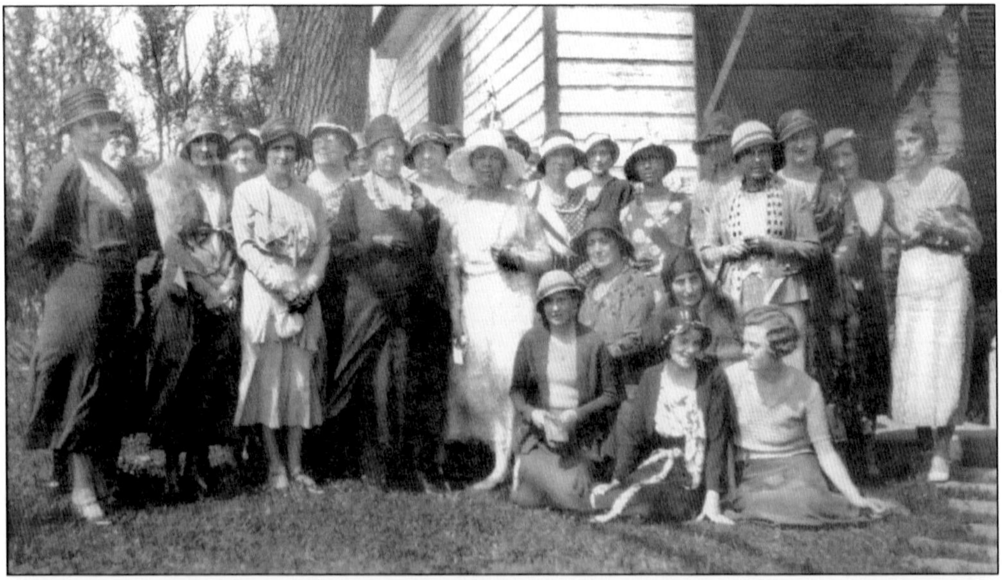

WOMAN'S CLUB OF ASHLAND. Founded in 1896, this club (originally called the Current Events Club) has as it motto "New Occasions Teach New Duties." The club was the brainchild of Esther Judkins and Hattie Lovell Scott. The group is still going strong—every Tuesday at 4 p.m.—for more than a century. (The Woman's Club of Ashland.)

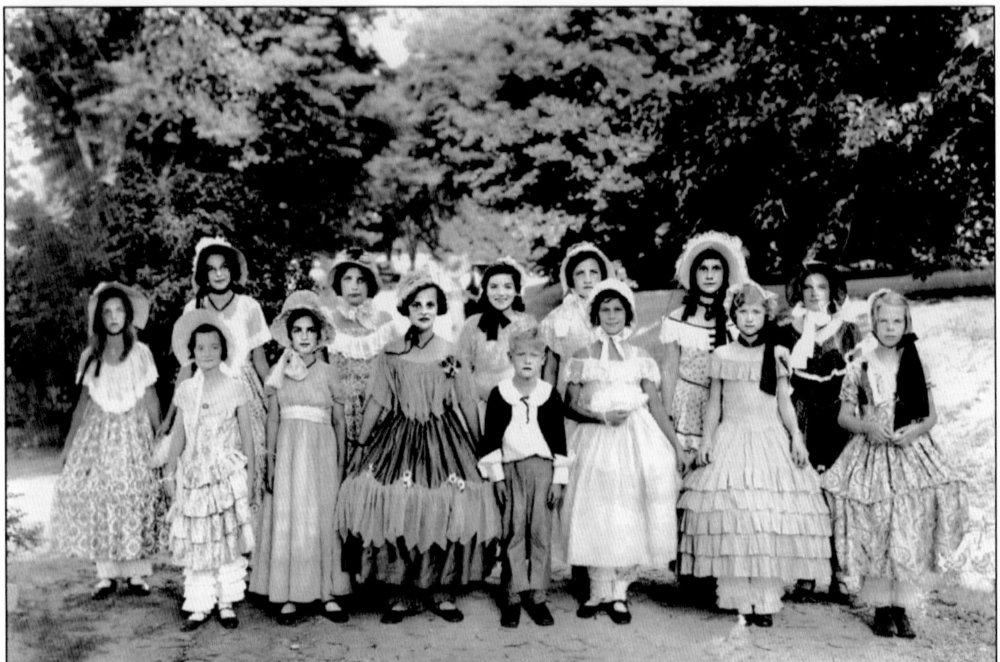

BETSY ROSS CHAPTER, CHILDREN OF THE CONFEDERACY (UNITED DAUGHTERS OF THE CONFEDERACY). Pictured here from left to right are, (front row) Mary Byrd Tucker, Elizabeth Hall, Mildred Saunders, Tommy Moncure, Clifford Booth, Mary Moncure, and Florence Temple Moore; (back row) Rosalie Saunders, Julia Gray Saunders, Byrd Harris, Frances Taylor, Helen Lee Wright, Virginia Sydnor, and Virginia Gordon Hall. (Sarah Jones Wright.)

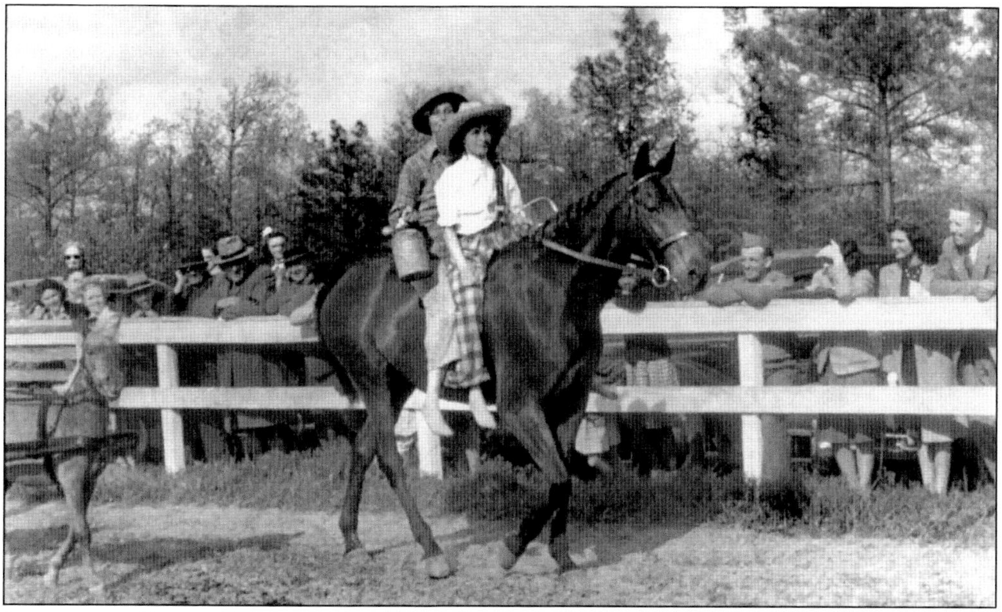

LANCE AND BRIDLE CLUB. Active for many years to support the interests in horsemanship in Hanover, the club held annual shows with up to 15 show classes. A regular show member of the American Horse Shows Association, Inc. in New York City, the club was effectively sponsored by most of the prominent businesses in Ashland. The 1946 show booklet read as a who's who of Ashland businesses. Elma Craddock (on the rear of the horse) joined Mary Barnes in a costume event. (Terry Barnes Shaw.)

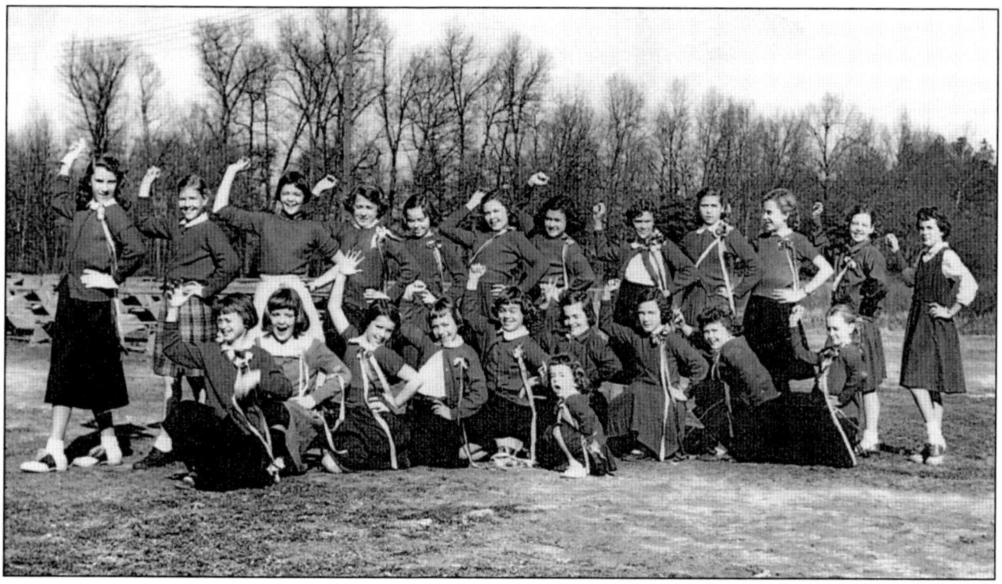

ASHLAND LITTLE LEAGUE CHEERLEADERS, EARLY 1950S. Shown here from left to right are (front row) Jo Ann Morris, Cecile Andrews, Elaine Lohr, Ann Ray, Nancy Leadbetter, Susan Sale, Linda Moore, Judy Waleski, and Jeannie Martin; (back row) Anne Maddox, Ann Winn, Melinda Luck, Betty Carol Wells, Carolyn Lee Davis, Joyce Gammon, Mary Ann Parr, Lanny Covington, Beth Ellington, Kay Ferguson, Ruth Hemingway, and Polly McLemore. Little Jane Waleski, the squad mascot, kneels in front. (Pen and Betty Carol Stevenson.)

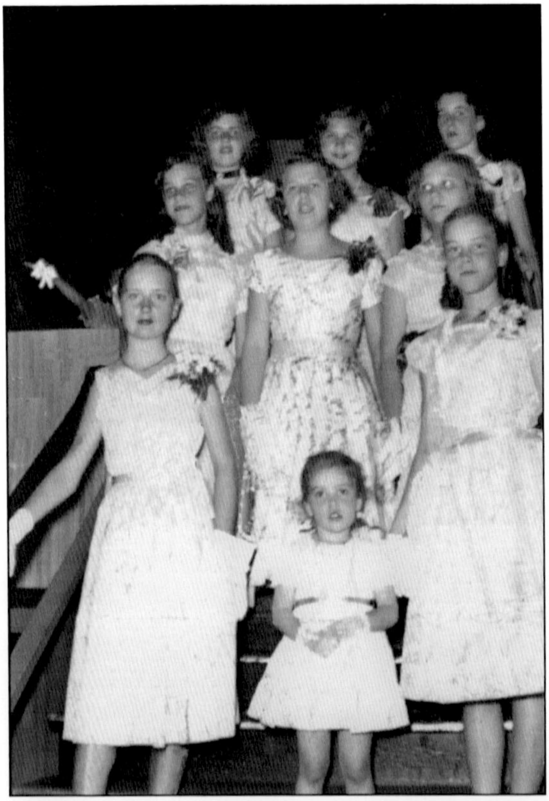

MRS. TRAYLOR'S COTILLION. In 18th-century England, young girls were introduced to society at balls featuring the French Cotillion. In 1953, special dance nights at Tantilla Gardens were still a way to get boys to dance with girls. Featured here from left to right are (front row) Mary Anna Tignor, Jackie Davis, and Carolyn Lee Davis; (middle row) Lanny Covington, Betty Carol Wells, and Janet Cobb; (back row) Mildred Fay Whitlock, Beth Ellington, and Emily Troxell. (Pen and Betty Carol Stevenson.)

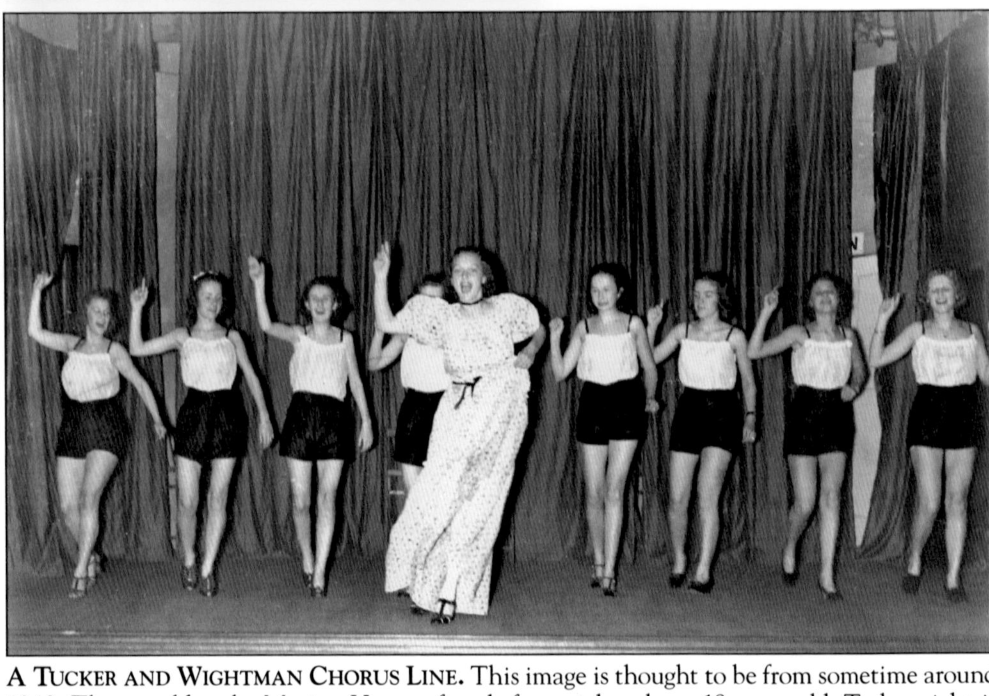

A TUCKER AND WIGHTMAN CHORUS LINE. This image is thought to be from sometime around 1940. That would make Marion Herget, fourth from right, about 18 years old. To her right is Libby Hall. To the far left is Dolly Carr. (Harvey "Todie" Grattan.)

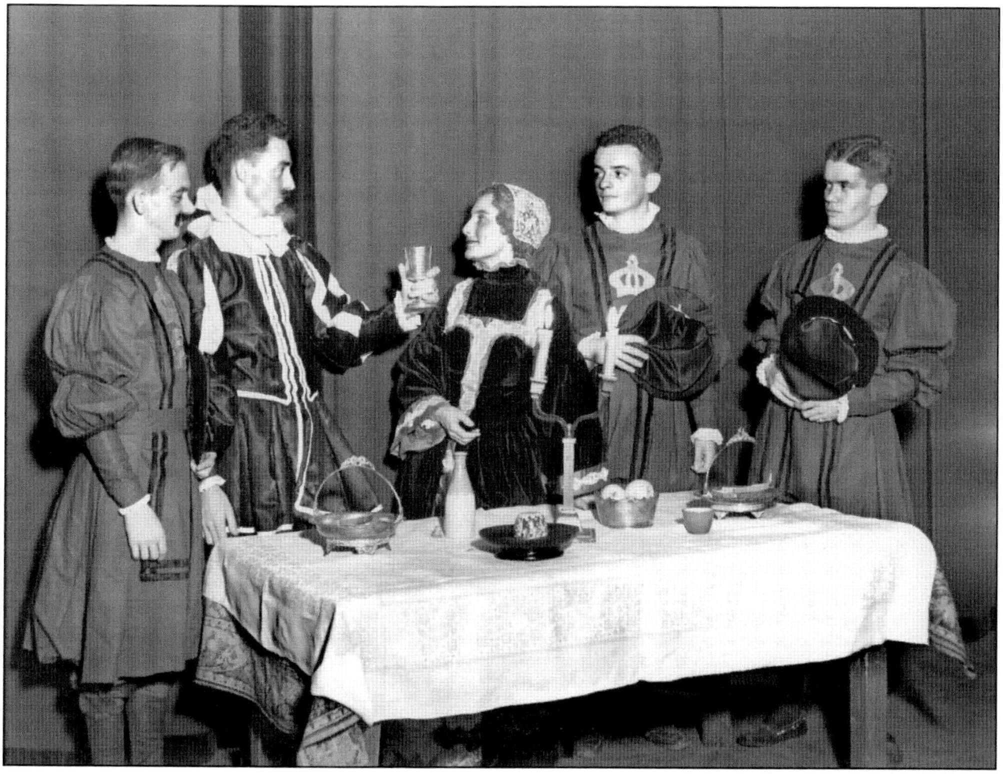

SCHOOL PLAY. Miss Rachel Smith (center) took the role of Lady Jane Grey in the Ashland High School alumni presentation of *Nine Days' Queen*, which was given as a benefit performance at the high school. Principals in the cast (from left to right) were Fritz Palmore, Knight Sanders, Smith, Floyd W. Tucker, and Drewry Kerr. (Harvey "Todie" Grattan.)

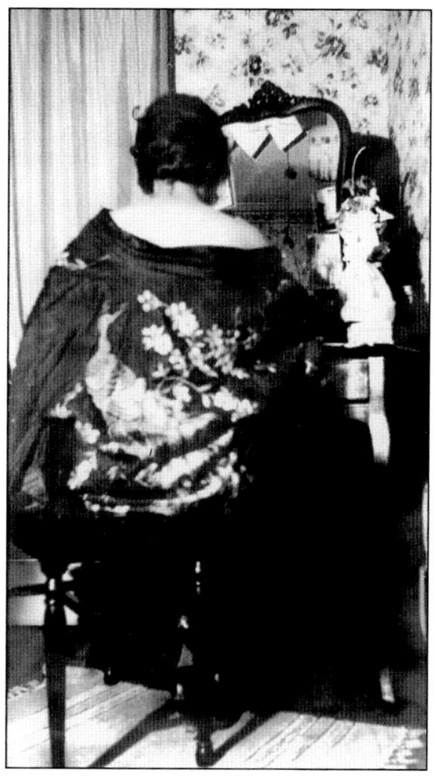

REBECCA KERR IN KIMONO. Getting ready to perform the Mikado, Rebecca Kerr carefully prepares her coif and costume. Active in local theater, Rebecca also played Sarah Shelton in the Patrick Henry Bicentennial to James Bell's Patrick Henry. She was a dedicated elementary school teacher. (Harvey "Todie" Grattan.)

PATRONIZE

THE HANGOVER NATIONAL BANK

"And get that morning after feeling."

See America First VIA THE Richmond-Ashland Bus Line	"Honor the Light Brigade, Oh, What a Charge They Made." *Virginia Electric and Power Companv*

PART III.

Five Minutes With

TUCKER & WIGHTMAN

PART IV.

PARCEL POST

or

"TOO BIG TO BE DELIVERED"

(A political farce in three short scenes)

Cast: Mayor, John Wightman.
Janitor: John Midyette.
Clerk: Fritz Palmore.
Inspector: Knight Saunders.
Councilmen: R. B. Coulter, Carter Ellis, Floyd Tucker, Harvey Hartman, Frank King.
Citizens: Mrs. Grattan, Anderson Bland, Drewry Kerr.

(Producer's note: Any similarity of names, places or events mentioned herein to any actual persons, places or events, is purely co-incidental and not based on fact.—ITPAH.)

Has Your New Car HYDRAULIC BRAKES? RAWLINGS MOTOR COMPANY	Buy A Chevrolet and WATCH THE FORDS GO BY. J. N. LUCK MOTOR COMPANY

DON'T LET THE RED LIGHT FOOL YOU.

Come in.

J. G. HUGHES

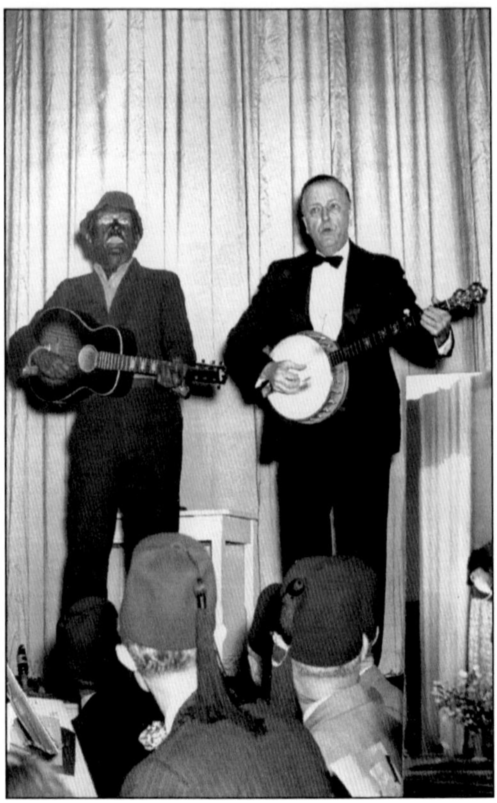

TUCKER AND WIGHTMAN. Marion Herget remembers the ever-popular Tucker and Wightman minstrels kept the town laughing and clapping for several hours as John Wightman played Mr. Interlocutor to Capt. Floyd Tucker's jokes. John Midyette always brought the house down with his singing of "Memphis Blues," and Rebecca Kerr was a perennial favorite with her rendition of "My Man I love Him So." (Woody and Susan Tucker.)

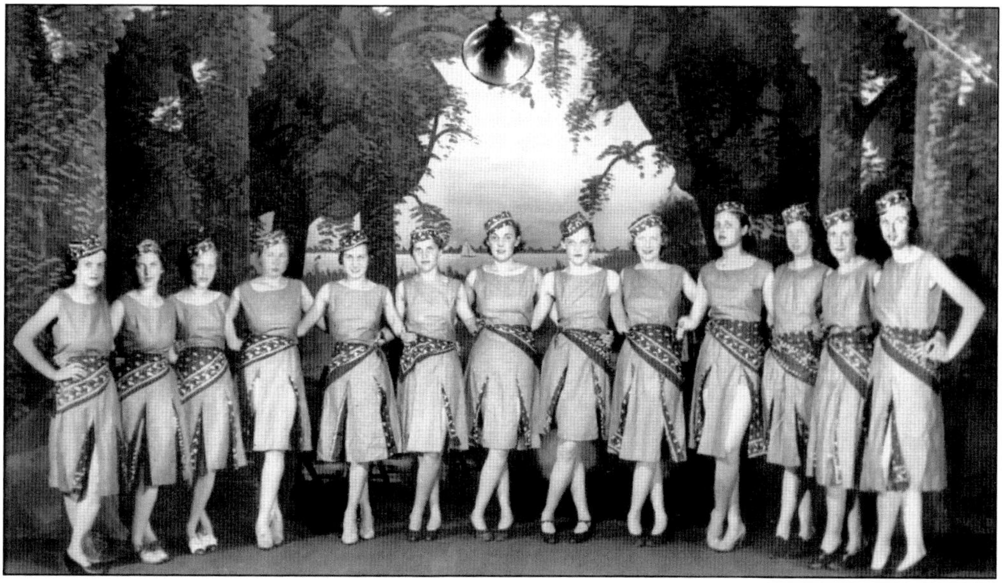

BECKY KERR'S DEVASTATING DAMSELS. The chorus at the Tucker and Wightman Minstrel Show in 1933 were, from left to right, Jane Pollard (Hartsook), Laughlin Smith (Spencer) Dorothy Bagby (Canada), Jo Luck (Ray), Dorothy Smeeman (Barnes), Conde Booth (Palmore), Mac Stiles (Carney), Isabelle Smith (Webb), Juliana Hartsook (Regester), Bec Campbell (Lewis), Mary Dozier Carter, Margaret Gilman, and Frankie Powell (Gilman). (Harvey "Todie" Grattan.)

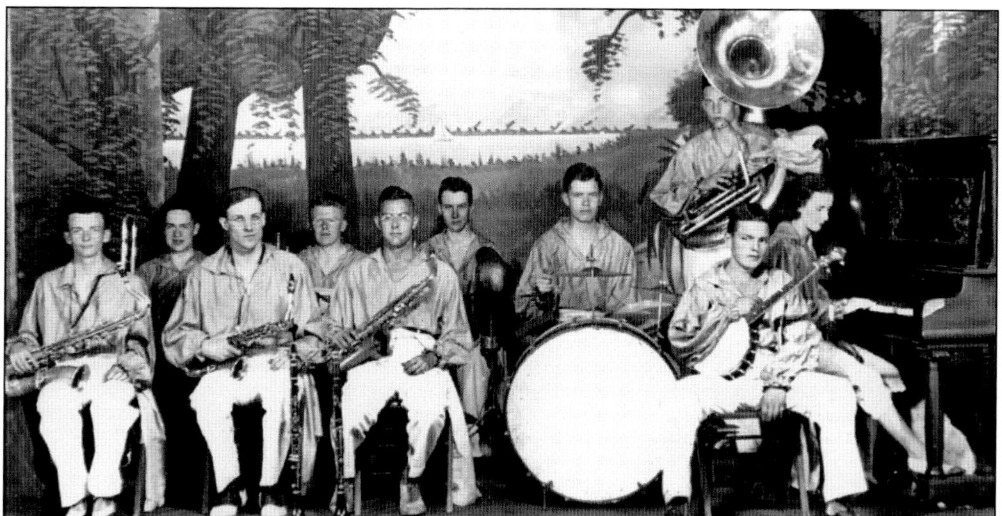

THE RACKETEERS. In 1931, a group of Boy Scouts, seniors at Henry Clay High School, decided to organize an orchestra. In 1932, the students enrolled at Randolph-Macon College and took the name "Racketeers." The group played for many dances and other functions in Central Virginia until it disbanded in 1936. Members were, from left to right, Floyd W. "Bootie" Tucker (soprano and tenor sax), Dr. J. Buell Weems (trombone), Dr. William C. Webb, J. Walton Hall Jr. (trumpet), George W. Carr (alto sax and clarinet), Virginius N. Vaughan (trumpet), H. Drewry Kerr (drums and washboard), W. Knight Saunders (tuba), Wilbur "Mickey" Lewis (banjo and vocalist), and Marie Wills Price (piano). (Woody and Susan Tucker.)

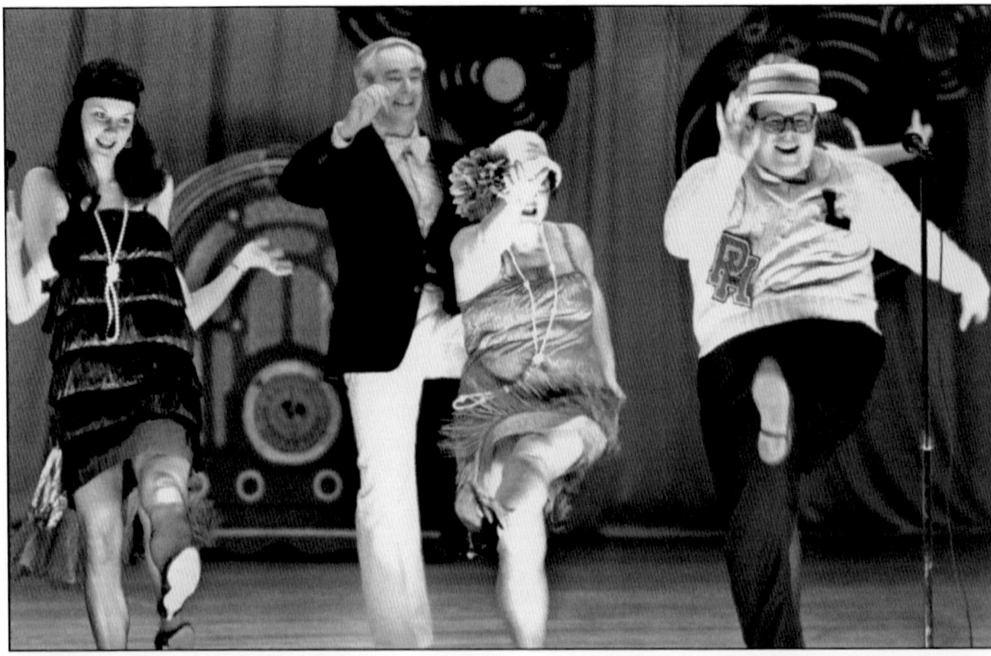

ASHLAND VARIETY SHOW. This show was an important part of Ashland's entertainment. Although not as old as the Tucker and Wightman events of the 1930s, these 1970s productions saw such local figures as Dick Gillis singing "Ashland, Ashland," written by Marion Herget and Dougee Zeno, which had been taken from the mayor's motto that Ashland was, indeed, the "center of the universe." (*Herald-Progess.*)

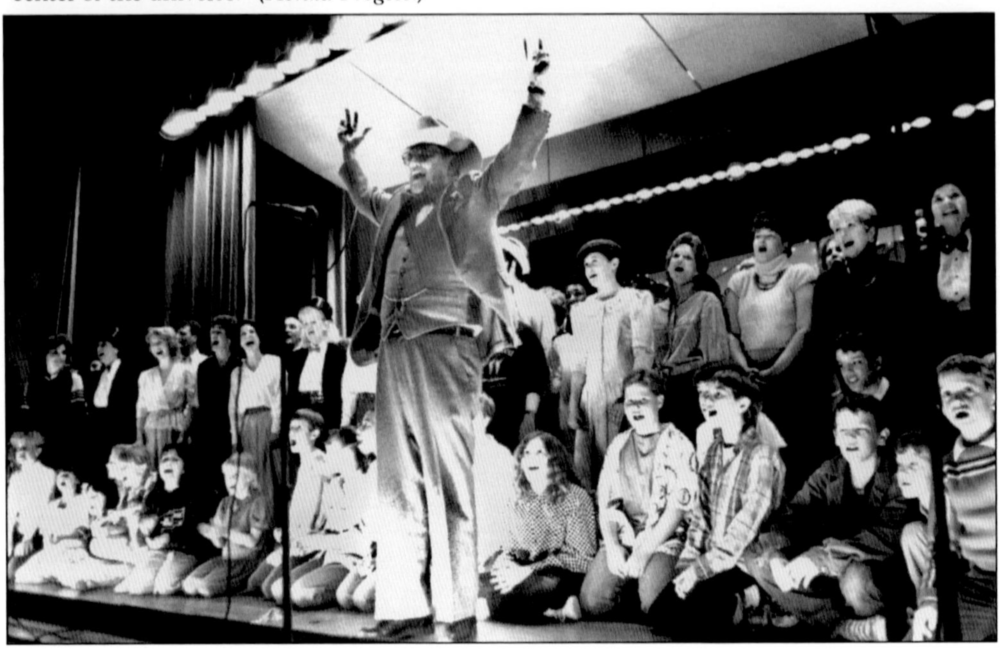

Nine

SOME FRIENDS

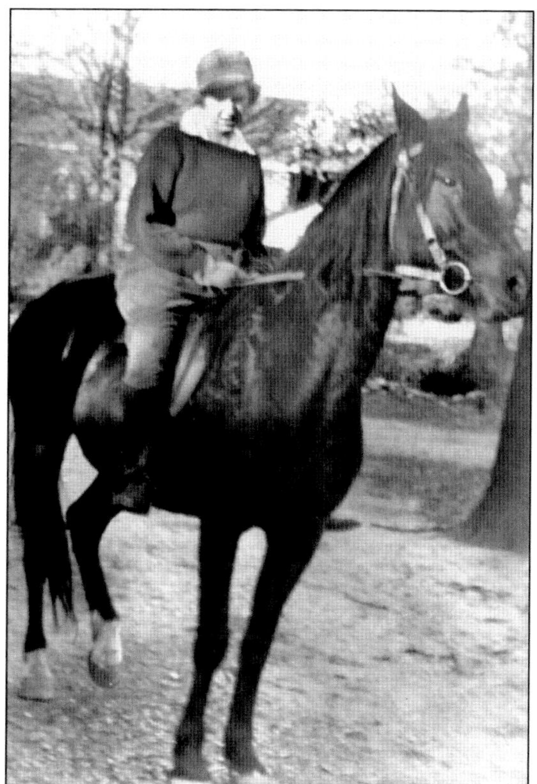

DR. DOROTHY GARDNER JONES. Born in 1912, Ms. Jones earned her bachelor's degree in Latin and Greek from Randolph-Macon College even when women were not officially admitted. She received a master's in sociology from the University of North Carolina at Chapel Hill. She did research for the Rockefeller Foundation and was on the faculty of Winthrop College. Ms. Jones was the first supervisor of the Hanover County Welfare Department. Here, "Dot.T" is going fox-hunting on a cold day in 1938 with Ed Gilman and Walter Cross. The men were bolstered by "Dutch courage," but she was not. When she stopped in a pine grove to get warm, her horse Blackie began whipping his head and biting at her boot, encouraging her to follow his line of sight. She saw a breathless fox, sunning himself in the same grove. Dorothy did not alert anyone to his position. (Dorothy Jones.)

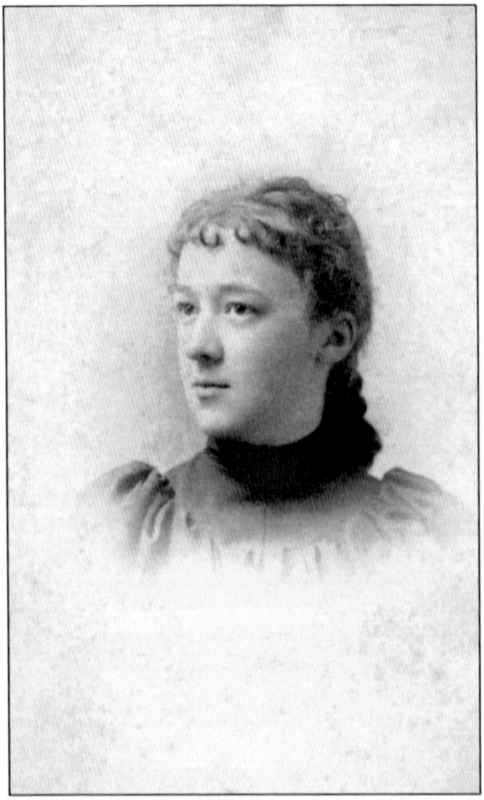

MISS JULIA WEISIGER, TELEPHONE OPERATOR, 1903–1937. Before public switched-telephone networks, operators manually connected calls. One would crank the phone and get Julia and ask for the party. She could find you a fourth for bridge, let you know who was expecting a new baby, and hustle you off a party line in case of an emergency. Rebecca Grattan remembered: "In case of fire we called Central. . . they would call out the horses from Luck's Livery stable . . . and hitch up the horses and start out with that old steam engine." (Sarah Jones Wright.)

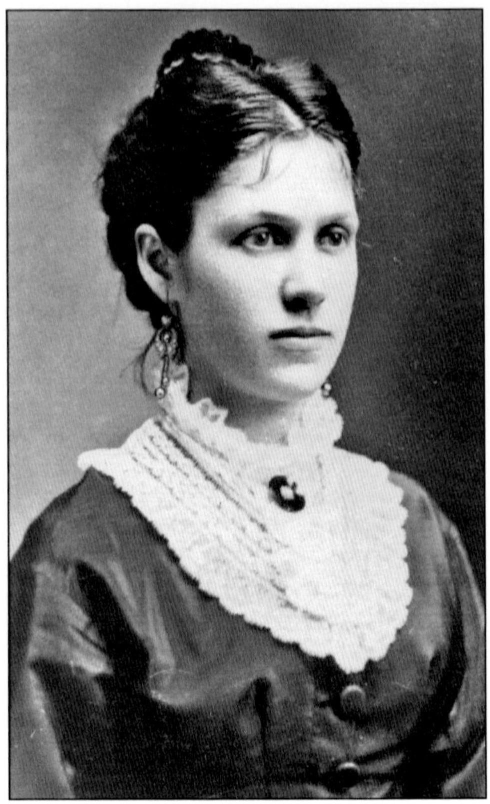

LUCY CHANDLER PENDLETON. Lucy was the daughter of Thomas Coleman Chandler of Fairfield, where Stonewall Jackson was brought when wounded during the Civil War. Jackson died there. Lucy was 12 years old when she witnessed his passing. She married Charles Kimbrough Pendleton and lived in Ashland for 40 years, the last few with her daughters, Elizabeth Pendleton Cox and Mamie Pendleton Carter. Descendants in town today are Hill Carter, J. Pendleton Stevenson and J.K. Cox. (Pen and Betty Carol Stevenson.)

ANNE DOSWELL JONES. The granddaughter of Thomas Walker Doswell of Bullfield and daughter of Bernard and Ellen Morris Doswell, Anne was born at "Hildene." She was a charter member of the Ashland Garden Club. Active in the Ashland Woman's Club, she was not only the "perpetual treasurer," but also had the distinction of being the only member of the club who never presented a paper to the club. She is photographed on the day of her marriage to Walter Kidd Jones wearing her sister's wedding gown. (Sarah Jones Wright.)

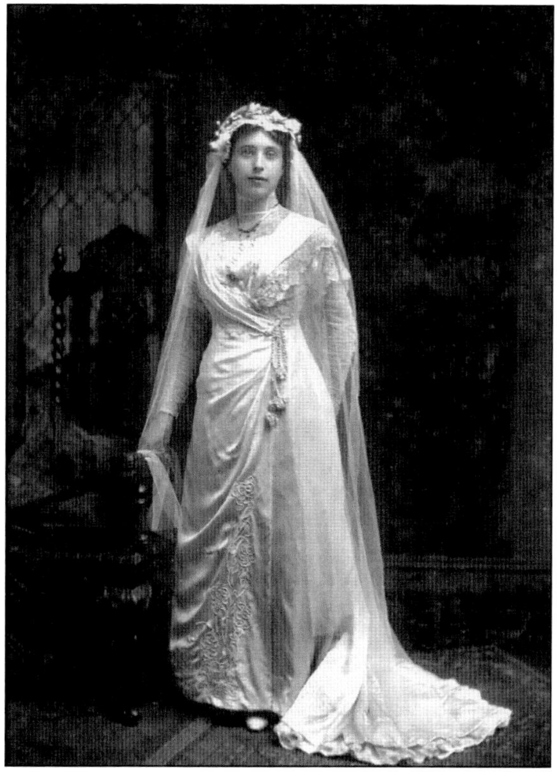

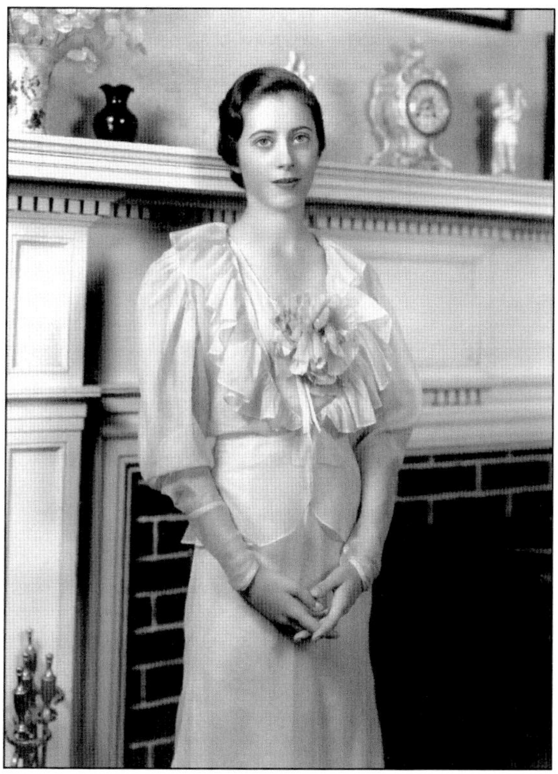

SARAH NEWMAN JONES. The daughter of Walter Kidd and Anne Doswell Jones, Sarah is pictured here on her high-school graduation day. She studied French and Spanish at Mary Baldwin College. Sarah married Arthur Henry Tuttle Jr., who was killed over the Atlantic in 1942 during World War II. She later married Louis A. Wright. Sarah is a longtime member of the Ashland Woman's Club and remains active in efforts to preserve Hanover County history. (Sarah Jones Wright.)

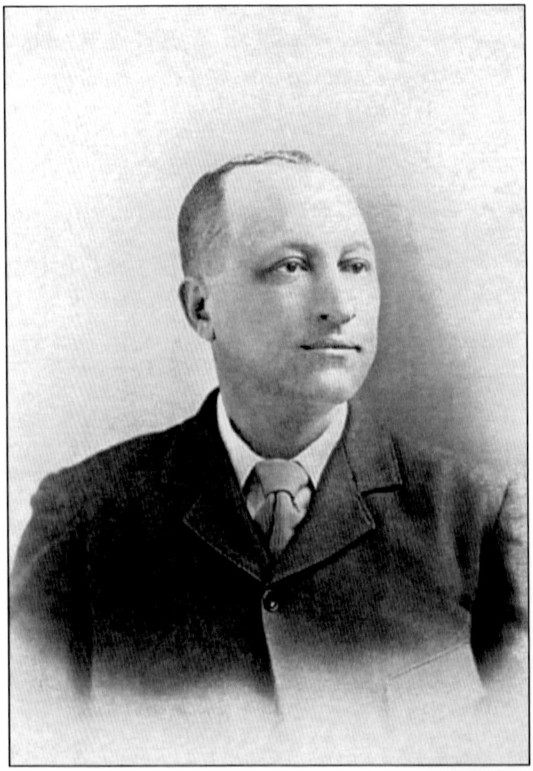

CLINTON WINSTON. The original owner of the Blacksmith Shop on Hanover Avenue, Winston was an important member of the Ashland community and continued his legacy by giving his shop to his son. (Inez Gray.)

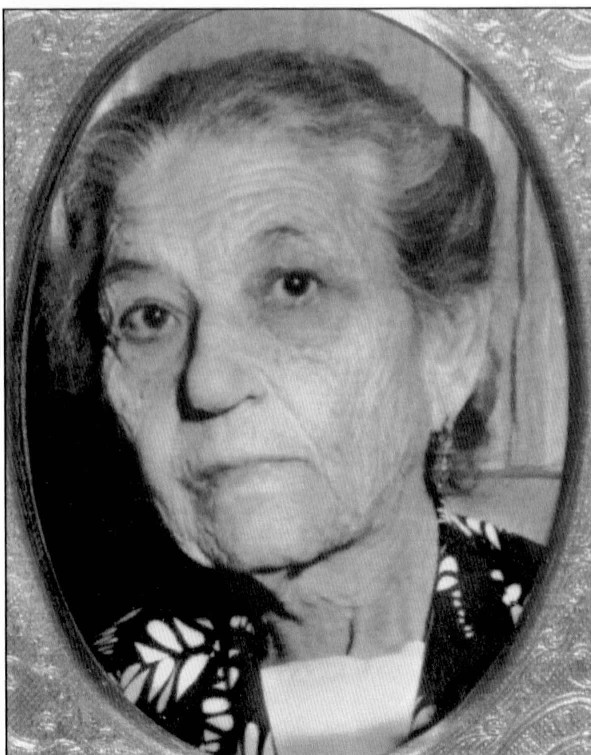

ANNIE LAURA PRICE WINSTON. Annie was Inez Gray's grandmother and the wife of Clinton Winston, who started the blacksmith's shop on Hanover Avenue in Ashland. (Inez Gray.)

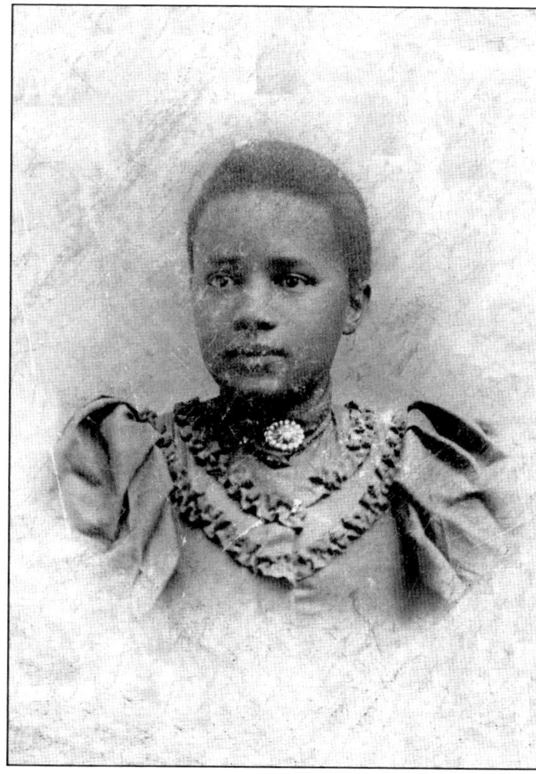

HATTIE WINSTON. Hattie was Johnnie C. Winston's sister and the mother of Elaine Beverly. Sadly, Hattie died as a young woman. (Inez Gray.)

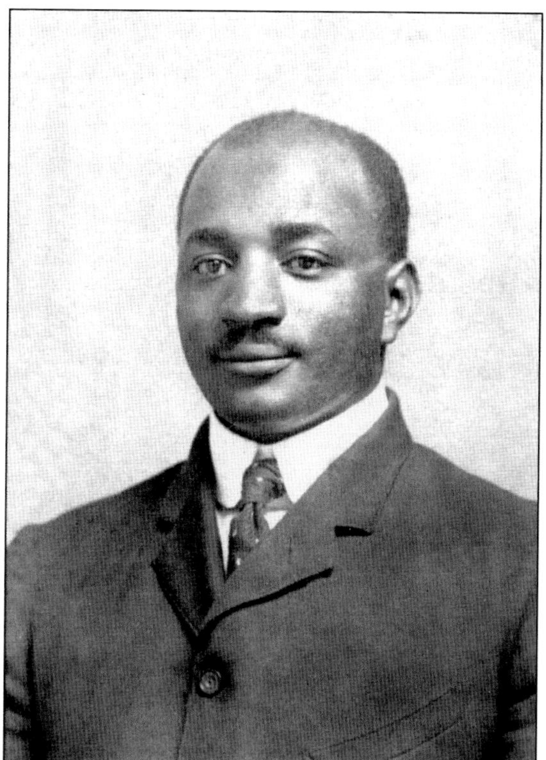

JOHNNIE CLINTON WINSTON. Son of Clinton and Annie Laura, Johnnie Clinton Winston sang with the choir all over Hanover County. He also owned and ran Clinton's Blacksmith Shop, carrying on his father's tradition. (Inez Gray.)

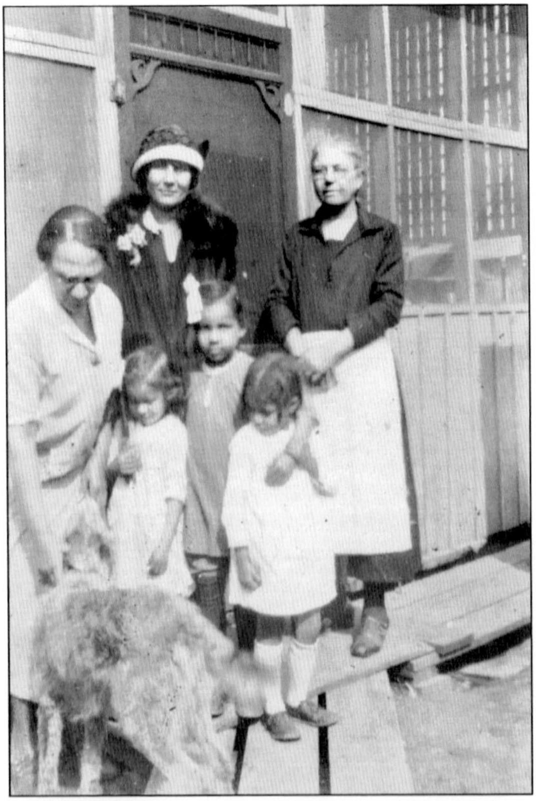

BEST FRIENDS. The three children are, from left to right, Louise Melton, Camilla Melton, and Virgie Beverly. The adults are, from left to right, Ethel Hicks (sister of Clinton Winston), Julia Melton, and Annie Laura Winston. The portrait of the friends was taken on the front porch of the Winston house, next door to Winton's blacksmith shop on Hanover Avenue. (Inez Gray.)

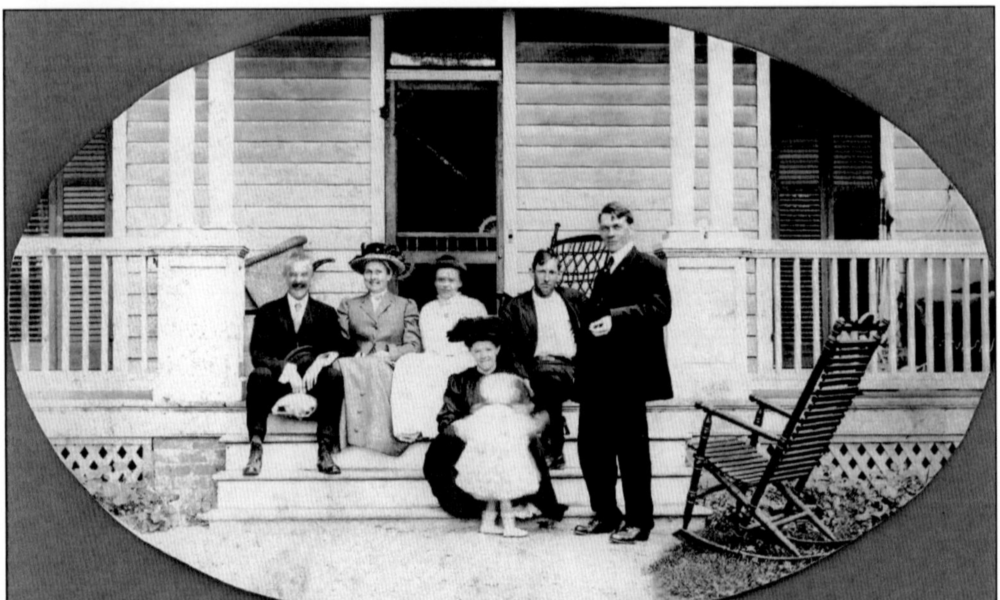

AT THE KERR HOUSE. Pictured here at the Kerr House is Louisa Ladew Kerr holding Rebecca Drewry Kerr, with behind her, from left to right, the Robbins couple, Bessie Henderson Ladew, and Hill Carter Jr.; standing is Henry Drewry Kerr. (Harvey "Todie" Grattan.)

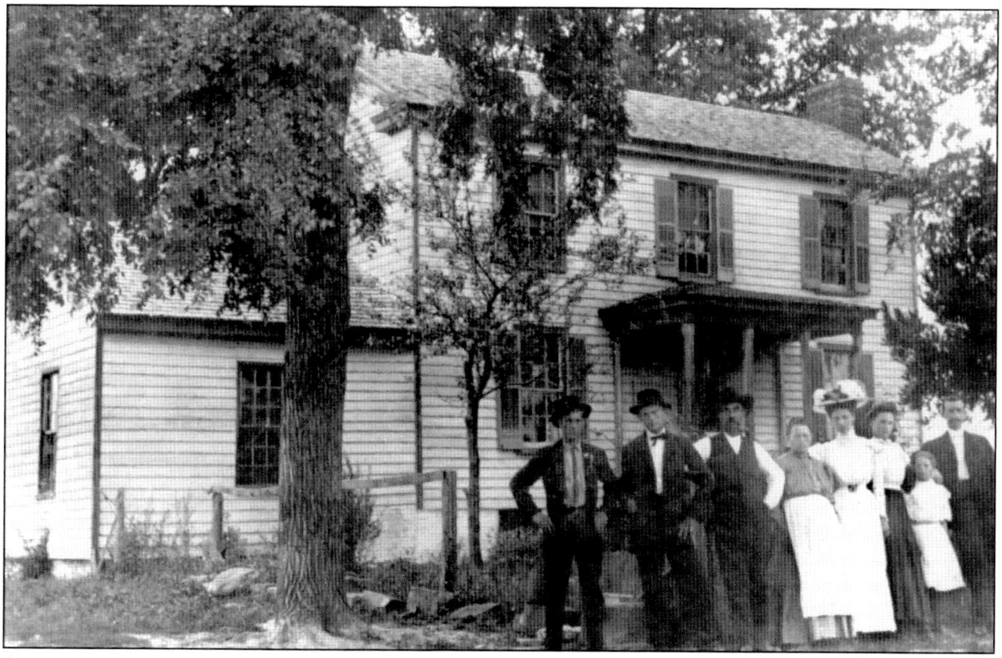

SMEEMAN FAMILY HOME. This home has been torn down, but it originally stood in Northern Hanover, across from Blunt's Bridge. This family portrait taken in the 1920s shows, from left to right, Harry Valentine Smeeman, Barney Smeeman, Mary Smeeman, Kate Smeeman (Lane), Lizzie Smeeman, and Joe Lane. The small girl is Mary "Mike" Smeeman. (Mildred Smeeman Davis.)

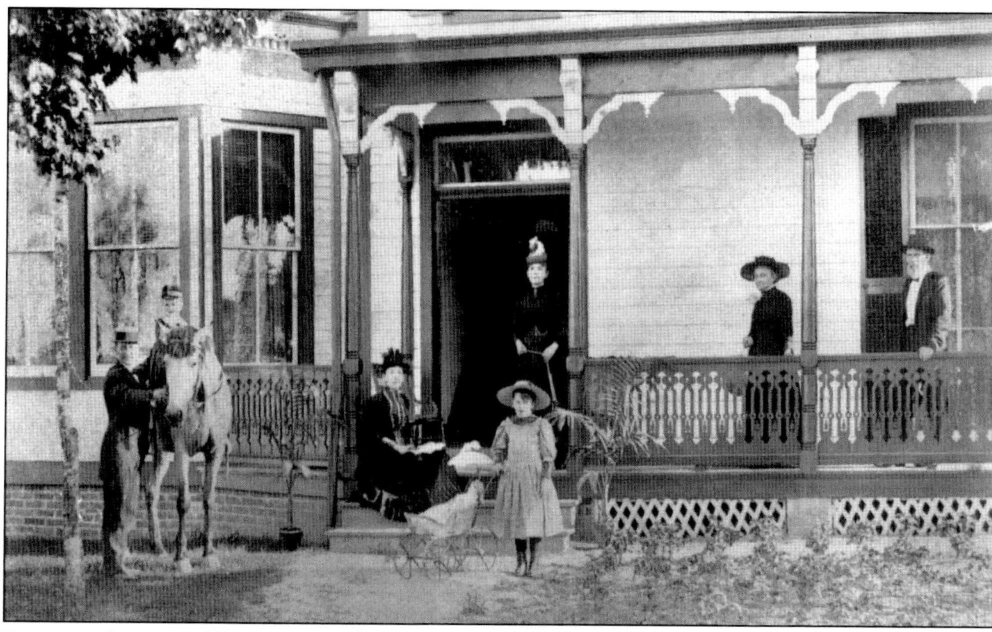

PALMER GORDON HOUSE. Standing at the left by the horse is J. Palmer Gordon, Ashland's first florist. Willie Gordon is on the horse. Ella Gordon is sitting on the steps. The small girl is Elizabeth Gordon, and standing on the porch from left to right are Sally Tinsley, Alverda Gordon, and John T. Gordon. (Pat Pace.)

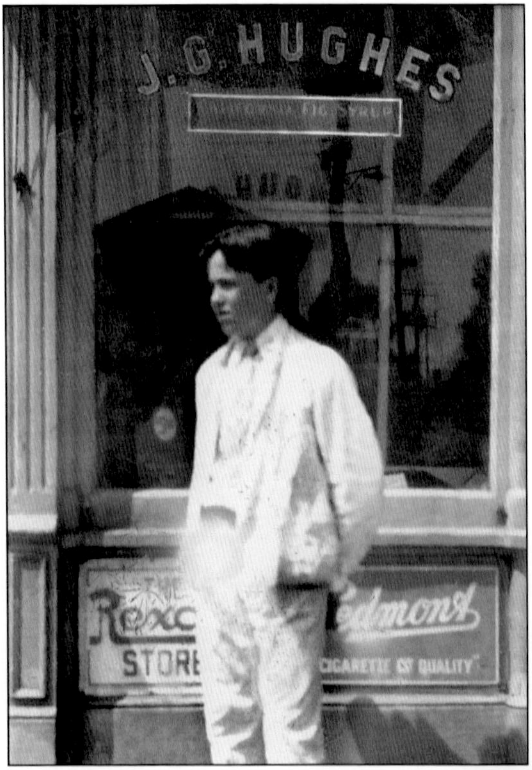

Dapper. Joe Schmierer worked as a soda jerk at Hughes Drug Store in the late 1930s and early 1940s. He had a twin brother who also worked in town. The two liked to play tricks on unsuspecting patrons. (Ann Curtis Palmore.)

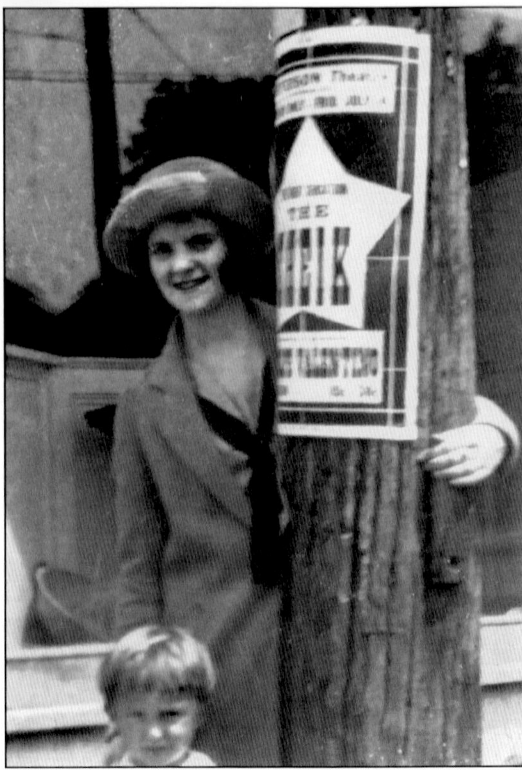

Evelyn Christian Hughes. Posed by an ad for Rudolph Valentino's *The Sheik*, Evelyn married "Doc" Hughes and worked as an editor for the *Herald-Progress* until she retired in 1956. (Hughes family.)

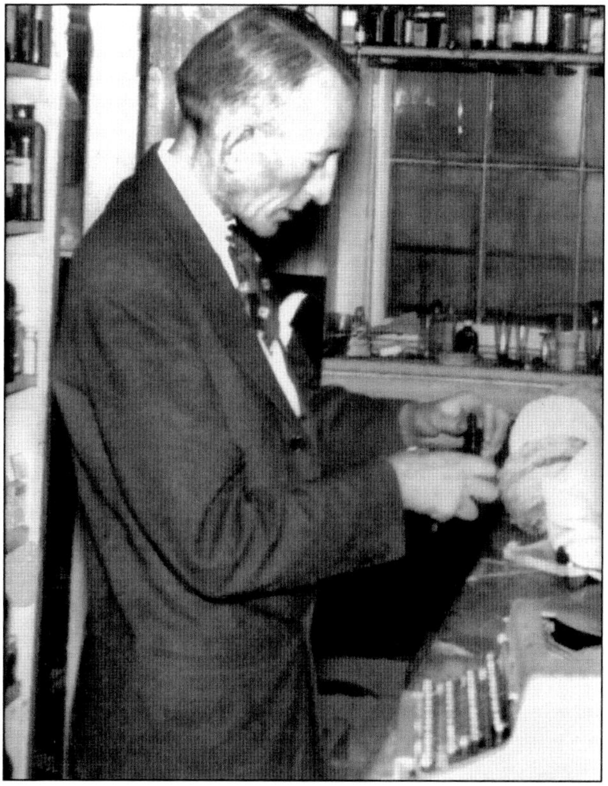

T.W.L. HUGHES. "Doc" Hughes, as most Ashlanders remember him, was called "Dot" Hughes in his high school yearbook. His fellow classmates said of him, "It has always been a mystery how Dot managed to 'vamp' all the girls. He manfully lives up to his motto, *Toujours l'audacious.*" (Hughes family.)

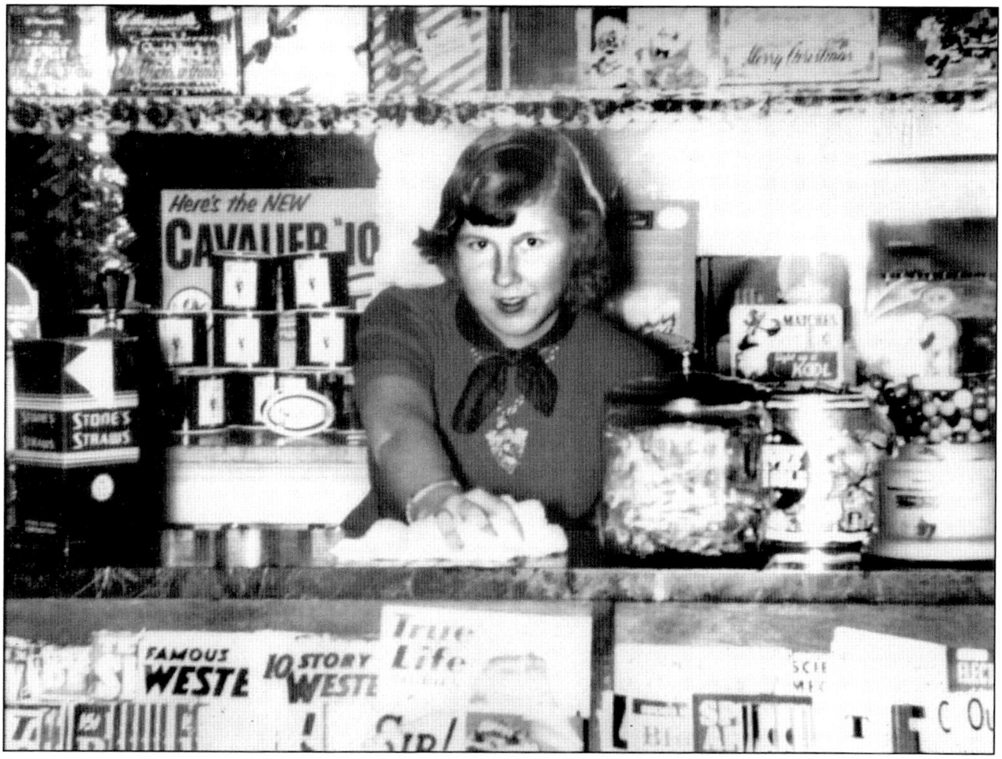

INSIDE HUGHES DRUG STORE. Connie Bull Hughes was a familiar sight behind the counter during the 1950s and 1960s. Later, she worked hard to develop the Slash Cottage neighborhood. (Ann Curtis Palmore.)

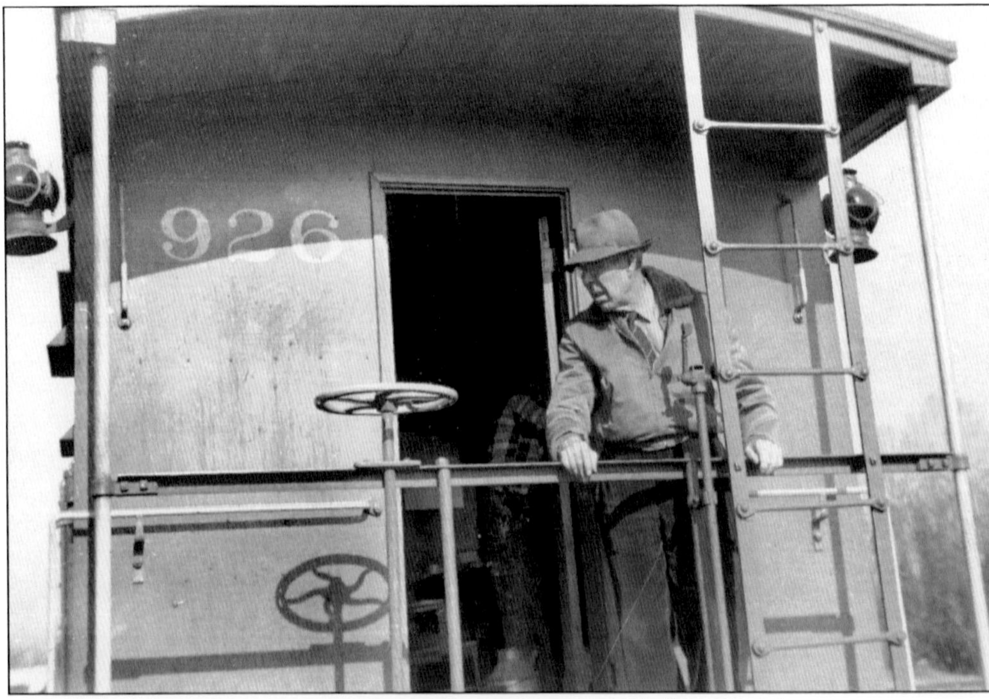

HE'S BEEN WORKING ON THE RAILROAD. Emmett V. Hall worked his entire career on the RF&P railroad. Many Ashlanders remember the special sound he was able to get out of the train's whistle when he passed his own house and through Ashland.(Woody and Susan Tucker.)

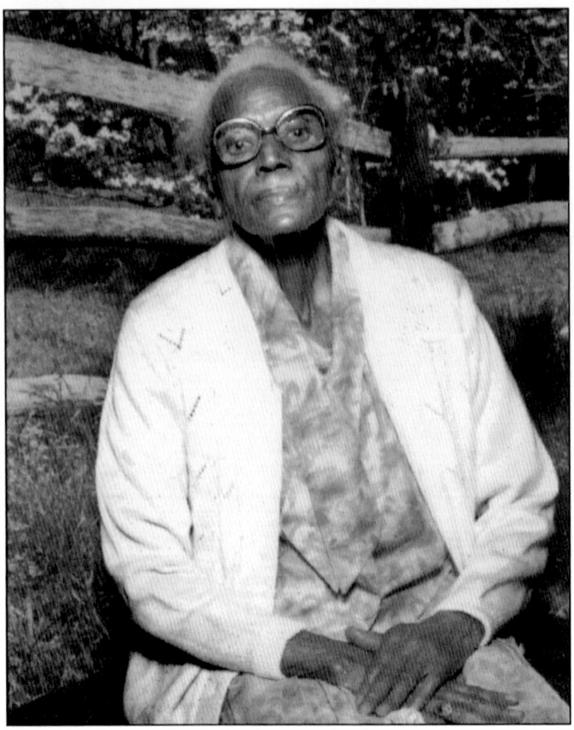

"MISS WINK." Winnie Davis is most remembered by her friends as an outstanding cook whose longevity practically made her an institution in Ashland. (Catherine Clark.)

THREE FRIENDS. Inez Gray (left), Eleanor Miller (center), and Pauline Miller (right) are pictured here on a Sunday in Clinton Heights, where families gathered for Sunday dinner and companionship. (Inez Gray.)

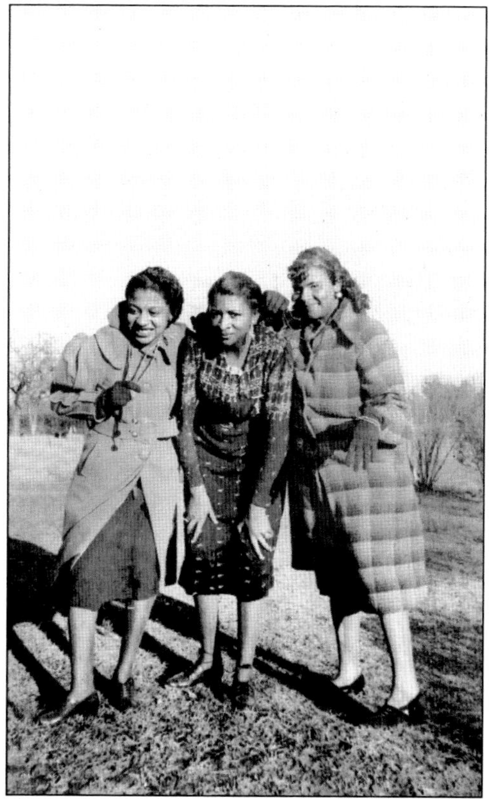

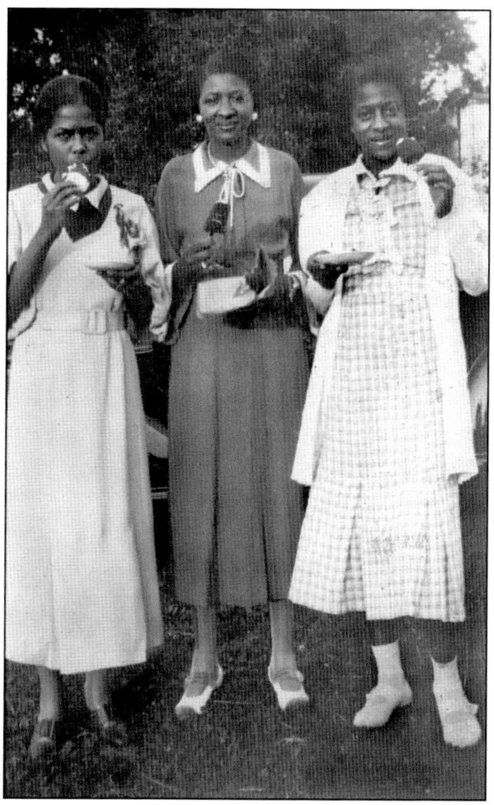

MORE SUNDAY FUN. From left to right, Sadie Fleming, Eleanor Winston Miller, and Gladys Inez Winston (Gray) eat a little ice cream on a warm Sunday afternoon. (Inez Gray.)

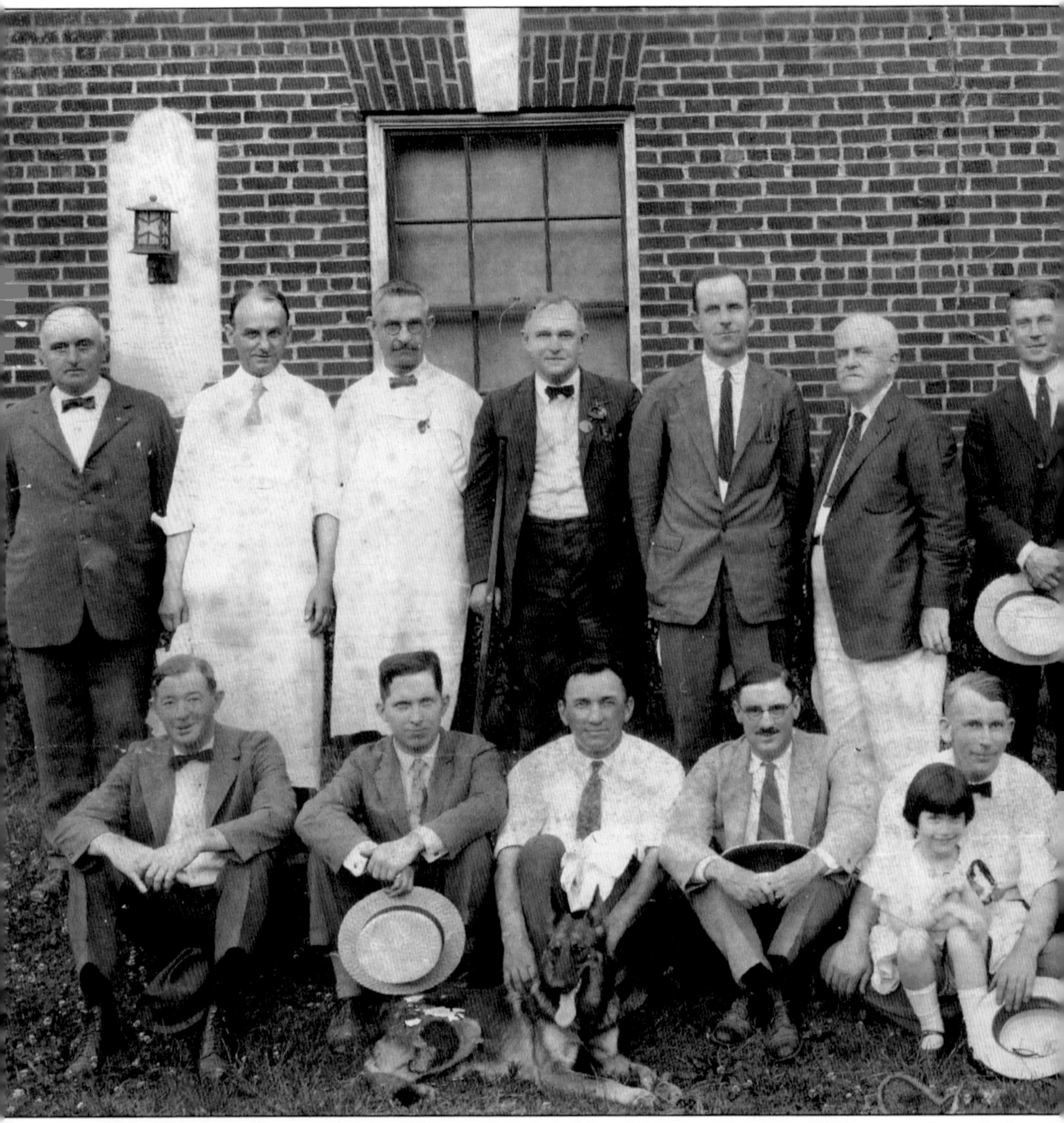

THE KIWANIS CLUB, 1920S. The pride of Ashland businessmen in 1922 were, from left to right, (front row) Walter Cross, J.M. Jones, Coach Welch, W. Walton Vaughan, Walter Sydnor, Robert B. Dugger, L.P. Hartsook, H. Laurie Smith, J. Walton Hall, S.C. Hatcher, and J.L. Anderson; (back row) Clyde Barnes, James M. Cox, W.H. Puryear, H. Carter Redd, Lewis Blanton, James F. Howison, J. Leitch Wright, Edward Rice, Lawrence Riker, George

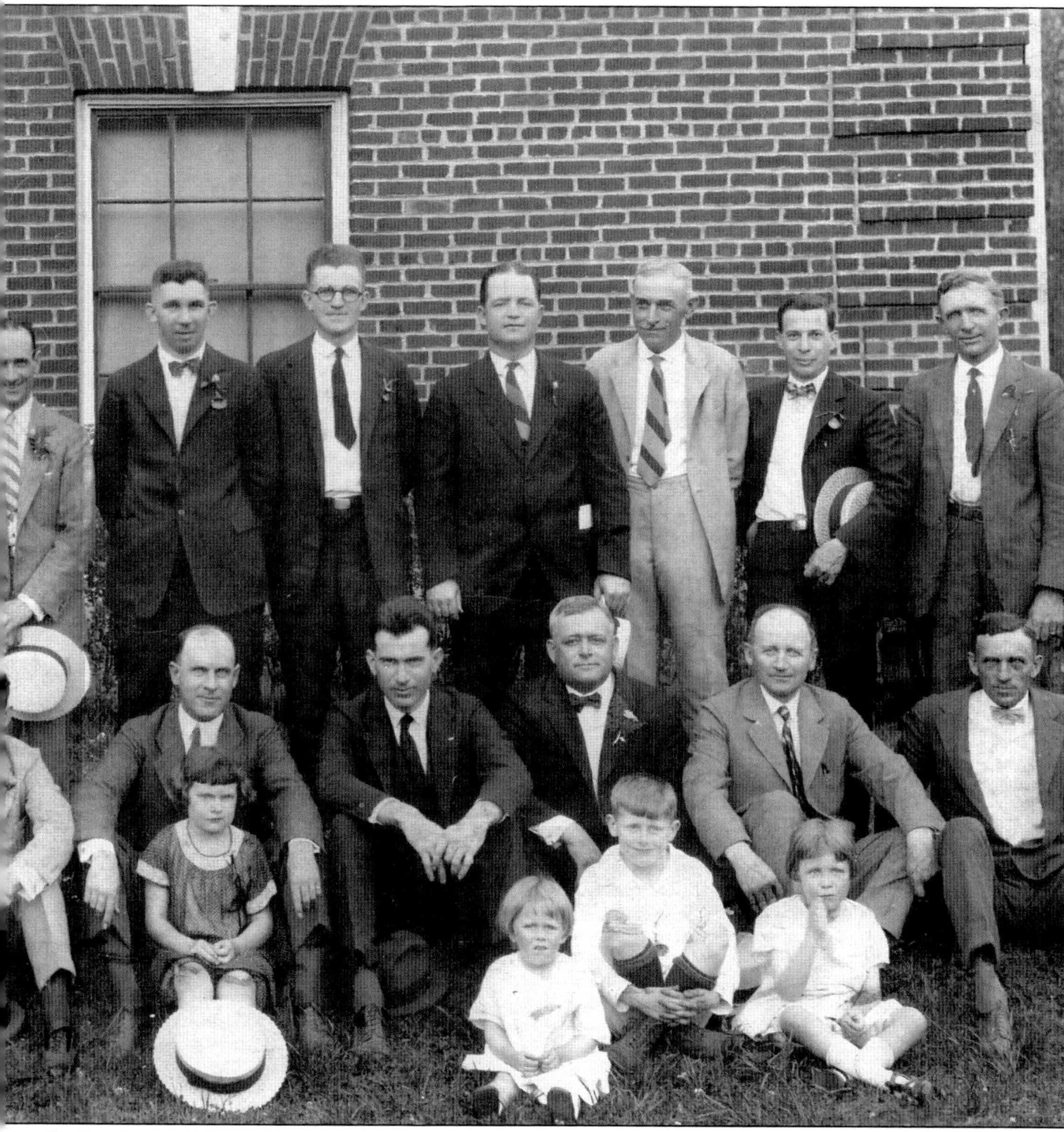

C. Rawlings, Edmund T. DeJarnette, E.W. Newman, Nelson Vaughan, James Luck. The children are Virgnia Sydnor, Juliana Hartsook, Elizabeth Luck, Walton Hall Jr., and Mary Luck. (*Herald-Progress*)

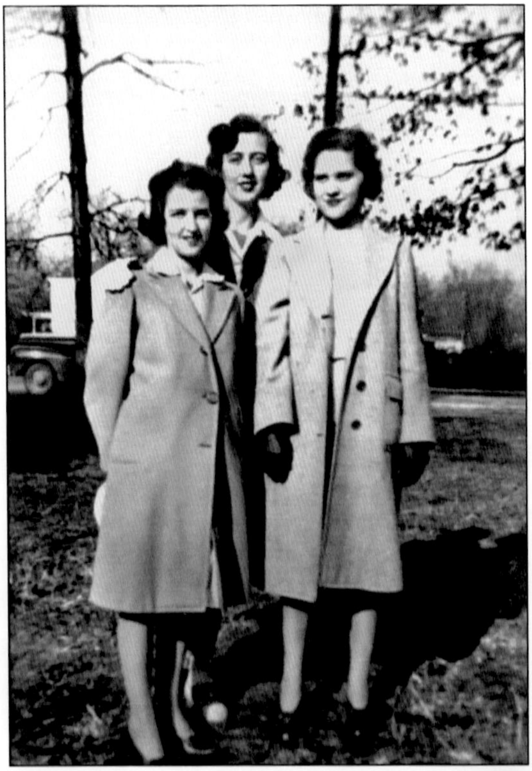

BEST FRIENDS. From left to right are Alma Earle Gilman Tucker, Frankie Powell Gilman, and Conde Booth Palmore. (Lelia Palmore Weyman.)

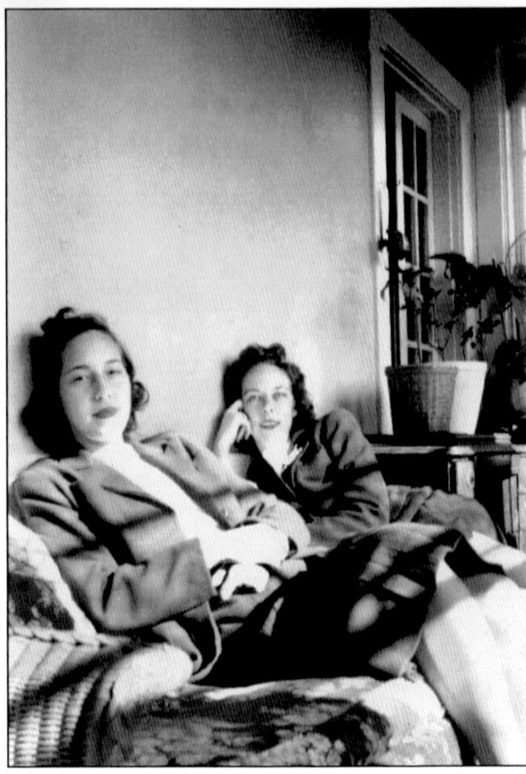

RELAXING ON THE PORCH. Kitty Carpenter (left) and Cary Gilman sometime around 1944 sit on the porch at Sarah Wright's house on Duncan Street. (Sarah Jones Wright.)

OUTSIDE HUGHES DRUG STORE AROUND 1940. From left to right are John Trevillian, unidentified, John Hawks, Jimmy Dawson, Anne Sledge Smith, and Clifford White. John Trevillian served in Italy and was wounded at the Battle of the Bulge. He eventually became a history teacher in Richmond. Anne Sledge Smith became a WAVE in World War II. Clifford became a state trooper and married Mary Hale. (Ann Curtis Palmore.)

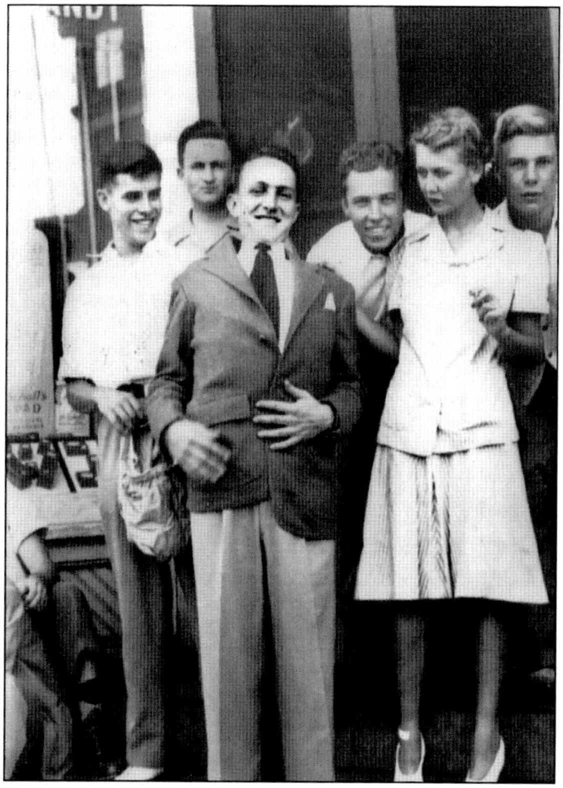

PALS. At Cross's Pond in 1939 were, from left to right, unidentified, Clifford White, Edgar Saunders, Aubrey Harlow, and Herbert Sledge. (P.K. Perrin.)

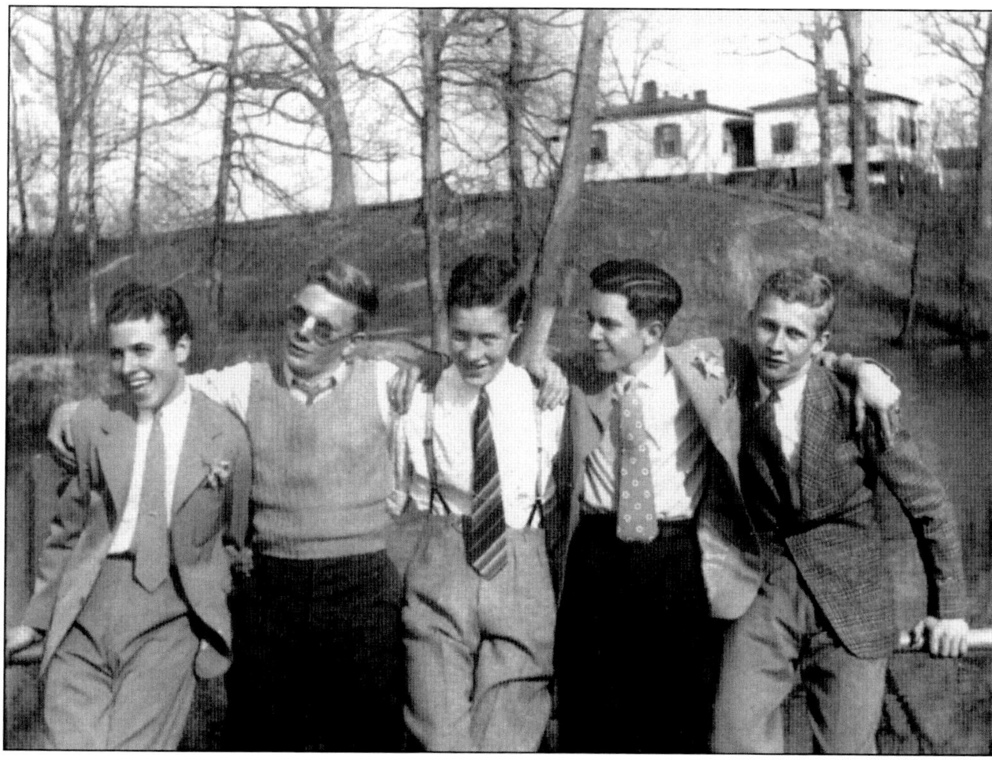

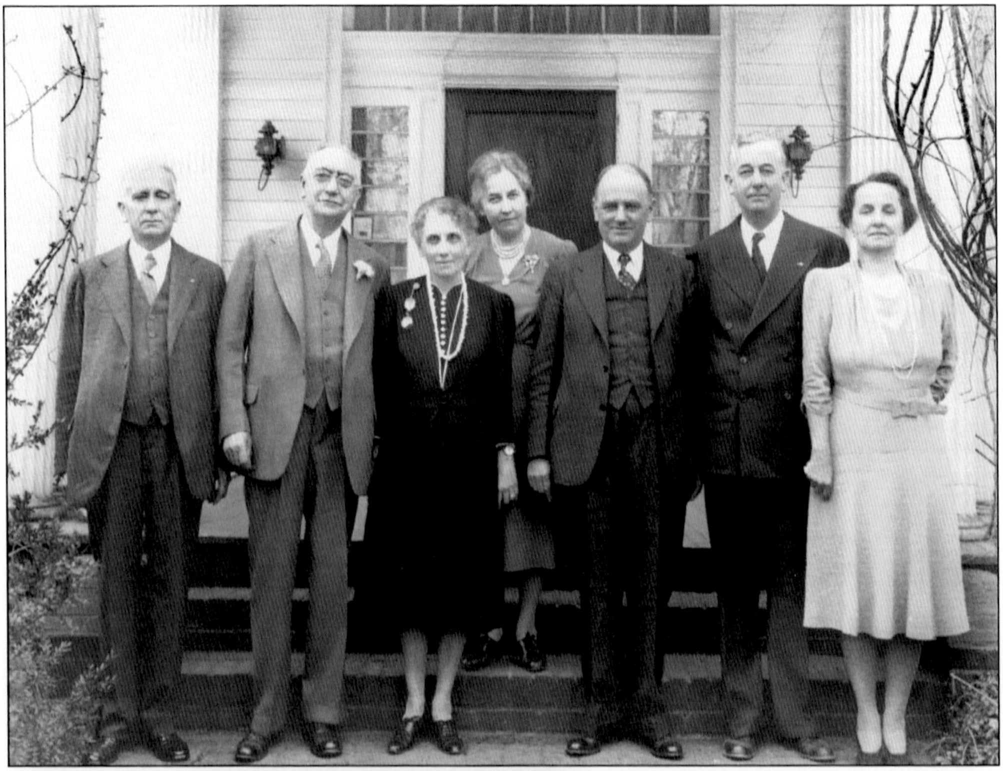

THE COX FAMILY. From left to right are Charles Curtis Cox, Joseph Edward Cox, Alice Cox Ellis, Louise Cox Fox, James Marcellus Cox, Frank Hallowell Cox, and Clara Cox Bell. The story of the Marcellus Cox family is a true success story of an Ashland family. Orphaned in 1882, the seven children took care of themselves and became prominent and successful citizens. (Pen and Betty Carol Stevenson.)

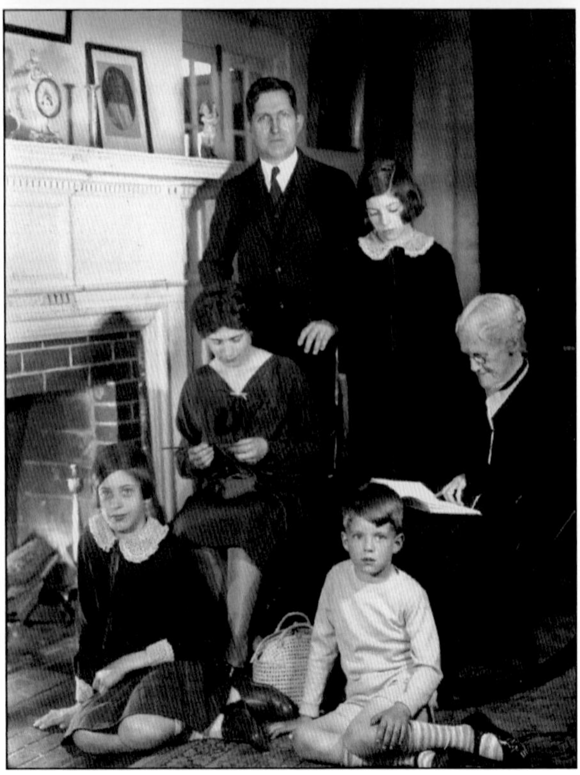

THE JONES FAMILY. This hearth-side photo was taken at 400 Duncan Street in the early 1930s. Seated from left to right on the floor are Sarah Newman and Walter Kidd "Brother" Jones Jr. Seated in the second row are Anne Doswell and Ellen Morris Doswell, with Walter Kidd Sr. and Ellen Morris standing behind them. (Sarah Jones Wright.)

HOUSE CALL. Dr. John Thomson Booth made house calls. As Marion Herget remembers, "If you could walk to the car, you went to your doctor's office." Dr. Booth, Dr. Vaughan, Dr. Ray, and Dr. Carter were the stalwart men who kept Ashland citizens healthy. (Lelia Palmore Weyman.)

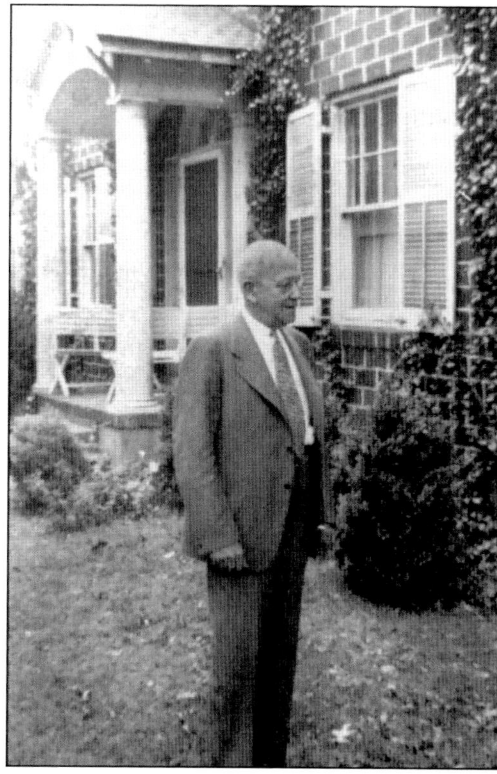

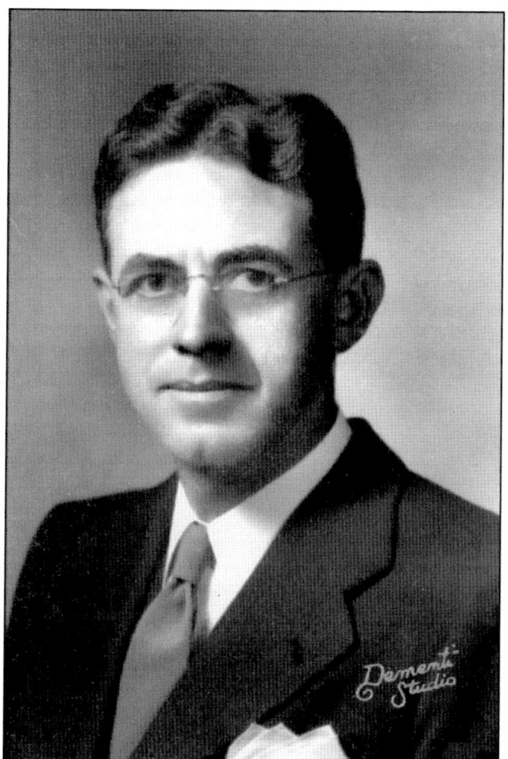

DR. VAUGHAN. Dr. Judson Vaughan began practice in 1929, right in the middle of the Depression, in a little white building on Thompson Street. His patients would often pay him in farm produce. After expenses, he made $23 that first year. For more than 40 years, Dr. Vaughan's office was in his home. (Judson Vaughan.)

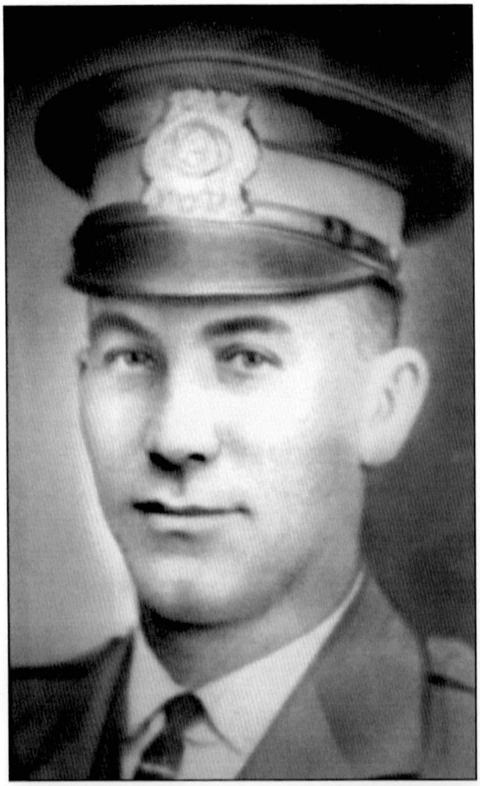

HARRY VALENTINE SMEEMAN. Born in South Dakota, Smeeman came to Ashland with his family as a youngster and grew up to be the town's only police officer in the mid-1920s. He and his dog Capsy were well-known figures around Ashland. On July 3, 1929, his body was found in a vacant lot in the rear of Cross Brothers Store, Ashland Pharmacy, and the county treasurer's office. His murder has never been solved and is still a subject of controversy in Ashland. (Mildred Smeeman Davis.)

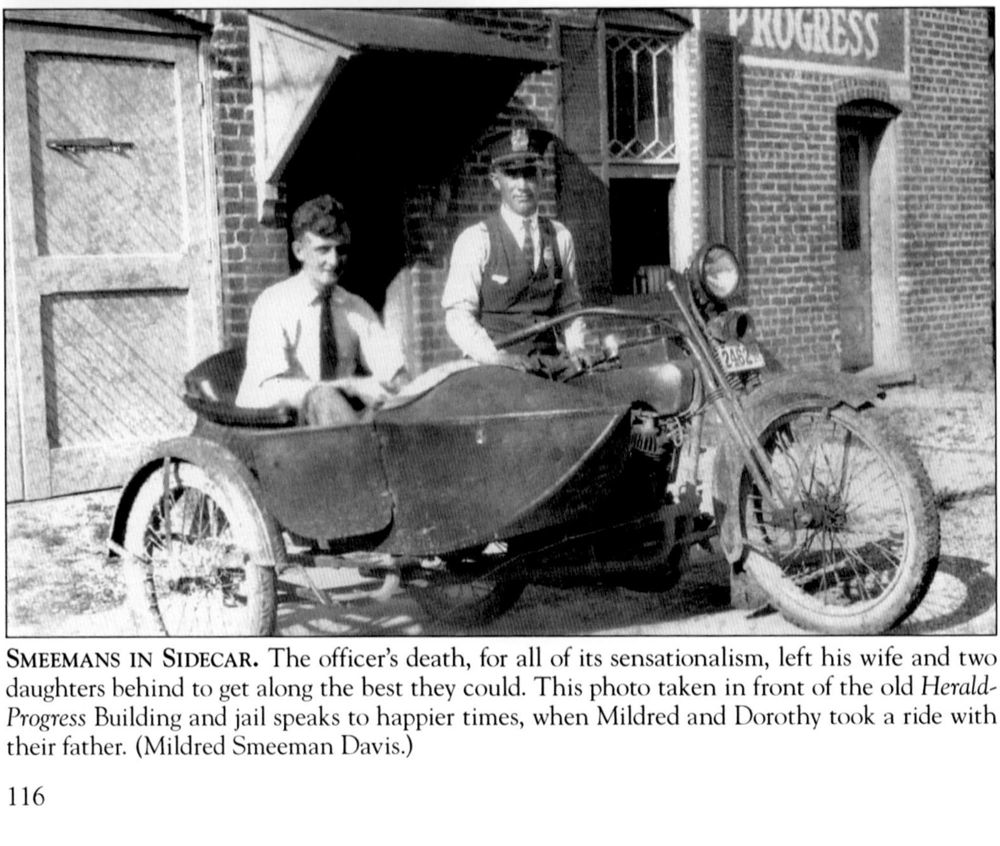

SMEEMANS IN SIDECAR. The officer's death, for all of its sensationalism, left his wife and two daughters behind to get along the best they could. This photo taken in front of the old *Herald-Progress* Building and jail speaks to happier times, when Mildred and Dorothy took a ride with their father. (Mildred Smeeman Davis.)

Ten

SOLDIERS

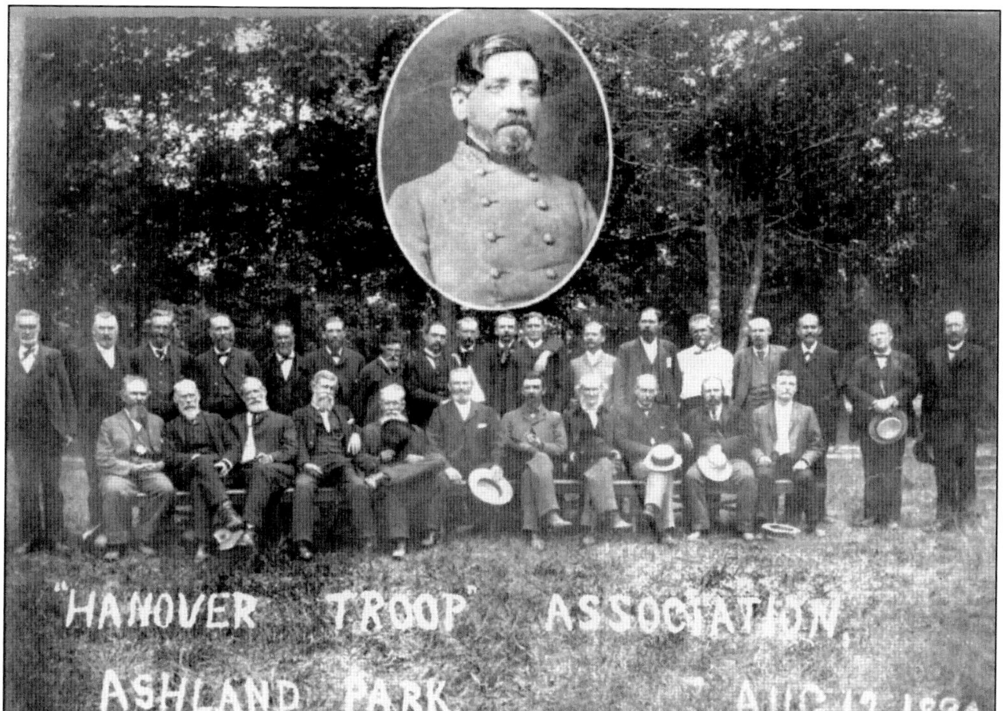

COMPANY G, 4TH VIRGINIA CAVALRY REUNION, 1890. This reunion photo shows, from left to right, (seated) Charles Coleman Taylor, Joseph Booth Brown, Walter Leake Wingfield, Peter Winston Wingfield, David D. Waldrop, Daniel Algernon Timberlake, John Lewis Greene, Martin Alpheus Waldrop, James Churchill Cooke, Asbury Watson Brock, and Luther Boxley Vauglun; (standing) John H. Blunt, Thomas Franklin Tylert, Jno. Henry Timberlake, Chastain Rufus Wingfield, Robert Lee Priddy, Alex Jackson, William Edward Carter, Charles Alexandria Taylor, John James Terry, John Lewis Talley, William Johnson Binford, Thomas Buchanan Dunn, J. Alexander Brown, Edmund Pleasant Winston, Francis Edgar Wright, John Richard Oilman, Judge Jno. Jeter Crutchfield, and Thomas Ellett Gilman. Gen. Williams C. Wickham is featured in the inset. (Woody and Susan Tucker.)

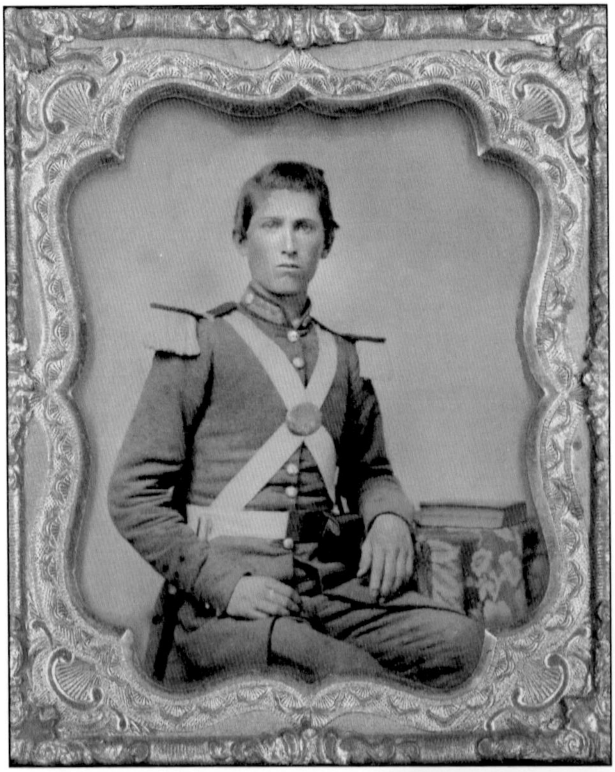

THE ASHLAND GRAYS. Callom B. Jones was a member of Company E, 15th Virginia Infantry, which saw action during the Civil War. He was paroled at Appomattox Courthouse in April 1865. Jones graduated from the Medical College of Virginia in 1869 and established a private practice in Ashland in 1882. (Woody and Susan Tucker.)

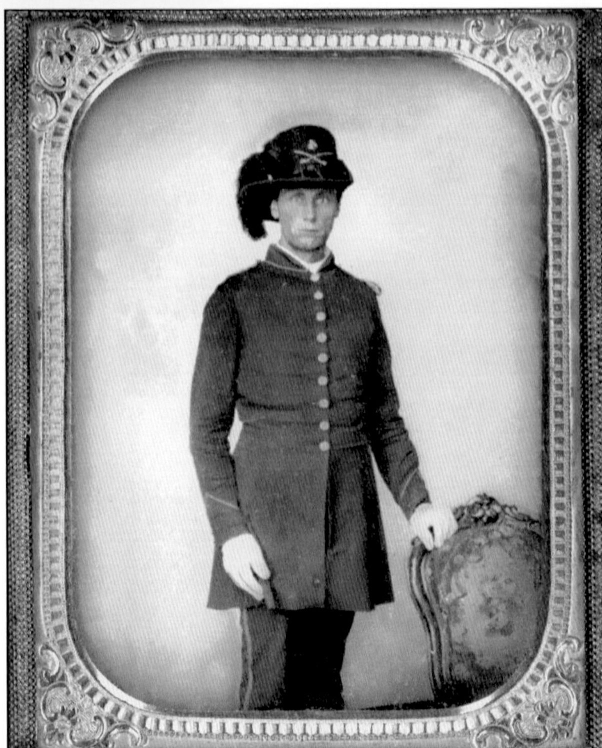

HANOVER LIGHT DRAGOONS. John Harris Blunt, whose father built Eagle Point Farm, was a member of Company G, 4th Virginia, during what Southern states called the War Between the States and Unionists called the Civil War. (Woody and Susan Tucker.)

CAPT. FLOYD WOODRUFF TUCKER JR. Tucker was active in the Hanover Grays, the Boy Scouts of America, and all things Ashland, including the famous and much-loved Tucker and Wightman Minstrel Show. (Woody and Susan Tucker.)

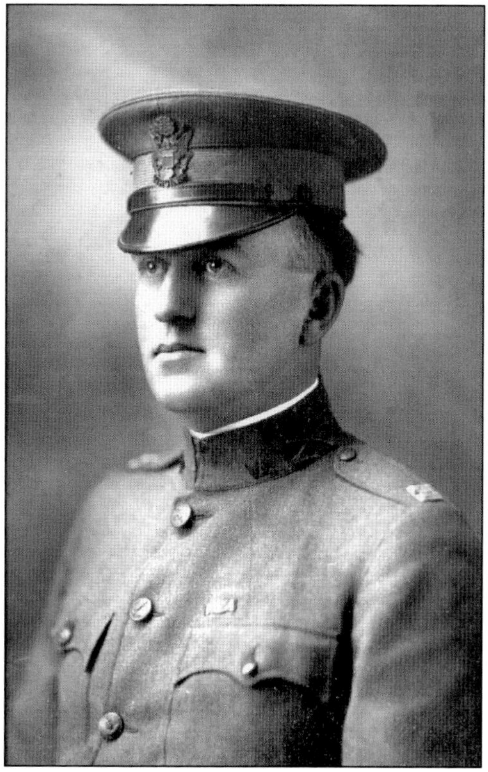

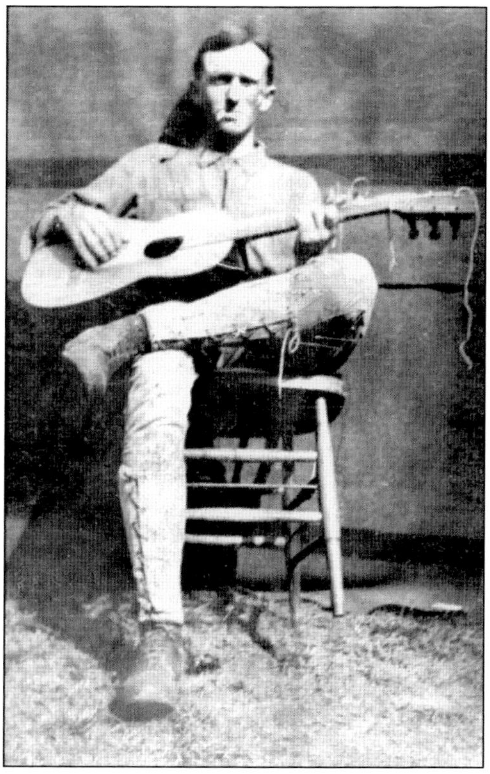

TUCKER IN CUBA. Tucker ran away to the army, underage and against his father's wishes. F.W. Tucker Jr. tried to enlist his father's help to get out of the deal when he found the romance of the idea did not match reality. His father refused. Here, F.W. is whiling away time in Cuba sometime around 1911. (Woody and Susan Tucker.)

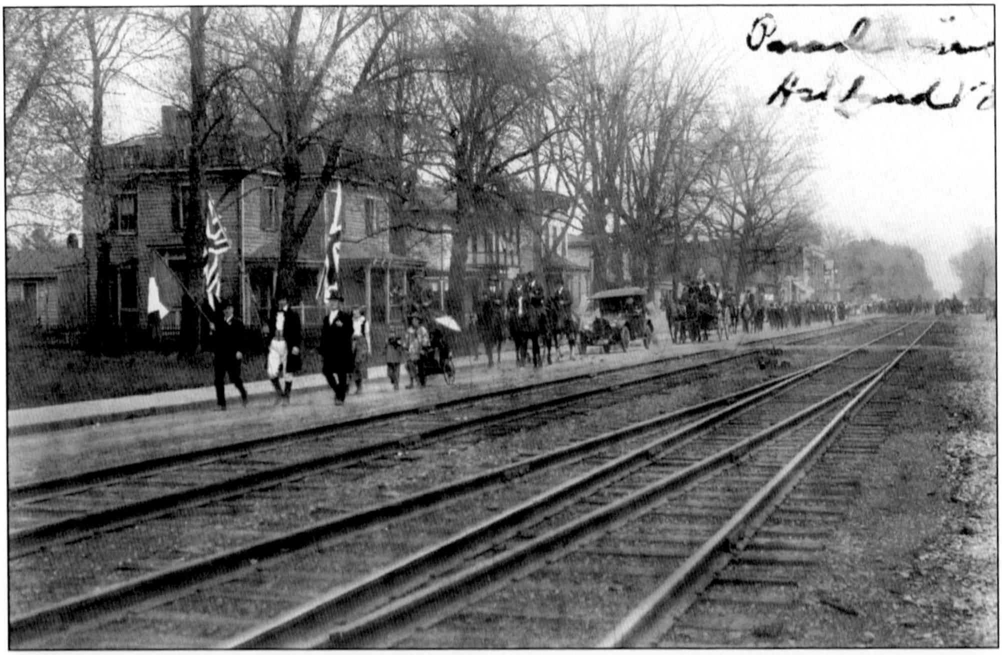

Liberty Day Parade. Recruitment events and bond drives were important events during World War I, and in Ashland it was no exception. Elaborate floats were made, and the entire town turned out. In April 1918, this parade was well attended and included, among others, F.W. Tucker and his Ashland Grays, six carriages of dignitaries, and the Boy Scouts. (Above: Lynn Taylor; below: Liz Stiles.)

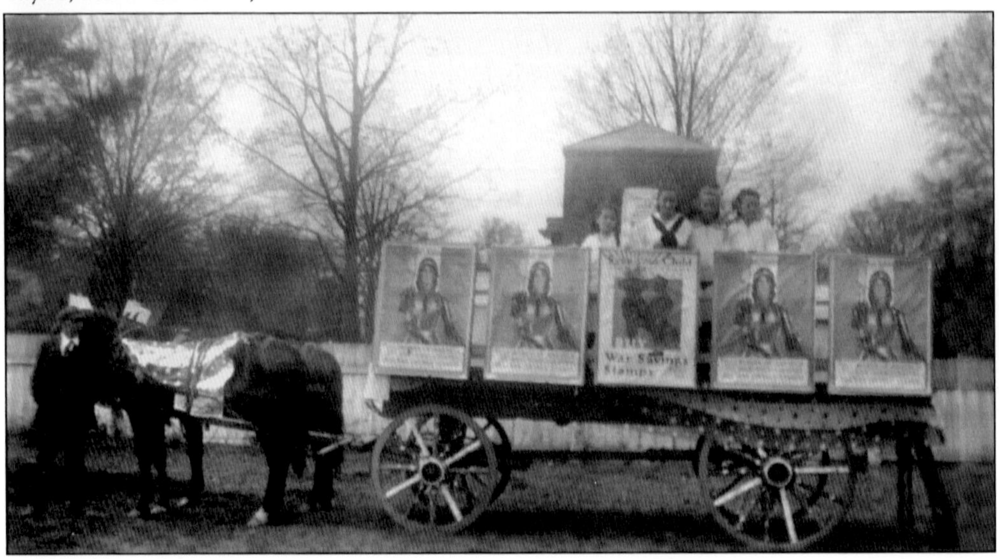

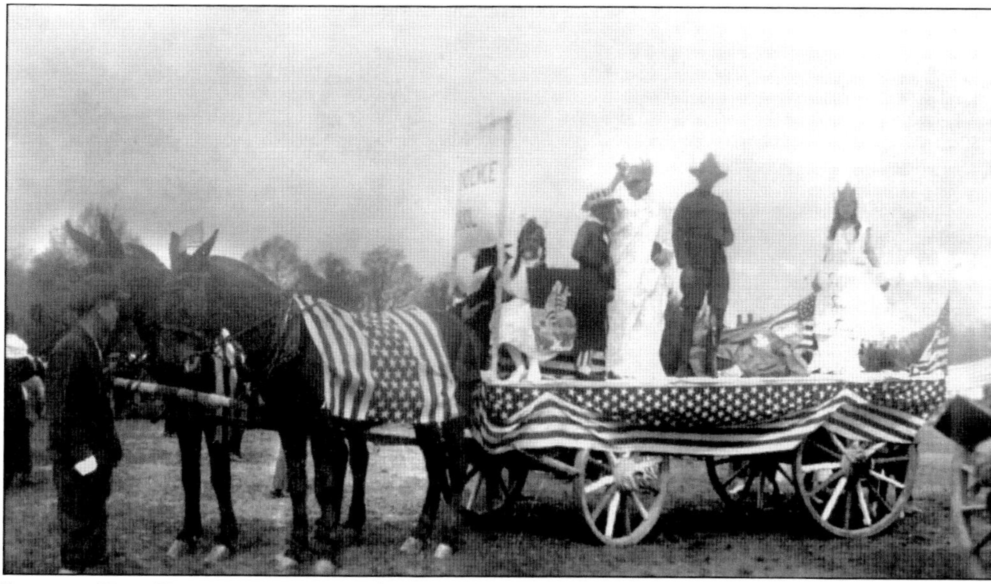

LIBERTY DAY PARADE, 1918. At the town lot, the Liberty Day Parade of 1918 ended with a speech by the Honorable Henry T. Wickham and Sen. Claude Swanson entertaining the crowd with patriotic speeches. The rally was closed with a vaudeville act—"Minnie the Wild Girl" and her snakes. (Liz Stiles.)

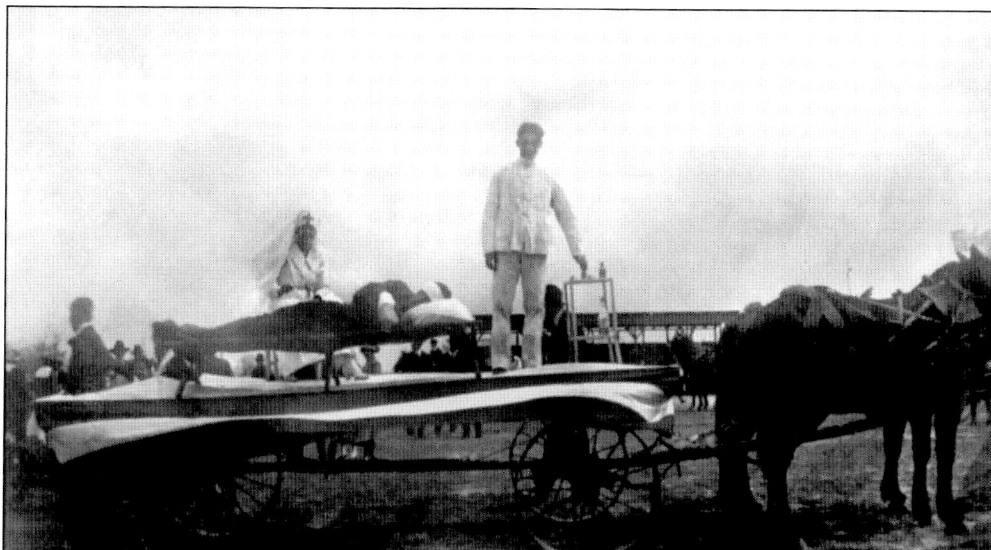

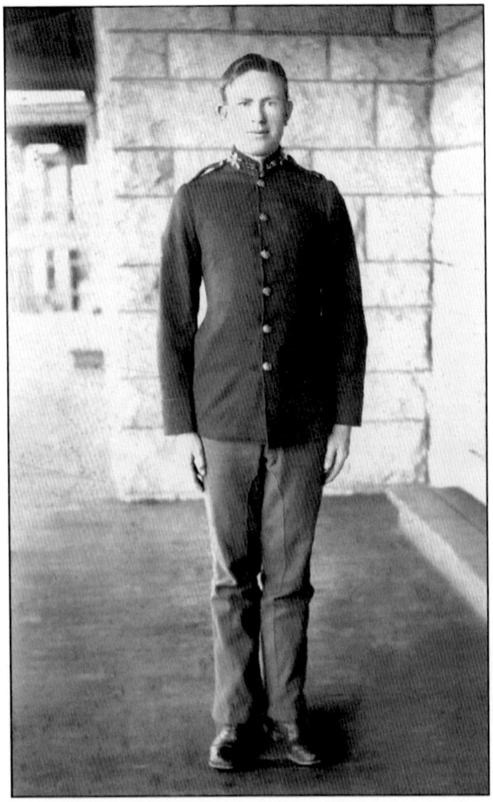

Patrick Pitman Perrin. In his new United States Army World War I uniform, Patrick Pitman Perrin stands at attention. (P.K. Perrin.)

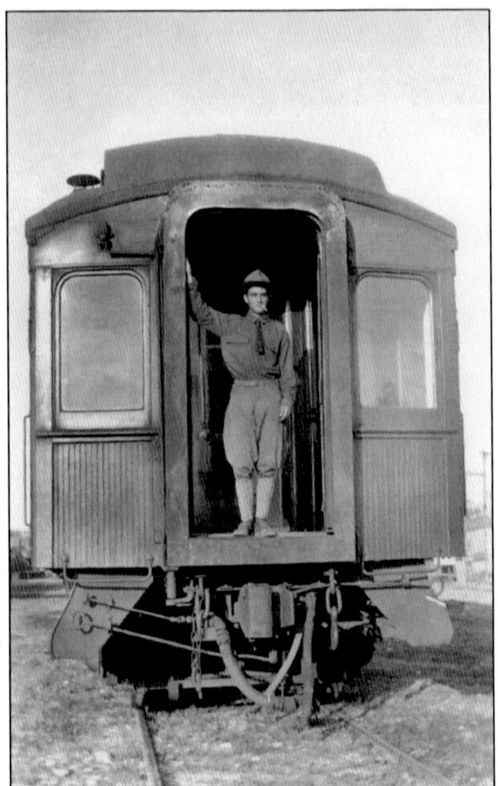

Saying Goodbye. This unidentified soldier is evocative of images many must have seen as soldiers departed Ashland for a war in Europe. (P.K. Perrin.)

PVT. CURTIS ALLEN PALMORE. Pictured with his father, Fred W. Palmore of Ashland, Curtis gave his life in action in Germany on February 20, 1945. Private Palmore was a graduate of Henry Clay High School and attended Randolph-Macon College. He was survived by two brothers: R. Vaughan Palmore, United States Army, who was fighting in the Southwest Pacific, and Lt. Fred W. Palmore Jr., United States Naval Reserve, who was stationed in New York. (*Herald-Progress.*)

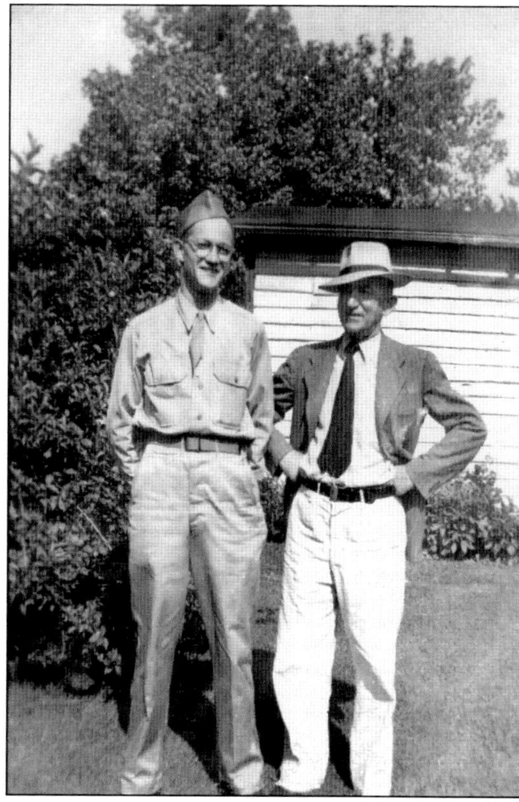

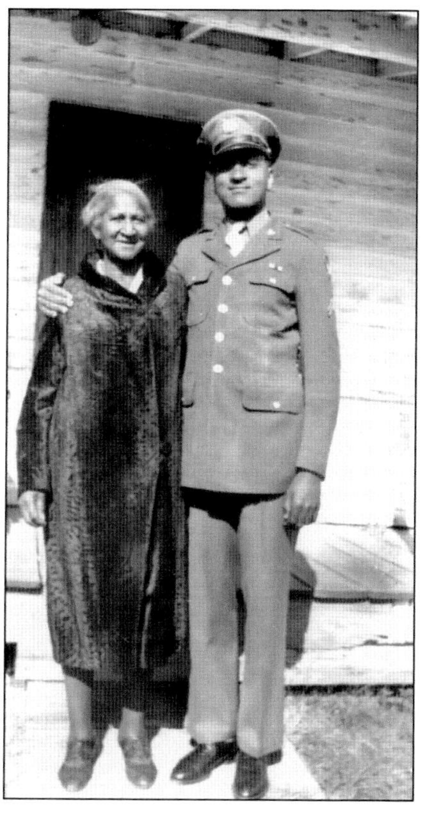

ROBERT CLINTON WINSTON. A proud member of the Winston family, Robert embraces his mother, Lillie Bell Winston, during World War II. (Inez Gray.)

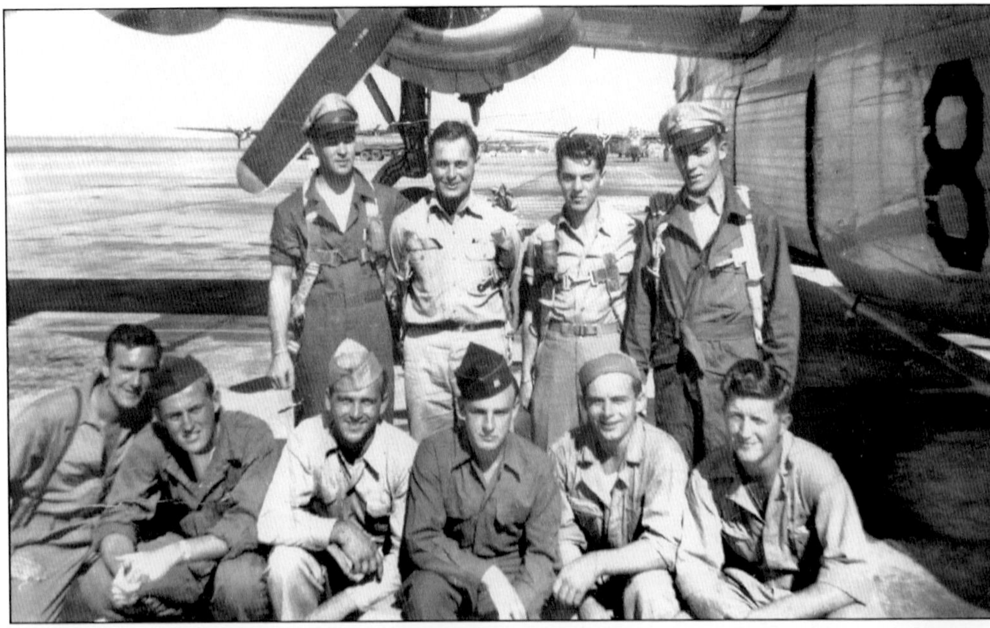

PIC PICCOLO AND CREW IN 1944. Shown here from left to right are (front row) Edward Pinner, (radio operator), Robert Drummond (gunner), Edward Wagner (nose gunner), Paul Oskowski (tail gunner), Robert Messner (ball gunner), and Russell Sage (engineer); (back row) Kenneth A. Wheeler (pilot), William B. Wivell (co-pilot), Robert H. "Pic" Piccolo (navigator and bombardier), and Cecil L. Pullen (navigator). (Eloise Piccolo.)

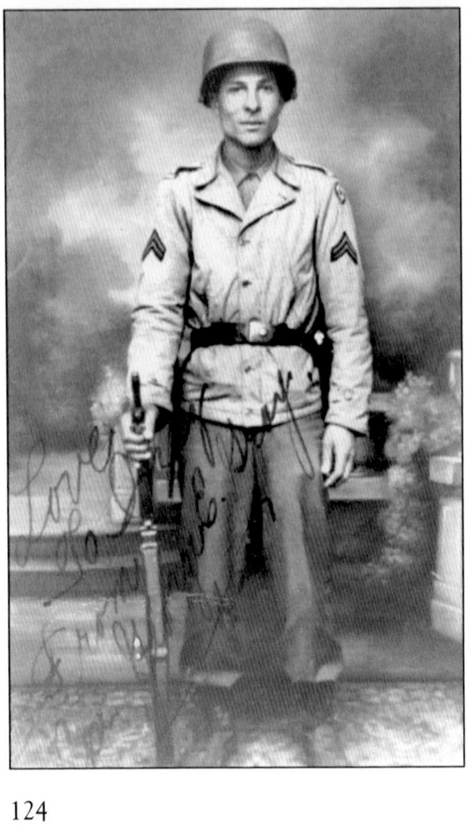

GEORGE GRAY. This image shows Cpl. George E. Gray Sr., United States Army, and was taken in 1945 when he returned after Victory in Europe Day on his way to Japan. Happily, he did not have to go the East. Born in 1915, he worked at Jacob and Levy Men's Store until 1974. He has been married to Inez Gray for 59 years. (Inez Gray.)

T.W.L. Hughes Jr. Doc and Evelyn Hughes's son, Tom, is pictured shortly after his graduation from the United States Military Academy at West Point. (Hughes family.)

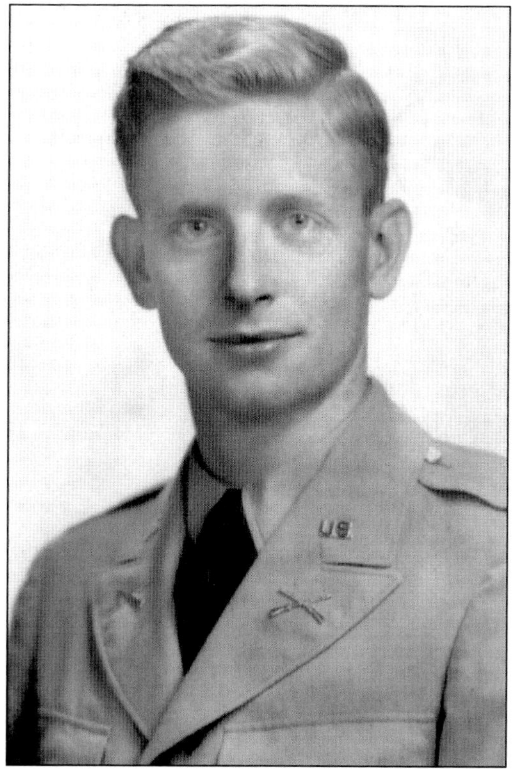

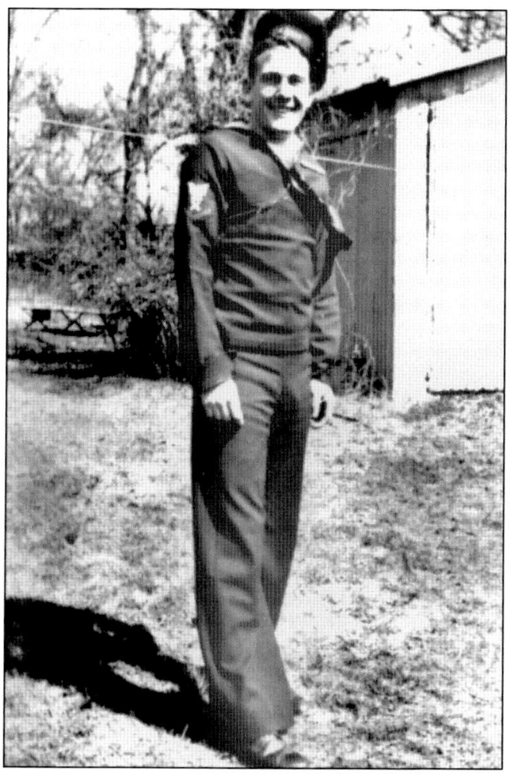

Ashland Sailor. Roland "Dick" Stone poses while home on leave from the navy during World War II. Sadly, Dick was to be killed in an auto crash. (P.K. Perrin.)

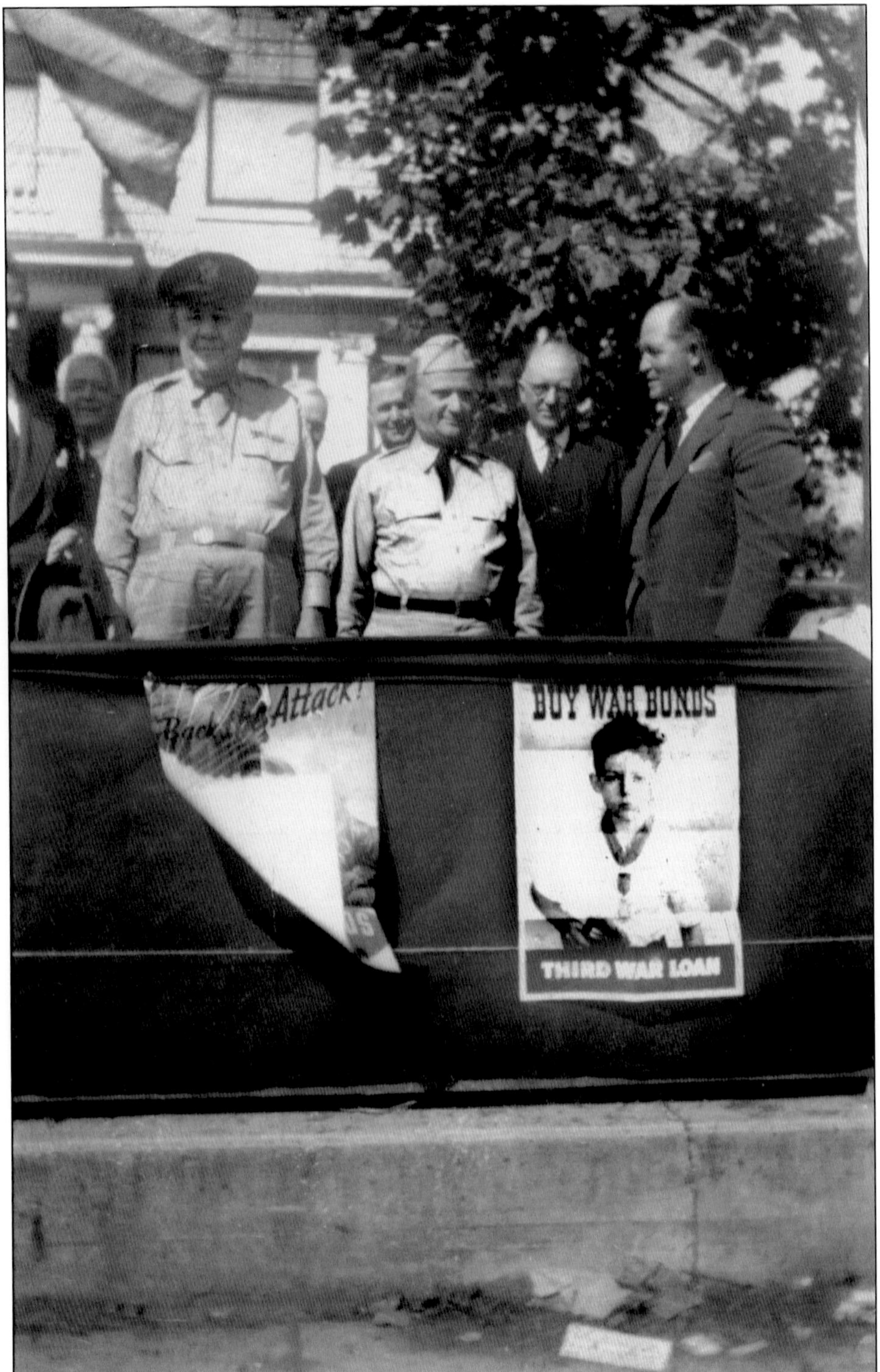

RAISING MONEY FOR THE WAR EFFORT. At a bond drive, Floyd W. Tucker Jr. (second from left) and Edmund DeJarnette (far right) rally Ashlanders to do their part during World War II. (Woody and Susan Tucker.)

Bibliography

Herald-Progress. 1881-1971 Commemorative Historical Edition. Ashland: *Herald-Progress*, 1971.

Herget, Marion. *The Watkins Years*. Ashland: *Herald-Progress*, 1981.

Manarin, Louis H. *15th Virginia Infantry*. Lynchburg, Virginia: H.E. Howard, Inc., 1990.

McKenney, Carlton Norris. *Rails in Richmond*. Glendale, California: Interurban Press, 1986.

Scanlon, James Edward. *The History of Randolph-Macon College*. Charlottesville: UVA Press, 1983.

Shalf, Roseanne Groat. *Ashland, Ashland: The Story of a Turn-of-the-Century Railroad Town*. Lawrenceville, Virginia: Brunswick Publishing Company, 1994.

Trains: The Magazine of Railroading. November 1977.